The Earles of Liverpool

The Earles
of Liverpool

A Georgian Merchant Dynasty

Peter Earle

LIVERPOOL UNIVERSITY PRESS

First published 2015 by
Liverpool University Press
4 Cambridge Street
Liverpool
L69 7ZU
UK

www.liverpooluniversitypress.co.uk

British Library Cataloguing-in-Publication data
A British Library CIP record is available

ISBN 978-1-78138-173-1 *cased*

Typeset by Carnegie Book Production, Lancaster
Printed and bound by CPI Group (UK) Ltd, Croydon CR0 4YY

Contents

List of Illustrations

Preface

This book aims to illuminate the social and economic history of Liverpool in the eighteenth and early nineteenth centuries by focussing on one important merchant family, the Earles. This was a very exciting period in the history of the city. The book starts in 1688, when Liverpool was a small town of little significance, and ends in the 1830s, by which time the Merseyside town had a population approaching 180,000 and was one of the greatest ports in the world. This period covers the whole of Liverpool's involvement in the notorious slave trade, from its tentative beginnings in 1699 until its abolition by Act of Parliament in 1807. It also covers the heroic years of the revolution in transport, which saw improvements in roads, rivers, canals, railways and finally the steamship transform the movement of goods and people, at first in Britain and then throughout the world. The eighteenth and early nineteenth centuries were also of course the years of the Industrial Revolution in which Liverpool, Merseyside and Lancashire were to have such important parts to play.

Social and economic historians tend to explain these great happenings in a rather impersonal way, by examining the movements of such abstractions as population, productivity and so on. Such an approach is clearly valuable, but it does tend to ignore the undoubted fact that in a capitalist society it is the capitalists who make the important economic decisions, such as whether to invest in this rather than that or not to invest at all. And, in a great port like Liverpool, it was the merchants who conducted overseas trades, such as those described in this book, who made these decisions. Why they made them is not often very apparent, but theory and common sense suggest that their main motivation was, in the short run, to make profits and, in the long run, to accumulate so much of these profits that it became possible to withdraw from the risky and rather vulgar world of commerce and live the life of a gentleman.

The fortunate survival of a collection of family papers makes it possible to explore both these themes, the extraordinary rise of Liverpool and, within Liverpool, the rise of one family, the Earles. This family attracted the attention of the writer, a Londoner, since they bore the same surname and many friends have assumed that they were his forebears. But this is probably not true. My family belong to another branch of the Earles, who were originally from Yorkshire and especially Hull, where they were shipowners and shipbuilders in the eighteenth and nineteenth centuries.[1] It is just possible that both the Liverpool and Hull Earles descend from a common ancestor in York but, if this is so, it is a remote connection and the main reason for the choice of this family of Liverpool merchants as the subject of this book was the survival of some of their papers.[2]

These papers were donated to Merseyside Maritime Museum in 1993 by Sir George Earle, the current head of the family, and are now known as the 'Earle Collection'.[3] The collection comprises 17 boxes of documents and other papers relating to the family's business, estate and personal affairs from the early eighteenth century to the 1930s. They constitute a rather mixed bag and seem to have been selected as an archive solely on the grounds of survival and in no way provide a full picture of the family's history. They include two very informative merchants' letter-books, each containing some 500 detailed letters, which throw much light on the business lives of their authors and indeed on eighteenth-century business in general. But they do this for only a few years in each case, so that the family's history during most of the 130 years covered in this book has to be pieced together from other sources. The collection also includes several loose letters to and from members of the family, some copies of wills and marriage settlements, a few travel diaries, the instructions from his employers for one slave ship captain and the logbook of another, partnership agreements and scattered papers relating to a very unsuccessful sugar plantation in British Guiana, but no accounts or other continuous series of papers. Much of this is enlightening and some of it is fascinating to read, but the book could certainly not have been written from the papers in the Earle Collection alone. It has therefore been necessary to supplement this by the use of standard sources for the study of mercantile and shipping history, some of which have been made available by two very

1 Bellamy, 1963.
2 Earle, 1890, pp. 15–25; Earle, 1929.
3 For a description of the collection and a catalogue see Reed, 2009.

helpful datasets[4] and, from 1756, the surviving copies of the Liverpool newspapers, which include a lot of material on shipping and commerce and on much else besides. Putting all this material together has been a bit like doing a jigsaw but, overall, the net result has been satisfactory and sufficient to write the economic and sometimes social history of an important Liverpool merchant family from the 1690s to the 1830s.

The main focus has been on six men representing three generations of the Liverpool Earle family, starting with John Earle of Warrington (1674–1749), the progenitor of the family who came to Liverpool as an apprentice in 1688. John Earle's life and business career is discussed in Chapter One and is followed by a general chapter about Liverpool in the second half of the eighteenth century, which is intended to set the scene for the rest of the book. Chapters Three to Seven and Nine examine the lives of the three sons of John who survived to adulthood, Ralph (1715–90), Thomas Sr (1719–81) and William Sr (1721–88), while Chapter Eight is about privateering during the American War of Independence, this being a very important activity for all Liverpool merchants and especially the Earles, and the source of much of their capital. The last three chapters of the book focus on the two sons of William Sr, Thomas Jr (1754–1822) and William Jr (1760–1839). Readers adept at mental arithmetic will notice that all six of these men lived long lives by the standards of the eighteenth and early nineteenth centuries and this was certainly a factor in their economic success since, other things being equal, men of the middle station accumulated more money the longer they lived and so were able to set their sons out with a larger starting capital.[5]

These six men were all merchants and, between them, they reflect very well the commercial history of Liverpool during these years. It is often assumed that Liverpool commerce was all about the slave trade, but this is a misleading generalisation. Liverpool merchants certainly invested in the slave trade and made profits from this activity; but they also invested in anything else which looked likely to make them a profit. William Earle Sr was the only one of these six men wholeheartedly involved in the slave trade; he was even the captain of a slave ship himself as a young man. But he was also very much involved in other trades, as will be seen in Chapter Five. Both of William's brothers

---

4 LTS and TSTD and see below pp. 45–46.
5 For an examination of this proposition for Londoners see Earle, 1986.

invested occasionally in the slave trade, but their main business was the trade to Russia and the Baltic conducted by Ralph and the trade with Italy carried out by Thomas, who lived for many years in the Tuscan port of Leghorn (Livorno) and set up a merchant house there in partnership with another Liverpool merchant. And finally, William's two sons inherited the businesses of both their father William Sr and their uncle Thomas Sr and so combined the slave trade with Italian trade and indeed many other trades, subjects discussed in Chapters Ten and Eleven. They were faced in 1807 with the need to adapt to a world in which the slave trade was now illegal and so, like the rest of Liverpool's merchants, they had to seek new horizons, a subject examined in Chapter Twelve. So, although three chapters are entirely concerned with the slave trade and this nasty business is described in considerable detail, the book also looks into many other trades, such as cotton, timber and linseed importing, the art trade from Italy, the wine trade, the emigrant trade to America and the two great fishing trades, Newfoundland salt cod and the export of cured fish from the Hebrides and the Shetland Islands, this last being a great favourite of the 'slave merchant' William Earle Sr. Most of the sources used relate inevitably to the business life of the Earles but, wherever possible, this has been set against the background of family life and every effort has been made to bring the women of the family into the story, most successfully perhaps with Mary, the wife of Thomas Earle of Leghorn, and her two daughters Maria and Jane.

My thanks are due to the libraries and record offices where I have done my research – The National Archives, the British Library and the Colindale Newspaper Library in London; the Merseyside Maritime Museum and the Liverpool Record Office in Liverpool; and the Archivio di Stato in Livorno. Many thanks too to my brother Robert, who has encouraged me in this project from the beginning and accompanied me on research trips to Liverpool, the Isle of Man, Livorno and on many occasions to the newspaper library at Colindale. His son, my nephew Lawrence, has also supplied important information from time to time. Thanks too for encouragement and enthusiasm to my son Jonathan, for computing advice and assistance to my son Nick and for continuous support, including reading and commenting on the chapters as they were written, to my old friend and colleague David Hebb. I would also like to thank the staff of the Merseyside Maritime Museum for their patience in helping me put much of the Earle Collection on memory sticks to be pored over back in London, and Xanthe Brooke of the Walker Art Gallery for her very helpful answers to my queries. Finally, I would like to acknowledge the support I have received from Sir George Earle of Crediton in Devon who presented his family's papers to the Merseyside Maritime Museum. It is a long time since his family has lived in Liverpool, but both my brother Robert and myself feel that Sir George's interest and response to queries have made the project seem more real.

Notes and Abbreviations

The notes refer to the surname of the author, or the first word or words of anonymous works, and the date of publication. Where two dates of publication are listed, the most recent one has been used. For full references, see the Bibliography, pp. 263–73. For abbreviations see below.

ADM	Admiralty papers in TNA
AHR	*American Historical Review*
AP	*Asta Pubblica* in ASL
ASL	Archivio di Stato di Livorno
B	Bankruptcy Court papers in TNA
BL	British Library
BLA	*Billinge's Liverpool Advertiser*
BM	British Museum
C	Chancery papers in TNA
CTB	*Calendar of Treasury Books*
CO	Colonial Office papers in TNA
D/DAV	Davenport papers in MMM
D/EARLE	Earle Collection in MMM
EcHR	*Economic History Review*
EJ	*Economic Journal*
FO	Foreign Office papers in TNA
HCA	High Court of Admiralty papers in TNA
IJAHS	*International Journal of African Historical Studies*
JAH	*Journal of African History*
JEEH	*Journal of European Economic History*
JEH	*Journal of Economic History*
LCBE	Liverpool Customs Bills of Entry in MMM
LG	*London Gazette*
LL	*Lloyds List*
LRO	Liverpool Record Office

LTS	Liverpool Trade and Shipping Dataset, 1744–86; UK Data Archive, University of Essex, # 2923
MM	*Manchester Mercury*
MMM	Merseyside Maritime Museum
NSL	*Nuovi studi livornesi*
RO	Record Office
SP	State Papers in TNA
T	Treasury papers in TNA
THSLC	*Transactions of the Historic Society of Lancashire and Cheshire*
TNA	The National Archives, Kew
TSTD	Transatlantic Slave Trade Database: www.slavevoyages.org
TY	Townley papers in BM
WELB	William Earle Letter Book, MMM D/EARLE/2/2
WLA	*Williamson's Liverpool Advertiser*

CHAPTER ONE

Origins of a Merchant Dynasty

> 'Liverpool is built just on the river Mersey, mostly
> new built houses of brick and stone after the
> London fashion ... The streetes are faire and
> long, it's London in miniature as much as ever I
> saw any thing.'[1]

Celia Fiennes's enthusiastic description of Liverpool as she saw it during
her 'Great Journey' of 1698 may seem rather surprising, as the Liverpool
she visited was a mere shadow of what it was to become. The population
of this 'little London' was perhaps 5,000 or 6,000 people at the time of
her visit, very little indeed when compared with the half million people
who lived in the metropolis. There were no docks, hardly a proper
port at all, but there was no doubt in the mind of observers that this
small town on the Mersey was destined for greatness. Daniel Defoe
called Liverpool 'one of the wonders of Britain' and enthused about its
rapid growth since his first visit in 1680. 'I am told', he wrote in the
mid-1720s, 'that it still visibly encreases both in wealth, people, business
and buildings. What it may grow to in time, I know not.'[2]

Liverpool had in fact grown quite phenomenally, from perhaps 2,000
at the time of the Civil War, to rather more than 5,000 by the beginning
of the eighteenth century, to 20,000 by 1750, and it was to quadruple
in size yet again by the time of the First Census in 1801, when the
population was said to be nearly 80,000. Such growth, heavily dependent
on Liverpool's prestige in trade and shipping, naturally drew in huge
numbers of migrants. Most of these were poor, destined to become
servants, labourers, sailors and the like, but there were amongst them
newcomers of higher social class. Commerce had become respectable
and so 'many gentlemen's sons of Lancashire, Yorkshire, Derbyshire,

1 Fiennes, 1982, pp. 160–61.
2 Defoe, 1968, ii, pp. 255–59.

Staffordshire, Cheshire and North Wales are put apprentices in the town.'[3] A new mercantile élite was created, men with surnames that were to become household names in the Mersey port – Molyneux, Tarleton, Blundell, Geldart and so on – most of whom began their careers in Liverpool in the 20 years or so either side of 1700.[4] One such recruit to the town's élite was John Earle, progenitor of the family of Liverpool merchants who are the subject of this book. Many branches of the Earle family were scattered through Lancashire and Cheshire in the years around 1700. They were mainly of the middling sort, lesser members of the rural gentry, country tradesmen, clergymen, people of reasonable education and some property but by no means rich. John's father, another John, was a maltster or brewer in Warrington in Cheshire, a prosperous market town about halfway between Liverpool and Manchester and the site of the first bridge across the Mersey.[5] He was therefore well placed to observe the rise of Liverpool and to have hopes of its future greatness, so in 1688 he despatched his 14-year-old eldest son John to serve an apprenticeship in the port, an auspicious year which ushered in the Glorious Revolution and was in many ways a key date in Liverpool's rise to glory. The revolutionary settlement not only guaranteed the triumph of commerce and the belief that it was an important function of government to promote it, but also committed England to the first of many wars against France, wars which nearly always benefited Liverpool and its merchants. 'The Liverpool of 1710', wrote the local historian Ramsay Muir, 'is almost unrecognizably different from the Liverpool of 1660.'[6] This was certainly true, and most of these changes occurred after 1688, during the first 20 years of John Earle's residence in the town.

John's master was William Clayton, one of the port's leading merchants who was also active in both local and national politics, becoming mayor the year after John's arrival and soon to be one of the two Members of Parliament for Liverpool. We know nothing about his relations with his young protégé, but he seems to have been an excellent choice. He was described by Thomas (later Sir Thomas) Johnson, his fellow MP for the borough, as 'very sensible ... and [he] has a very good notion of most

---

3 Muir, 1907, p. 139.

4 For population etc. see Muir, 1907; Marriner, 1982; Clemens, 1976; Ascott et al., 2006.

5 For Warrington at this date see Sellers, 1998.

6 Muir, 1907, p. 135.

Figure 1. John Earle (1674–1749), portrait, British school, 1710–1720

business and a good memory.' And, when he died in 1715, his monument in the church of St Nicholas, the only church in Liverpool when John arrived, described him as 'a great encourager of trade.'[7]

Apprenticeship was defined by the author of a guidebook for young apprentices as 'that genteel servitude which by a few years' service faithfully and diligently performed towards their masters, lays a certain foundation for attaining riches and honour in this world, and by God's grace everlasting happiness in the life to come.'[8] John Earle entered into

7   Cruickshanks, 2002, iii, p. 615.
8   Burton, 1681, p. 2.

this servitude in 1688, as has been said, but we know nothing of the conditions of his apprenticeship since his indentures have not survived. It was usual for apprentices to merchants at that date to serve for seven or eight years and there is little doubt that his father would have had to pay a high premium to place his son in the service of one of Liverpool's leading merchants, but this was unlikely to have been a problem for John Sr, who seems to have been a fairly wealthy man and was assessed for rates higher than anyone else in Warrington.[9] Premiums for merchants' apprentices in London in the late seventeenth century were mostly between £200 and £500 and, although Liverpool premiums were no doubt smaller, this outlay would still have been a substantial expense for his father in a world where weekly wages were rarely more than £1 or £2 a month.[10]

The master paid for the apprentice's keep during his period of service but, once that was completed, there would be an even greater outlay to provide the young man with his initial trading capital. A writer in the middle of the eighteenth century claimed that at least £3,000 to £4,000 was needed to engage in foreign trade to any great advantage. Some of this start-up capital might be borrowed, half according to William Stout, a shopkeeper of Lancaster, 'the other half being ready money, as was then [late seventeenth century] usual to do of any young man beginning trade'. Finding this ready money might or might not have been a problem for a Warrington brewer but, whatever the particular situation, the provision of a young beginner's trading capital was a major rite of passage for the fledgling merchant as parents, relations and friends clubbed together to set him up in business, often aided by the dowry of some suitable young lady.[11]

'His apprenticeship is … a school to him', wrote Daniel Defoe in his *Compleat English Tradesman* published in 1726.[12] Just what the apprentice actually learned at this 'school' obviously varied from master to master. Nearly all merchants of the late seventeenth and early eighteenth centuries wrote neatly in an easily readable hand and this might be learned from the master himself or more likely from his clerk or at one of the many writing schools which were set up from the 1660s

---

9 Earle, 1890, pp. 28–29.
10 Earle, 1989, p. 94.
11 Collyer, 1761, p. 107; Marshall, 1974, p. 112.
12 Defoe, 1987, p. 15.

onwards. Such schools also taught double-entry bookkeeping and other accounting skills and there seems little doubt that John would have been educated in this way. He was in all likelihood already quite well educated when he started in Liverpool at the age of 14, for his younger brother Peter was schooled to become a clergyman and eventually became a Fellow of Brasenose, so it is unlikely that John was educated any worse. He would also learn the mechanics of trading, how to draw up an invoice or bill of lading, how to do business at the customs house and so on. One very important skill, which must have taken years to acquire, was the ability to judge the quality, age and saleability of the goods being traded. Nearly all merchants' correspondence has comments on this subject, usually in the form of complaints that they are being sent poor quality goods.

Since merchants engaged by definition in overseas trade, many masters arranged for their apprentices to learn a relevant language or languages and often sent them abroad to learn foreign ways. Most Liverpool trade in the late seventeenth century was with Ireland and the American and West Indian colonies, so maybe there was less emphasis on foreign languages, though both William Clayton and later John Earle had an interest in trade to Spain and Portugal which might well have been instigated by a visit. Just what the business of William Clayton was when John Earle joined his employ in 1688 can be discerned from the Liverpool port books, many of which survive for the late seventeenth century and the first three decades of the eighteenth. These books were kept by the customs officers and list all the cargoes coming in and going out, giving the name and destination or place of loading of the various cargoes and the names of the merchants involved. Any such document must be treated with caution since all merchants were keen to keep as much as possible hidden from officialdom and the merchants of Liverpool were notorious in their skill in this respect.

Bearing this in mind, it is still possible to get a very good idea of Liverpool's trade and William Clayton's part in it from the port books of the late seventeenth century. The main axes of Liverpool's overseas trade at this time were the import of tobacco from Virginia and Maryland, sugar from the West Indies, especially the smaller islands such as Montserrat, Antigua and St Kitts (Saint Christopher), and general trade with Ireland, which was probably the largest element in the town's trade. William Clayton, and hence John Earle, were involved in all these trades, especially tobacco, which required the assembly and despatch of a very mixed cargo to satisfy the tastes of the colonial population. Similar cargoes were sent to the sugar islands and included all sorts of woollen, cotton, linen and silk textiles; blankets, rugs and other coverings for beds; clothing such as stockings, hats, small clothes; haberdashery; a wide variety of metal goods; leather wares; earthenware; hoops and staves for making casks and barrels; saddlery and other equipment for horses; nails; cartwheels; window glass; cane chairs; and, at the bottom of the hold, some heavier goods such as bricks, coal and salt. In amongst all this utilitarian stuff there would be luxuries and trifles to lighten the lives of colonists: fans and masks for dancing, feather-beds and curtains, periwigs, playing cards and tobacco pipes and such useful things as starch, beeswax, goose quills, paper and ink. Exports to Ireland were similar, though they included large quantities of coal and especially salt, this last being the most important export from Liverpool, in volume at least. Salt came by water from Cheshire, both white salt, which was the product of evaporation using coal as a fuel, and rock salt, which had been discovered in Cheshire in the late seventeenth century.[13] There were big wholesalers called warehousemen who specialised in the assembly and sale of these colonial cargoes, but a smart operator like William Clayton would want to bypass such men if possible and so take their profits for himself, and one can imagine that much of John Earle's work as an apprentice and later as a merchant involved dealing with manufacturers and specialist suppliers all over the country, but especially in such manufacturing centres as London, Manchester, Sheffield, Birmingham and the Black Country and in the ring of textile and metal manufacturing towns that were expanding rapidly in south Lancashire and Cheshire.

Imports from the colonies were much less complicated. Virtually nothing but tobacco came from Virginia and Maryland, though one finds the occasional exception such as the *Dolphin* from Maryland, which arrived in March 1695 carrying some 50,000lb of tobacco for William Clayton but also some products of the chase, the skins of foxes, otters, minks, muskrats and bucks. And from the sugar islands came of course sugar but also, in smaller quantities, rum, indigo, molasses, lime juice (essential for punch) and dyestuffs such as fustick and logwood. These colonial exports could be obtained through professional intermediaries but it was usually more profitable to work through agents on commission or factors. These

13 Liverpool port books for 1665–1750 in TNA, E. 190/1337/16 to /1406/3.

were often employees of the importers and were particularly important in the tobacco trade, where one of the keys to Liverpool's success was the use of factors who sold the incoming cargo direct to customers and at the same time accumulated in warehouses a cargo ready for shipment home, thus cutting down on turnaround time.

Liverpool's trade with Ireland was a very important element in the port's success. As we have seen, outward cargoes were similar to colonial cargoes but with a heavy emphasis on coal and salt. The return cargo, which became known throughout Europe and the colonies as an 'Irish cargo', was mainly the product of the island's agriculture – salt meat, butter, cheese, hides, tallow and so on – though there was a fair amount of iron exported from Ireland as well, not to mention *usquebaugh* or, as we would say, whiskey. Much of this was exported to Liverpool and then redistributed, but much was shipped from Ireland to some other destination so that an Irish cargo might be an important component of a cargo going to the colonies where it would compete with similar goods from New England and the middle colonies. Irish cargoes were also quite likely to end up in southern Europe or the Mediterranean. Liverpool's coastal trade was rather similar to her Irish trade. Small ships sailed to every port, some of them minute, on the west coast from Cornwall via Wales to the north-west and Scotland. Nearly every one of these ships carried salt and often coal as well, but they also redistributed colonial goods, and returned with whatever was the product of the region – fish, grain, malt etc. Playing a special role in this system was London, far and away the biggest city and biggest port at this time. Liverpool's great export to London was Cheshire cheese, often several thousand cheeses on a single ship, and back from the metropolis came heterogeneous cargoes which rivalled the outgoing cargoes to the colonies in their complexity. In March 1689, for instance, the *Brotherhood* arrived from London with soap, iron, apothecary's wares, hemp, hops, anchovies, oilmen's wares (dyestuffs etc.), spirits and brandy, whalebone, brimstone (sulphur), paper, painters' oil and colouring, a chest of Florence wine and so on. London was to Britain what Liverpool was to Ireland, Wales, western Scotland and the north-west of England, a source of all those good things which made life worth living.

William Clayton dealt in all these trades. He also had a number of other interests which show up in the port books and elsewhere from time to time. He was, for instance, one of several Liverpool merchants who benefited from supplying King William's army during his invasion and conquest of Ireland. Clayton was a major source of tobacco for the soldiers, no doubt one good reason why William won the Battle of the Boyne. However, military contracting, though potentially the most profitable of all mercantile activities, was rather hazardous since the government was notoriously slow in paying its bills and we only learn about this business from a dispute over payment between Clayton and the Treasury.[14]

Clayton probably made more money out of his voyages to Spain and Portugal, ventures which were later to attract the young John Earle. Clayton traded with Alicante, Cadiz, Bilbao and most importantly Oporto, much of this trade being conducted in a ship called the *Adventure* which was probably his own. In February 1694, the port book notes the arrival of this ship, captained by William Middleton, her usual master. She was carrying 50 chests containing 25,000 oranges and lemons, bags of sumac (used in tanning and as a black dye), almonds and chestnuts, corkwood, Portuguese oil and port wine. A year later, she was back with a similar cargo. There are few records of her outward voyages, but they were probably roundabout trading journeys which might involve a voyage to Ireland to pick up an Irish cargo or to Newfoundland for a cargo of salt cod, both of which were very saleable in Portugal, Spain and the Mediterranean generally. The *Adventure* and other Liverpool ships also sailed to Bilbao to bring back prunes (used mainly in distilling) and rosin, products which normally came from France and were probably smuggled to Bilbao during the war, as well as the iron and steel for which Bilbao was famous. The only other trades engaged in by William Clayton during this period were to Scandinavia, to Norway with a cargo mainly of salt to exchange for Norwegian deals (fir or pine normally sawn into planks) and train (whale) oil and to Stockholm for iron, pitch, tar and hemp.

None of these trades was very important compared with Clayton's bread and butter business with Ireland and the American and West Indian colonies. But they did show his willingness to be an innovator or a 'fast follower', that is someone quick to follow useful leads made by others.[15] This can be seen again in a much more significant way in the voyages of the *Liverpool Merchant*, which sailed from the Mersey on 1 December 1699, and the *Africa*, which departed in July 1700. Both

---

14   *CTB* vol. 10/2, p. 646, 8 June 1694; Hancock, 1995, pp. 224, 237–38.
15   For the concept of 'fast followers' see Hancock, 1995, p. 14.

these ships are clearly recorded as slave ships in the records of the Royal African Company, which had a theoretical monopoly of English slaving until 1698. And both of them were owned by John Earle and William Clayton in partnership, so it seems that John's very first ventures as a fully fledged merchant were as a partner in the very first ships from Liverpool to engage in this trade which was to make the port so rich and so notorious in the course of the eighteenth century. These were powerful ships, each of 200 tons burthen and each carrying 20 guns when they received letters of marque (privateering licences) when the war with France broke out again in 1702.[16] There seem to have been two more, possibly three, Liverpool ships engaged in the slave trade in these years which saw in the new century – the *Dragon*, the *Union* and the *Blessing*, Thomas Brownbill, master, whose instructions from his owners have survived in the Norris papers.[17] But this brief flurry was a false dawn, as there were no more slaving voyages for nearly a decade and it seems probable that these ventures were unprofitable.

John Earle's apprenticeship as a merchant was therefore quite varied and interesting. His name occasionally appears in the port books when he made an entry for his master, as in November 1695, when he loaded saddles, gunpowder, shot, chairs and various other goods on the *Elizabeth & Anne* bound for Virginia or, perhaps more excitingly, when he supervised the loading of some of the cargo of the slave ship *Union* on 18 November 1699. Earlier that year, he had made his first entry as a merchant in his own right when, on 24 May, he appears as the consignee of one cask of muscovado sugar (i.e. unrefined) on the *Supply* coming in from Montserrat. John is normally described as coming into his freedom as a merchant in 1700, but this small shipment may well have been a sort of token celebration, for his former master is credited with 99 casks of sugar on the same ship. One hogshead is not much, but John was now a fully fledged merchant in the most rapidly expanding port in Europe, indeed in the world. And he was also a shipowner, a slaver and a privateer as other members of his family were to be in the course of the eighteenth century.

John was 26 in 1700 and he celebrated his freedom by getting

16 Data on slave ships here and elsewhere in the book taken from TSTD; TNA, T70/349 f. 75; T70/351 fols 46, 51, 52; HCA 26/17, 29 July and 16 December 1702. For the Royal African Company see Davies, 1957.

17 16 October 1700, LRO 920/NPR 2/179.

married at St Nicholas church on 10 December of the same year. His bride was Eleanor Tyrer, the daughter of a fellow merchant and shipowner, Thomas Tyrer. John and Eleanor set up home in Chapel Street, at the very heart of the early development of the port, and on 6 June 1702 their first and, as it turned out, only child Thomas was born. Just a few weeks later Eleanor was dead and, in February 1703, baby Thomas died too, a sad history that was only too common.

John now focussed on building up his mercantile business. This was slow at first, some small shipments of tobacco from Virginia and sugar from the Leeward Islands, but one can see him slowly gaining confidence and also keeping an eye open for the main chance. In the summer of 1704, for instance, he was engaged in organising the salvage of a ship from the West Indies which had wrecked on the Isle of Man. From this wreck John was able to bring into Liverpool cedar wood, fustick and braziletto, woods valuable for the dyes which could be extracted from them. In the following year, he concentrated on Portugal. In February, the *Terra Nova* arrived from Oporto with delicacies for the table for John and his partners, described as '& Coy' in the port book. There were 45,000 lemons and oranges, raisins, chestnuts, corkwood, brandy and substantial quantities of port wine. In May, the *Happy Return* arrived from Lisbon with more of the same and 35 hundredweight of figs. In 1706, the *Terra Nova* was back again, having completed a roundabout voyage typical of the period. She had sailed from Liverpool via Ireland for Newfoundland with a cargo of salt, nails, haberdashery, leather, linen, tobacco pipes and ale from Liverpool and provisions from Ireland. A cargo of salt cod was then despatched to Lisbon, where the ship loaded up with the usual Portuguese cargo. Meanwhile, John was also extending his sugar and especially tobacco imports with shipments of tobacco from Virginia consigned to him in seven different vessels in 1709. There are no surviving accounts or business correspondence to give depth to this bald statement of John's interests, but on the face of it he was doing pretty well for a beginner.

While John was building up his business and acquiring a reputation as an enterprising and sometimes innovative merchant, he was also becoming well known in the town as one of the governing élite. In 1703, he was persuaded, somewhat against his inclinations, to join the council of 40 men who ruled the town. This council was dominated by merchants who had won a famous victory in 1695 over the landowners who had previously decided what should be done in Liverpool. In 1708, John was one of a group of 12 large-scale traders in the council, each with an average of 34 shipments in the port books, and in the following year he was elected mayor at the age of 35.[18] His year in office was chiefly notable for the council's successful application for an Act of Parliament to enable the construction of the first of the port's docks, the world's first enclosed wet dock. This came into use six years later on 31 August 1715, the occasion being marked in the diary of Nicholas Blundell of nearby Little Crosby: 'I went to Leverpool and saw the Mulbury, the Batchlor and the Robert all in ye Dock, they came in the morning and were the first ships as ever went into it.' Previously, ships had to anchor in the river, where there was just 'a pier forming a kind of open harbour'. The dock made use of a tidal pool off the Mersey, which was enclosed with quay walls and protected from the river with locks which were opened at high tide to allow the ingress of ships and water and then closed with up to 100 vessels inside at anchor.[19]

John's success as mayor was followed in 1710 by his success in choosing a second marriage partner, Mary Finch, only child of Ralph Finch of Chester. She was one of several heiresses to marry members of the Earle family during the eighteenth century, this being a very important way for Liverpool or indeed any merchants to build up their trading capital. We do not know the size of her dowry, but it must have been substantial for John seems to have had much more capital to back his projects after his marriage than before. John and Mary were to have a long marriage by the standards of the eighteenth century, 39 years till John's death at the age of 75 in 1749, Mary dying two years later. Four of their children were to survive them, Ralph (born 1715), a second Thomas (1719) and William (1721), whose activities will be discussed in the following chapters, and Sarah, who was born in 1717.

In the next few years John built up a very considerable business importing wine, so much so that he justifies the description of wine merchant he was sometimes given, though he continued to trade in sugar, tobacco and much else besides. In 1713, the port books show that he was involved in at least ten ships importing Spanish, Portuguese and French wines from Cadiz, Gibraltar, San Sebastian, Bilbao, Bordeaux, Lisbon, Viana and Fayal in the Azores. These ships also brought in

18 Power, 1997, p. 322.
19 Hyde, 1971, pp. 13–14; Gibson, 1895, p. 137.

for John the other specialities of their regions, oranges, lemons, raisins and brandy from Bordeaux, corkwood from Portugal and iron from Bilbao. This wine business was to continue to expand, and in 1717 the *Hart & Goodwill* brought in from Rotterdam 43 gallons of Rhenish wine as well as a consignment of wainscoting (wooden panelling used for lining walls and an absolute must for the fashionable houses of the period).

One ship which appears prominently in John's wine business is the *John & Mary* and this was probably his own, built and named in honour of his marriage to Mary Finch. Another ship which was certainly his own, or rather the property of a consortium of which he was head, was the *Earle Galley*, which first appears in the Liverpool port books in August 1712, when she arrived from Antigua with a typical cargo for John Earle & Company of sugar, molasses and cotton. A couple of months later, on 27 October 1712, the *Earle Galley* is recording as departing for Madeira. This was a common first call for ships sailing for the West Indies, the local wine being very popular in the Caribbean. But there is something a little suspicious about the *Earle Galley*'s voyage as she was loaded with pewter, copper manufactures, wrought iron, nails, linen and aqua vitae, all products shipped to pay for slaves, as we shall see in a later chapter. It seems probable that John and his partners were concealing the fact that the ship was actually sailing for the coast of Africa as well as Madeira in order to avoid attracting the attention of the Royal African Company, the former monopolist group which was entitled to lay an imposition of ten per cent on the cargoes exported by 'Separate Traders', that is slave traders who were not members of the Company. Such suspicions would seem to be confirmed when the cargo of the ship's return voyage from Antigua is listed, since it included, in addition to sugar, molasses and other West Indian goods, 'elephants' teeth' and redwood, two products which were carried on most ships coming from Africa and certainly not from Madeira, an island not famous for its elephants.

The *Earle Galley* was in fact a slaving ship of 160 tons burthen. She was built in Liverpool in 1710, the year of John's marriage, and she carried six guns and a crew of 20 men.[20] She was one of at least 17 Liverpool ships engaged in the slave trade to Antigua, Nevis, Jamaica and Barbados in the middle years of the 1710s.[21] This trade, which had remained dormant since the very beginning of the century, was now thriving and John Earle, newly flush with capital from his wife's dowry, was at the forefront of this development. The *Earle Galley* made the trip via Madeira and Africa to the West Indies, mainly Antigua, almost every year from her first appearance in the port books and in June 1718 was recorded in the returns of the Barbados Naval Officer as arriving in that island with 182 slaves. John can also be identified as either consigning on or receiving goods from at least seven other slavers He may normally have been described as a wine merchant, but to us he might seem remarkably like that vilified species of trader, a slave merchant.

The port books record John as a very active merchant for every year from his marriage in 1710 until the last years of the decade. Some of these records are badly affected by damp and virtually illegible, but one can read enough to know that John Earle was a busy man, still active in the slave trade, engaged in the Newfoundland fish trade, importing colonial staples from the West Indies and Virginia, and trading with many places in Europe such as Portugal, Ireland, Scandinavia and the Low Countries. But towards the end of the decade this busy, busy life seems to have become somehow disturbed. He dropped out of the slave trade in the second half of 1718 and engaged in very little trade at all for 1719 and absolutely nothing for the early years of the 1720s. He makes a brief reappearance in the port book for 1726, the last year for which they have survived, but this is on a very small scale compared with his former glories. It is clear that something had gone seriously wrong with John's career as a merchant.

There are no surviving business papers for John Earle, no newspapers for this period and few other records to throw light on his apparent

20 Such details about ships can sometimes be obtained from the colonial Naval Officers' shipping returns, in this case CO 33/15, 10 January 1717, for an entry from Barbados and CO 157/1, 20 July 1713, for one from Antigua. See also TSTD.

21 A list of ships coming into Barbados with slaves in the years 1716–26 can be found in CO 33/15. Other slave ships can be deduced by the presence of elephants' teeth in the incoming cargoes of ships from Nevis, Antigua and Jamaica.

downfall. There is a strong hint, however, in the brief biography written by his descendant, T. Algernon Earle, in 1890. 'John Earle's life was a busy one', he wrote, 'and his fortunes were somewhat chequered; sometimes he was successful; sometimes – and especially towards the close of his life – he seems to have suffered considerable losses and disappointments ... He died a comparatively poor man ... but left his family settled and in prosperous circumstances.'[22] We shall see in the next few chapters that the last part of this statement is absolutely correct. All three of John's sons got off to a good start in the Liverpool business world and, if their father was comparatively poor, their mother and her family were comparatively rich and no doubt provided the funds to launch the sons in their careers. And it is in fact from one of these sons, William, who died in 1788, that we get the first clear information as to what had happened to their father. In William's will, dated 10 October 1782, there is a clause requiring 'that two thousand pounds be paid into trustees' hands for the equal payment of my late father's creditors, so far as it will go to the discharge of his debts owing on his book in 1737 and not in his former bankruptcy in 1714 as happened before I was born.' So, nearly 40 years after John's death in 1749, some or possibly all of his creditors would be paid out of the fortune accumulated by his son, a successful slave trader and general merchant, a gesture which might be described as truly filial though also a reflection of the shame which debt and bankruptcy carried in that age.[23]

Bankruptcy, as a result of bad luck, poor judgment or cash flow problems so serious they could not be resolved, was the greatest fear of the eighteenth-century businessman, whose activities depended on a great chain of credit given to or by him. Just one failure of one link in this chain could cause large numbers of business houses to collapse, so the fact that John Earle went bankrupt is not particularly surprising or reprehensible. The actual process of bankruptcy was governed by legislation of 1706 which was remarkably lenient for the age. Commissioners examined bankrupts who surrendered themselves and made a full and honest declaration of their affairs and a dividend, say a payment of ten shillings in the pound, would be declared and the creditors paid this much out of the surviving assets, while the bankrupt was entitled to be given back five per cent of his net estate,

22 Earle, 1890, pp. 35–36.
23 MMM D/EARLE/10/3 – will of William Earle of West Derby.

to a maximum of £200. The bankrupt was then given a certificate discharging him of the balance of his former debts, so long as four-fifths of the creditors agreed to give it. So, providing the debtor could prove that he was honest, if perhaps misguided, there was life beyond bankruptcy.[24]

Although there is no doubt that John Earle suffered two bankruptcies, not just one, it would seem that his son William had been misinformed as to the date of the first, 1714 having been a year in which John was fully active in trade. It was in fact five years later, on 31 January 1719, that a commission of bankruptcy was awarded against him, the chief creditors being two London merchants. These and other creditors managed to gather in some of the assets formerly belonging to John but soon ran into a problem as the bulk of his assets were either in Liverpool or were still abroad or at sea. So a year later, on 25 February 1720, John's leading Liverpool creditor, the merchant Henry Parr to whom he 'was indebted in £20,000 and upwards', petitioned the Lord Chancellor for a new commission to be awarded, with commissioners appointed in both London and Liverpool to gather in John's assets, an arrangement which would not only reduce costs but would make it more difficult for John to conceal or embezzle his former property. This was agreed and a couple of weeks later, on 15 March, an advertisement appeared in the *London Gazette*, the official government newspaper, announcing this new commission and appealing to creditors in and about London to come and prove their claims at the London Guildhall at three in the afternoon of 24 March, and creditors in and about Liverpool to do the same on 11, 14 and 18 April at Liverpool Town Hall. Meanwhile, John was required 'on every of the said three last days to surrender himself to the said Commissioners to be examined ... and make a full discovery of his estate and effects.'[25] No doubt this was a humiliating experience for a man who had once been Mayor of Liverpool in that same Town Hall, but this we can only surmise as no comments have yet been discovered to enable us to determine just how Liverpool reacted to the downfall of one of the port's leading merchants and citizens, an alderman and a former mayor as well as a dealer in wine, slaves and many other cargoes besides, a man whose credit had only recently been so good that he had been trusted with the huge sum of '£20,000 and upwards' by his

24 Duffy, 1980; Earle, 1989, pp. 126–30.
25 TNA, B 1/5, pp. 258–59; B 4/3, pp. 35, 113; *LG*, 15 March 1720.

biggest creditors and lesser sums by other creditors both in Liverpool and London. These large sums would be much reduced once John's ships arrived in the Mersey, but they are still large and give some indication of John's standing in the Liverpool mercantile community just 20 years after he first became a merchant.

Why and how John went bankrupt in the late 1710s is not clear, since none of his business records or the detailed records of the Bankruptcy Court have survived. He certainly greatly expanded his trading activities in this decade, as has been seen. And he was simultaneously, like other Liverpool merchants, taking advantage of a unique opportunity to speculate in the town's real estate. The Moore family, the most important landowners in the seventeenth-century town, had fallen on hard times, and their mortgaged estates were put on the market by their London creditors (also confusingly called Moore) from 1712 onwards. The biggest purchaser was the Earl of Derby, but John Earle was also described as 'a considerable purchaser'. His interest was focussed on the northern end of the town, at that time the pleasantest and most salubrious part of Liverpool, and amongst other building ventures he arranged for Earle Street to be laid out as part of a fashionable residential quarter close to the centre. This monument to his vanity was to prove a poor speculation, as the fashionable centre of gravity shifted further south to the area round the dock and it seems likely that expenditure on purchasing this land and laying it out for building contributed to his bankruptcy.[26]

John was trading again by 1726, albeit on a much-reduced scale, so it is clear that he was in fact discharged after his examination in 1720. But his attempt to reinstate himself in the Liverpool trading world did not last very long and he was soon in trouble again. No mistake was made this time by his son William in naming the date of his father's second bankruptcy. The commission was awarded on 20 May 1737 and the notice appeared in the *London Gazette* on 31 May. The examinations were to take place this time on 'the 9th and 13th June next, and on the 12th of July following at ten in the forenoon, at the house of Mrs Margaret Turner in Liverpool aforesaid, commonly called the Merchants Coffee-house.' There seems to have been no question of John's honesty

---

26   Picton, 1907, ii, pp. 39, 230. My thanks to an anonymous reviewer who drew my attention to John Earle's building speculations.

and, once agreement had been reached as to the dividend to be paid to the creditors, John was given his discharge.[27]

John was now in his sixties and made no further attempts to reinstate himself during the remaining 12 years of his life. He retired from the bustling port where he had once been a great man and went to live in Prescot, a small town eight miles east of Liverpool. Prescot had an international reputation as a centre for the making of watch parts and movements and of various tools, especially 'small files, the best in the world', which were made by workmen who combined their manufacture with the operation of small farms scattered over the countryside.[28] But the town's main economic significance was that, together with nearby Whiston, it lay on the south-western end of the Lancashire coalfield. The local collieries were the nearest to Liverpool and so able to benefit from the huge expansion of the demand for coal as the port grew and from the growth of various local coal-using industries, especially salt refining and glassmaking. Cheap transport was the key to the exploitation of coal and local production was given a great boost by the construction of a turnpike road from Liverpool to Prescot in 1726, though not everyone saw this as a benefit. Samuel Derrick noted in a letter written in 1767 that travellers from Liverpool to this 'very pleasant market town … are often incommoded by the number of colliers' cars and horses.'[29]

During these years, the collieries of Prescot and Whiston were the largest and most technologically sophisticated on the south Lancashire coalfield and they were also the most profitable, having a near monopoly of the Liverpool market until the opening of the Sankey Navigation from St Helen's to the Mersey in 1757. But in fact so insistent was the rise in demand that neither this nor the opening of the Leeds and Liverpool Canal in 1774 did more than check the profits accruing to the owners of these mines so close to Liverpool and the Mersey. These profits in turn attracted mercantile capital from Liverpool, including several members of the Clayton family and their commercial partners, the Cases, all of course well known to John Earle. But, most important from his point of view was the Willis family, who since 1684 had controlled most of the collieries in Whiston from their base in Halsnead Hall. This wealthy family were cousins of John's wife Mary and were destined to play a

27   TNA, B 4/9 p. 23, 20 May 1737; *LG*, 31 May and 20 September 1737.
28   Aikin, 1795, pp. 310–12.
29   Derrick, 1767, pp. 29–30. On coalmining in general see Langton, 1979.

very important part in the fortunes of the Earle family, as will be seen at the end of Chapter Nine. It seems quite likely that they provided John and Mary with a home when they retired to this part of Lancashire. John died in Prescot in 1749 and was buried in the local church. He left three sons, Ralph aged 34, Thomas 30 and William 28, whose careers as merchants shall be considered in later chapters. But, first, the scene will be set by looking at the extraordinary history of Liverpool in the first 40 years after John's death.

CHAPTER TWO

This Very Opulent Town[1]

> 'The town is exactly like London. Hackney coaches
> ply in the streets, the shops are numerous and
> elegant; the town is well lighted, and the bustle,
> noise and confusion that reigns throughout,
> offer to the traveller an exact epitome of the
> metropolis.'[2]

Just under 100 years after the visit of Celia Fiennes in 1698, John
Manners, Duke of Rutland, echoed her words in his enthusiastic
description of Liverpool following a visit in October 1797. Liverpool
was still a 'little London', but it was a lot less little than it had been in
1698. Just four years after the duke's visit, the population was counted for
the first census and found to be 77, 653, over four times larger than in
1750, an astonishing rate of expansion. Such rapid growth could only be
achieved by very considerable immigration, from all the north-western
counties and from Scotland and North Wales, and also from Ireland,
though this Irish immigration was not yet as vast or as desperate as it
was to be in the nineteenth century.

Liverpool's association with the African slave trade was reflected
in the appearance of a few black faces. Some of these were there of
their own accord or that of their parents, the children of some of the
wealthier slave sellers in West Africa being sent to Liverpool to learn
the language and the customs of their main customers. Numbers were
fairly small, perhaps 60 or 70 at any one time, but there was a larger
community of black men serving aboard the ships which used the port,
mariners recruited in both West Africa and the West Indies. Some of
these sailors were free men, but most were probably slaves, such as the
'stout negro young fellow, about twenty years old' who was offered for

1 Derrick, 1767, p. 9.
2 Manners, 1805, pp. 368–69.

sale in the local newspaper on 24 June 1757. 'He has been employed for twelve months on board a ship and is a very serviceable hand.'[3]

Visitors to Liverpool rarely mentioned the blacks in their midst, but there were plenty there, mostly young men or women or children employed as household servants, though a few had a trade, such as cooper or barber. Numbers are not known but there were certainly a few hundred black people in Liverpool by 1800, maybe a few thousand. We usually hear about them when they were offered for sale, like the 'negro boy, about 12 years old, that hath been used since September last to wait at table' or the 'very fine negro girl, about eight years of age, very healthy and hath been some time from the coast', or, more commonly, when they ran away, as did 'a black boy, short, about 16 years of age ... the property of the Rev. Mr. Gwyn of Prescot.' Where these runaways hid themselves is usually unknown though there is sometimes some information, as in the case of the 'extream good looking black' belonging to the merchant Thomas Seel. 'He spoke of going to the Forest of Delamere in Cheshire,' a very large forest which might well make a good place of refuge for an African.[4]

Just occasionally the black youngsters of Liverpool appear in a way which gives them a little more humanity, such as the 'black boy belonging to Mr Edmund Jenney called Liverpool'. We hear about him in a report of a near tragedy in which he and three white friends were playing in a boat which was carried out to sea by the ebb tide.[5] Black people also appear in some contemporary paintings and engravings. The most moving is by Joseph Wright of Derby, who spent a few years in Liverpool painting portraits of the town's worthies. Some of these are very fine, such as his portrait of Sarah Clayton, daughter of John Earle's master and herself the greatest female entrepreneur in Liverpool. But the picture that really catches the eye is called 'A Conversation of Girls', exhibited in 1770. This shows two white girls with their black servant, a beautiful girl whose enigmatic pose, down on her right knee and looking up at them, foreshadows the famous medallion produced by Josiah Wedgwood in 1787 with the emancipation movement's slogan, 'Am I not a Man and a Brother?'[6]

3   *WLA*, 24 June 1757.
4   *WLA*, 24 June 1757, 17 September 1762, 11 March 1763; Williams, 2004, p. 476 and see, in general, Costello, 2001.
5   *WLA*, 2 June 1758.
6   Parsons, 2007.

• • •

The main cause of the rapid population growth in Liverpool was of course the expansion of the port's trade and shipping. This was quite extraordinary. Shipping tonnage, to take just one measure, rose from 19,000 tons in 1751 to nearly 130,000 tons in 1801.[7] The geographical spread of trade remained much the same as in the first half of the eighteenth century, with coasting and the Irish trade still very important, probably the most important, trades, followed by the sugar and tobacco trades and of course the slave trade. Liverpool had already overtaken Bristol and London as a slave-trading port by 1750 and was completely to eclipse them later in the century. Between 1791 and 1800, for example, the Lancashire port sent out 910 slave ships to Africa, over three-quarters of all the slave voyages from Britain, and they were to carry over a quarter of a million slaves to America and the West Indies.[8] By this date, the trade and Liverpool were already facing an increasing barrage of criticism, which was to lead to Abolition in 1807. This miserable but profitable trade will be considered in detail in later chapters since John Earle's youngest son William and William's two sons, Thomas Jr and William Jr, were among the port's leading slave merchants.

Other areas which saw a higher than average growth were the trades to the Baltic and the Mediterranean, both of which already existed in 1750 but were to grow considerably in the next half century. All the Earles were involved in these trades, but especially the eldest son Ralph, who concentrated mainly on Russia and the Baltic, and the second son Thomas, who set up a merchant house in Leghorn (Livorno) in Tuscany in partnership with another Liverpool merchant, Thomas Hodgson. One completely new trade which does not seem to have attracted any Earle investment was whaling. English whaling was focussed on Greenland and the Davis Strait at this time and the first Liverpool whaler to sail to these icy seas set out in 1753. Numbers fluctuated in the next half century, peaking in the late 1770s, when 10 to 20 Liverpool whalers sailed north each year, each with crews of 40 or 50 men, but decline set in fairly quickly and whaling had virtually vanished from Liverpool by the beginning of the nineteenth century. Whaling was traditionally an east coast (or even more, Dutch) trade

7 Chalklin, 1974, p. 49.
8 Morgan, 2007, pp. 15, 25.

and it seems probable that Liverpool's interest was mainly generated by the bounties offered by the government to ships engaged in the trade (rising from 20 to 40 shillings per ton), shipowners 'fitting out for the sole purpose of catching, not the fish, but the bounty', as Adam Smith put it in *The Wealth of Nations*.[9] But, whatever the reason, there is no doubt that there were Liverpool whalers in the second half of the eighteenth century, thus completing a full house of ungreen trades in the port, ranging from the slave trade and the trade in elephant tusks which accompanied it, whaling and of course those two really sinful activities, the import of sugar and tobacco.[10]

While Liverpool merchants took advantage of national legislation in their favour and ignored or evaded as far as possible those laws which were not, they were the first to benefit by the laws and orders issued by their own town council. This self-appointed group of 'forty and one honest and discreet men' had a firm control of elections to their number and consisted mainly of Anglican merchants, an élite in the town amongst whom the Earle brothers were prominent, especially Ralph, who emulated his father by becoming mayor. Analysis of the commercial interests of this council makes it abundantly obvious why the port was hostile to the abolition of the slave trade since, in 1787, at the start of the abolitionist campaign in Parliament, 37 of the 41 councillors had investments in slave ships or were suppliers to the trade.[11] This local government, though clearly not very democratic, was certainly beneficial to the growth of Liverpool since there was little or no opposition to measures designed to improve the general fabric of the port. The most important of these was the continued expansion of the system of docks initiated during the mayoralty of John Earle in 1709. A second dock, Salthouse Dock, was opened in 1753 and this was followed by the North Dock (later called George's Dock), the Duke of Bridgewater's Dock and the King's and Queen's Docks, this last being opened in 1796. All visitors were bowled over by the size and splendour of the docks, even the curmudgeonly American loyalist Samuel Curwen, who spent a few hours in Liverpool in June 1780 and wrote a very hostile account of the port. 'The Docks, however,' he had to admit, 'are stupendously

---

9 Adam Smith, 1961, ii, p. 25

10 Enfield, 1773, p. 72 reports the import of 6,855 elephants' teeth in 1770. For more on the trade in ivory see below p. 57.

11 Sanderson, 1977, p. 66.

Figure 2. Liverpool from the Cheshire Shore, water-colour by J.T. Serres, 1798

grand.' And so said everyone else, stressing their huge size, the forest of masts, the sight of ocean-going ships in the midst of houses and the overflowing warehouses, 'a scene of business scarcely to be equalled in the port of London.' 'It is certainly the most convenient port in Great Britain', wrote the more friendly American visitor Jabez Maud Fisher, 'and there is perhaps none superior to it elsewhere.'[12]

Expansion of the docks led to specialisation, as can be seen in the interesting guide to Liverpool produced in 1797 by Dr William Moss. He noted that the Old (i.e. first) Dock served the West Indian and African trades, as well as ships trading to Europe and Ireland; Salthouse Dock specialised in handling the cargoes of the corn and timber ships; St George's dealt mainly with West Indiamen; the King's Dock with American (especially tobacco) and Baltic shipping; while the Queen's Dock also welcomed American ships and was the main berth for the whalers. So one knew where to go to seek a passage or cargo space and it was also possible to know in advance what ships were coming into the river, thus giving merchants more time to prepare for them. This was done by a signalling system on the lighthouse on Bidston Hill on the Cheshire side of the river and a guide to the signals was available from booksellers.[13]

More information could be garnered in the places where merchants congregated, in the Exchange (or Town Hall) in Castle Street, a 'handsome square structure of grey stone, supported by arches', which was completed in 1754 and had on the ground floor an area for the merchants to congregate. But 'it is so very dark that little or no business can be transacted in it; and the merchants assemble in the street opposite to it, as they used to do before it was erected.'[14] In the same central location there were several 'highly respectable' coffee-houses, the Merchants Coffee-house in St Nicholas Churchyard, which had a good view of the signalling station across the river, Pontacks (a good London name) and the Exchange Coffee-house in Water Street, and many more, where merchants could do deals with other merchants or shipowners, auctions and meetings could be held and news, so vital in trade, could be picked up from gossip and in the well-equipped newsrooms which, from 1756, included amongst the papers on display

12 Curwen, 1972, p. 628; Manners, 1805, p. 369; Morgan, 1992, p. 81.
13 Longmore, 2006, pp. 156-67.
14 Manners, 1805, p. 373.

Williamson's Liverpool Advertiser, the town's first newspaper. The Duke of Rutland was impressed by the Hotel in Lord Street, where 'we amused ourselves in the coffee room, which is a very grand place, full of newspapers from every corner of Europe and always crowded by the principal people in Liverpool.'[15]

Communications by land were very poor in 1750. There were no stagecoaches and travelling from London to Liverpool by road was quite an adventure. It was necessary to travel by horseback and in large companies as a protection against highwaymen, so that the normal practice was for a company of travellers to assemble every Friday morning in London at the Swan with Two Necks in Lad Lane, from where, accompanied 'with a gang of horses', they slowly made their way north and west, reaching Liverpool on Monday evening. But this, almost medieval, mode of travel was soon to change. Advertisements in the local paper and information in the town directories, which were published every few years from 1766 onwards, mark the progress of improvement. Regular wagon and coach services to London, Manchester, Birmingham and elsewhere were established, and the journey time from Liverpool to London was reduced from three days in the 1760s to just 36 hours (or even less) by the Royal Mail Coach, which set out from Liverpool every evening in 1792 from the Talbot Inn in Water Street at five in the afternoon and arrived at the Swan with Two Necks (if all went well) at five in the morning on the second day. By the 1830s, it was possible to do the journey, very expensively, in just 23 hours, but such performances were soon to be eclipsed by the railway.

Running parallel to the improvements in roads was the development of the river and canal system serving Liverpool. This involved engineering works even more impressive than those necessary to build the docks and were on such a scale that, by the end of the century, Liverpool was connected by very slow but very cheap water transport with the coal mines of south-west Lancashire, the salt mines of Cheshire and such centres of business and industry as Manchester and Birmingham. There were connections to places even further afield as the Mersey was linked to the Severn at Stourport in 1772, the Trent in 1777 and the Thames in 1790. The first real canal was the Sankey Brook Navigation, whose promoters 'had no difficulty in enlisting the sympathy and practical support of the Corporation in their undertaking.' This canal opened in

15 Touzeau, 1910, p. 498; *WLA*, 5 July 1774.

1757 and enabled the coal and industry of the area round St Helens to be linked with the Mersey and so Liverpool. A much more ambitious scheme was started in 1770, the ultimate aim being to link Liverpool by a roundabout route across the Pennines to Leeds, but progress was understandably slow. But progress there was and, on 21 March 1774, the first 20 miles of the Leeds and Liverpool Canal was opened, 'this much-wished-for event being welcomed with ringing of bells, a band of music, the firing of guns ..., the shouts of spectators and all the marks of satisfaction that so important an acquisition merits.'[16]

Impressive though this achievement was, the real star of the north-western canal system was the Duke of Bridgewater's Canal. This was built by the famous engineer James Brindley to connect the centre of Manchester with the duke's coal mines at Worsley, a few miles to the west, an immediate success which halved the price of coal in Manchester when the canal opened in 1763. This canal was really spectacular, starting with a tunnel which led right into the mines and later carried across the River Irwell on an aqueduct 39 feet high. 'The scene is really beautiful', wrote Jabez Fisher: 'One river crossing over another so high above and boats sailing in each has a pretty effect.' Such success led to a decision to extend the canal to Runcorn, from where a 'pretty stair case' of ten locks took boats down to the Mersey. The main function of this extension was to transport coal and other goods cheaply to Liverpool, but it was also popular with passengers. From Liverpool, a coach would be taken to the top of the staircase of locks and then a canal boat to London Bridge just outside Warrington. Samuel Curwen travelled this way in 1780 and found it 'pleasing beyond description', pulled by a single horse at four or five miles an hour. He sat in the 'foremost apartment, roofed with glass windows, and allotted to better company', where he was able to enjoy a picnic lunch of 'a cold roast chicken, some ham and two bottles ale.'[17]

The cheap coal brought in by this impressive canal and river system was mainly destined to warm the homes of Liverpool's rapidly rising population. But some of it was employed as a source of power for industry, and engravings and maps of the town show many conical chimneys belching out smoke, as well as many windmills which, together with water, provided the main source of power in these last few years

16 Morgan, 1992, pp. 83, 233; Curwen, 1972, pp. 627–28.
17 *WLA*, 28 May; Enfield, 1773, p. 88.

before the introduction of steam power. Many industries focussed on the processing of imports, such as tobacco refining, snuff manufacture, salt evaporation and sugar refining. There was no industrial zoning and these industries were often sited right in the middle of otherwise residential parts of the town, such as the 'large commodious sugar-house' put up for sale in May 1756 in Hanover Street, at that date just about the smartest location for merchants' houses in the whole of Liverpool. By the time William Enfield wrote his *Essay towards the History of Leverpool* in 1773, there were eight sugar houses in the town refining 6,000 hogsheads of sugar annually.[18]

Other industries emitting a lot of smoke included the evaporation of salt, glass making, soap making, pottery, herring curing, brewing (40 breweries by 1797 producing rather poor beer according to William Moss) and copper smelting, a works being set up in 1767 by Charles Roe & Co. of Macclesfield to smelt Anglesey copper and produce copper and brass articles for the slave trade.[19] But smelly, smoky and often noisy as all these industries were, none could compare for unpleasantness with the 'building for extracting the [whale] oil … provided with boilers' in Greenland Street near the Queen's Dock where the whalers berthed. As even William Scoresby, the very readable writer on whaling had to admit, 'the smell of oil, during its extraction, is undoubtedly disagreeable.'[20]

Not all of Liverpool's industries were smelly. Watchmaking was clean enough, the Liverpool industry specialising in watch movements and other components, which were often purchased by London watchmakers and finished off there. And one of the largest of Liverpool's industries could hardly be called offensive. This was shipbuilding, nearly all of which was carried out on the shelving sandy beaches of the Mersey, mostly in the area between the river and the docks which shipbuilding shared with timber yards. Here too were various smaller industries ancillary to shipbuilding – rope walks, sawpits, foundries for anchors and other metal components of ships.

Engravings and paintings of the town were often taken from the Cheshire side of the Mersey and show the shipyards with rows of half-finished vessels propped up with balks of timber. Roger Fisher, a

18 Moss, 2007, p. 137; Marriner, 1982, pp. 52–53.
19 Scoresby, 1820, ii, p. 407.
20 Fisher, 1771, p. 46–47; Stewart-Brown, 1932, pp. 22–23.

Liverpool shipwright, claimed in his book *Heart of Oak*, published in 1763, that in 'the flourishing town of Liverpool ... there has not been less than 1,000 sail of ships built in the last 50 years' and, by the 1780s, there were 14 or 15 yards producing over 40 ships a year, numbers which were to decline rapidly in the next few decades as the growth of the docks took over the space previously occupied by shipyards and forced the industry to cross the Mersey into Birkenhead.[21] The Liverpool yards produced every sort of vessel, from 1,000-ton monsters destined for the Norwegian timber trade to slave ships, sloops, coasters and canal 'flatts' to service the expanding waterway system. Liverpool's greatest pride was, however, the 36 ships built for the Royal Navy, most of them built during the War of Austrian Succession and the American War of Independence, when the yards in the Thames and on the south coast were severely stretched.

There was always a party to celebrate the launching of vessels, large and small. When HMS *Liverpool*, a frigate with 28 guns and 12 swivels, was completed in 1758, she was 'esteemed one of the most beautiful and best ships that has hitherto been built in this port ... and most of the neighbouring gentry are expected to be at the launching and assemblies in the evening.' There were also plenty of people at the launch in February 1793 of the *Watt*, a vast three-decker ordered for the Jamaica trade by the wealthy West Indies and slave trading firm of Walker & Watt: 'The tide was very high, the launch very fine, and having a large band on board playing martial tunes, the whole proved highly gratifying to a vast concourse of spectators.' The launch in 1775 of the *Mary Ellen*, a slave ship built for his father and named after his mother was about the first thing that the 'nonagenarian' J. Stonehouse remembered and wrote about in his *Recollections of Old Liverpool*, published in 1863. He claimed to remember everything since he was six years old, and so maybe he really could recall the huge cheer when the ship moved off the runway and into the water and the great festivity and hilarity that followed the launch. Liverpool certainly enjoyed a party.[22]

One of the most striking aspects of Liverpool to the visitor and indeed to the historian was the fact that the place was one huge building site. A population which quadrupled in the second half of the eighteenth

21 Longmore, 2006, pp. 156–57.
22 *WLA*, 9 February 1758; Stewart-Brown, 1932, p. 124; Stonehouse, 1863, pp. 8–11.

Figure 3. A Plan of the Town of Liverpool by John Eyes, 1768

century had to be housed. The anonymous author of the guidebook called *The Stranger in Liverpool* liked to play with figures and he calculated from maps and plans of the town that the area covered with streets and buildings had increased from 1 million square yards in 1765 to 4 million in 1790. Much of the land was owned by the Corporation or landed families and these were only too happy to enrich themselves by giving leases to merchants and others prepared to organise and finance the building process, the Earle family playing its part in this generally profitable exercise.[23]

The Mersey runs roughly north–south at Liverpool and the waterfront remained much the same length through the second half of the eighteenth century, from Queen's Dock in the south to the outlet of the Leeds and Liverpool Canal in the north, a distance of about a mile and a half. To the east of the waterfront, the town formed a very rough half-moon and slowly advanced into the countryside in a generally eastward direction, away from the river and up steadily rising land so that many of the new streets and houses had pleasant views. In 1787, for instance, 'a large new-built house and garden' were advertised for sale in Hope Street, at that date on the very edge of the built-up area. 'It commands a full view of the town, the entrance into the port, with a view of the river ... being only a mile from the Exchange'.[24]

There was no overall planning before the Corporation began to take a hand in the 1780s and the result was a predictable muddle. There were some shop-lined streets with fine houses in which merchants and other wealthy people lived, such as Hanover Street, the 'habitat of the mercantile aristocracy who erected noble mansions and made to themselves gardens and orchards', or the half dozen or so London-type squares, some with central gardens. But there were also innumerable cellar dwellings and tiny court tenements, these homes of the poor not being so obvious in the eighteenth century as they were to become in the nineteenth.[25] Even the nicest streets and squares took time to build, so that there was always much unfinished business with the dust and noise that building inevitably creates. Great George Street, for instance, lying on the southern fringe of the town and offering fine views down to the river and beyond, was only partly developed in the late 1780s, with

23 *Stranger*, 1816, pp. 31–32. For the building process see Chalklin, 1974.
24 *WLA*, 22 January 1787.
25 Picton, 1907, ii, p. 152; Chalklin, 1974, p. 211.

the west side 'open to the fields and completely unbuilt, the east side partly built.' In 1787, the delightful Liverpool diarist Hannah Lightbody admirably captured the emotions which such a sight aroused: 'Walked up town with my Mother and felt a mingled sensation of melancholy and admiration at the appearance of present devastation and the prospect of future grandeur it exhibited.'[26]

Visitors to Liverpool were divided in their opinions of 'this very opulent town', as Samuel Derrick, a generally favourable observer, described the flourishing port. Nearly everyone agreed that the town was dirty, though not as dirty as Manchester according to the Duke of Rutland, who was very positive in his opinion of Liverpool. The American Jabez Fisher was also a Liverpool enthusiast on the whole, but he was forced to admit that 'the town itself is dirty, irregular, illy paved, and in general but indifferently built, though there be some good streets and squares.' There was general agreement that the streets were too narrow, poorly paved and poorly drained, at least until the 1770s and 1780s, when the council began to enforce improvements, with street widening orders from 1774 and, in December 1785, the appointment of an 'improvement committee ... to meet every Thursday till further notice to consider of the best methods of improving the town.'[27] Water supply remained a serious problem, as John Aikin observed. 'Good water is ... more of a rarity here than could be wished', he reported in his description of Liverpool, and he noted the presence everywhere of carts bringing water into the town. But, on the other hand, he thought that the Liverpool Corporation was 'beyond most in England ... active and liberal in promoting places of public interest ... and street widening.' Harold Ackroyd, the historian of the Liverpool stage, sums up rather nicely the appearance of Liverpool at the end of the eighteenth century: 'There were pleasant landscapes, fruitful gardens and picturesque windmills dotted here and there within a mile of the Town Hall ... but the town was badly paved, drained and lit.'[28]

Some writers find it tempting to seize upon the more negative aspects of Liverpool's environment, such as its dirtiness, together with its situation as the world's most flourishing slave-trading port, to paint

26 Lightbody, 2008, pp. 15, 69; Brooke, 1803, p. 486. For more on Hannah Lightbody see below pp. 37–42 and Sekers, 2013.
27 Manners, 1805, p. 376; Morgan, 1992, p. 232; Picton, 1886, p. 258–59.
28 Aikin, 1795, pp. 358, 363; Ackroyd, 1996, p. 13.

an equally negative picture of the social, artistic and intellectual life of the town, the assumption being that merchants and especially slave merchants were philistines who could not appreciate the finer things in life. But this is a very unhistorical way of looking at a society. Where does it say that slave merchants have no culture?

Liverpool merchants were certainly interested in making money and were prepared to devote a lot of time and effort to the work necessary to accumulate wealth, but they were also interested in enjoying themselves and living in as pleasant an environment as possible. The provincial towns of Georgian England were famous for being civilised places which went to considerable effort and expense to make life enjoyable for their inhabitants, especially those who were better off, and Liverpool in the second half of the eighteenth century was no exception. As Jane Longmore has written, in an excellent reply to the critics of slave-trading Liverpool, 'commercial growth and politeness were far from mutually exclusive.' A perusal of the local newspaper and a look at what is left of the eighteenth-century built environment are sufficient to establish that Liverpool shared what Peter Borsay has styled 'the English Urban Renaissance'.[29] Urban renaissance is perhaps not quite the best epithet for Liverpool, which, being such a new town, had nothing which could be reborn. But every development described by Borsay can be found in the then Lancashire town, rather later than in many southern towns. Nevertheless, by the third quarter of the eighteenth century, Liverpool had 'all the characteristic features of cultured urban life.'[30] But, sadly, this would be only a brief window of culture and civility as further population growth swamped the town and some of its most pleasant amenities from the 1780s and 1790s onwards.

The most visible aspect of the urban renaissance were the houses themselves, the smarter ones nearly all built in the London fashion, what we call 'Georgian', brick-built on three or four storeys with pleasing proportions, flat-fronted with sash windows, similar indeed to a house being let in March 1759. This was suitable for a gentleman or merchant and comprised 'a sashed dwelling-house ... with a yard and counting-house adjoining ... genteely hung with paper, and has grates in every room with marble and other chimney pieces.'[31] Inside

---

29 Longmore, 2007, p. 7; Borsay, 1989, *passim*.
30 Stobart, 2002, p. 473.
31 *WLA*, 16 March 1759.

would be everything that might be expected in a similar London house, heavy window curtains, fine linen and tableware, jewellery, paintings, engravings and other works of art, lots of mirrors, wallpaper as in the advertisement or walls plastered and painted, and a fine display of two very fashionable materials, mahogany from Jamaica and Honduras, and marble from Italy, both of which were imported by the Earle brothers among others.

Gardens were an important aspect of the more substantial houses and these fairly small town gardens might be supplied by seedsmen such as John Slater, who advertised that he had in stock 'flower roots, greenhouse plants, a good assortment of dwarf fruit–trees for walls or espaliers; as peaches, nectars, apricots …' There were also some public gardens, the best known being Ranelagh Gardens, opened in 1759, in direct imitation of the well-known pleasure gardens of the same name in London. These were very attractive, with scented flowerbeds, fishponds, paths for strolling and little alcoves or bowers for dalliance. Refreshments and drinks were available as visitors listened to a band playing in a Chinese temple in the centre, while on gala nights there would be fireworks and other extravaganzas. But, after only 20 years, the onwards march of building required the gardens to be broken up, to the great sorrow of contemporaries.[32]

Public walks were another attractive feature of the urban renaissance. These were created in Liverpool by the council, who laid out the walks and employed someone to maintain them at public expense. These walks are mentioned favourably by practically every visitor to the town, especially the two Ladies' Walks at the southern and northern ends of the town, which had gravelled walks lined with Lombardy poplars with seats underneath. The walk at the south end was 400 yards long and had a very fine view across the town and the river and beyond: 'on the left arise the distant mountains of Flintshire … on the right flows the Irish Sea, while, in front, the luxurious fields of Cheshire, skirted by the curving Mersey, relieve the eye.' One old man, recalling his youth 80 years or so before, remembered these walks with great affection and was very sad that they had been overtaken by the building process. 'On fine evenings', he recalled, 'all the gay and fashionable world of Liverpool used to take the air.'[33]

32 *WLA*, 25 September 1761; Stonehouse, 1863, pp. 13–18.
33 Troughton, 1810, pp. 368–69; Stonehouse, 1863, p. 67.

While we are outside, we can consider the sports available for the men and women of late eighteenth-century Liverpool. There were four bowling greens and a court for real tennis, which the Gentlemen Tennis Players were informed was now ready for the new season on 26 March 1762. The Corporation kept a pack of hounds, 'commonly called the Town's hounds', which were paid for by subscription, 'for the diversion of the gentlemen of this town', and sale advertisements for hounds appear frequently in the paper, such as the 'couple of stout, strong, bonny hounds with musical mouths' which were put up for sale in October 1761. Shooting was also popular, hardly surprisingly when open farmland was so near at hand. In September 1787, it was reported that the local farmers were 'suffering greatly by the number of shooters trespassing on their land' and would in future bring prosecutions against transgressors.[34]

Horse racing meetings throughout Lancashire and Cheshire were often advertised, but the first meeting at Liverpool itself was in August 1774. The races were held at Crosby Marsh, 'a very fine turf' on the seaside a few miles out of town, and attracted huge crowds for the first few years, 40,000 in 1777 according to one account. Apart from the races themselves, 'the horses are in view every foot of the way', there were 'stands and theatrical booths which covered one side of the race ground with colours, streamers, and standards flying', while beyond them with views as far as Snowdon lay the open sea, 'covered with sails, sloops, wherries and boats, loaded with passengers.' But, strangely enough, this splendid event failed to attract the expected support in later years and the meetings were abandoned in 1786.[35]

Maybe the punters preferred something rather more violent. A 'main of cocks' was fought at the New Cockpit near the North Shore Coffee House during the Race Week in 1774 and cockfighting was the most frequently mentioned sport in the local paper. There were matches or mains between counties, Cheshire v. Lancashire, between towns, Warrington v. Liverpool, and between individuals. Really magnificent prizes might be offered to the winners. On 9 June 1758, a cockfight was advertised, 'a Welch main of 32 cocks', and the winners were to receive 'a pleasure boat ... very elegantly furnished and gilt, with an awning, sash windows and six pictures in the cabin.' Thirty years later,

---

34 *WLA*, 2 October 1761, 10 September 1787; Picton, 1886, pp. 129–30.
35 *WLA*, 5 July 1774; Baines, 1852, p. 445; Brooke, 1803, pp. 268–69.

one sees a new form of fighting making its first appearance in the north-west. 'The boxing furor has at length reached this part of the kingdom', announced the *Liverpool Advertiser* in 1788 with the report of a crowd of 300 to 400 spectators assembled at a fight across the river in Cheshire. A few years earlier there appeared in the *Manchester Journal* the first known reference to a cricket match in Lancashire. But there was as yet no mention of football in Liverpool and the only reference to the beautiful game in the local paper up to the 1780s was in a bizarre story reported in the issue of 24 February 1764. This related to the captain of a slave ship who kept a tame tiger on board and a negro boy, 'his playfellow and particular favourite', to look after it. But, alas, one morning the captain heard a noise and, 'looking out of his hammock, perceived the tyger playing a football with the negro's head.'[36]

One last activity, half indoors, half outdoors, should be mentioned as it appears to have been very popular. This was sea bathing or at least saltwater bathing, an activity which was given a boost by George III's enthusiastic bathing at Weymouth. Both Hoylake on the Wirral and Southport with its mile of beach to the north of the Mersey were being developed as sea bathing resorts in the 1790s. Seawater baths at Liverpool itself go back at least to the early 1760s, when a range of bathing activities at the north end of the town were advertised, hot and cold seawater baths and a *bagnio* or sweating room, i.e. a Turkish bath. These were maintained by the Corporation and are mentioned by most visitors. In 1794, the baths (suitably in Bath Street) could offer hot and cold seawater baths, separate public baths for ladies and gentlemen and six private baths for each sex, with doors that could be fastened on the inside. There was also access through a passage to the open river where bathing machines were available, 'far from being despicable', according to *The Stranger in Liverpool*, 'though the promiscuous bathing of the sexes … and the consequent public exposure will not, however, recommend them to persons of real or affected delicacy.'[37]

Indoor amusements followed the pattern established by many towns in southern England. The most important institution was the Assembly, which combined elegant entertainment with civic and neighbourly

36 *WLA*, 9 June 1758, 24 February 1764, 23 June 1788; *Manchester Journal*, 1 September 1781.

37 Marriner, 1982, pp. 73–75; *Stranger*, 1816, pp. 138–39; Brooke, 1803, pp. 409–10.

bonding, as everyone who was anyone was likely to attend. The assemblies, from 1754 to 1795, when it burned down, were held in the new Exchange or Town Hall, which had been built by John Wood the Elder, famous for his buildings in Bath. The assembly room was upstairs, a grand and finely illuminated space where people met for dancing and card playing once a fortnight from October to June. Samuel Derrick, who visited in 1760, assured his correspondent, the Earl of Cork, that you could find there 'some women elegantly accomplished, and perfectly well dressed.' Provision was made to bring the men up to the standard of their womenfolk. In February 1776, for instance, a Mr Vincent advertised his dancing school in Williamson Square, 'an evening school for those gentlemen who choose to practice for the Assemblies', and from time to time he gave a ball so that they could demonstrate their improved skills. William Moss reported that the assemblies were 'generally pretty well attended' and, on special occasions, there could be huge numbers present. When the new Exchange first opened in September 1754, 'there was a most magnificent ball at which no less than 242 ladies were present who made a most brilliant appearance,' and even this was exceeded at the Grand Corporation Ball on 16 April 1789. 'Eight hundred well dressed persons of both sexes, commodiously sat down to an elegant supper, *all* at *one* time, in *one* superb room, splendidly illuminated with 10,000 lights.'[38]

Liverpool was famous for its theatre, most of the players being engaged from the Theatre Royal in London while the theatres in the capital were shut for the summer. This made for a fairly short season, starting in the first week of June and playing three or four times a week, but it did mean that the standard was high and the Liverpool audience could see such famous actors as Mrs Siddons, who played Hamlet dressed in a black cloak, or her brother John Philip Kemble, who in 1789 played Romeo and Macbeth amongst other parts. The Liverpool stage also had its own darlings, such as Betsy Farren, who made her début at the age of 15 and was so beautiful that she caught the eye of the Earl of Derby and became his countess, and was painted by Sir Thomas Lawrence. Up till the early 1770s, the theatre was in Liverpool's own Drury Lane, where the critical Samuel Derrick 'saw several pieces really well done', but on 5 June 1772 a

---

38 Derrick, 1767, p. 12; *WLA*, 2 February 1776; Moss, 2007, p. 129; Longmore, 2006, p. 148; Lightbody, 2008, p. 94.

new theatre called the Theatre Royal was opened on the north side of Williamson Square, still more or less in the country at that date. The £6,000 needed to build this 'large and handsome building' was raised in shares of £200 each and all the money was subscribed in less than an hour after the list was opened.[39]

Music (very often with refreshments) accompanied virtually every event in eighteenth-century Liverpool, sometimes provided by the Town Music, who were maintained by the Corporation to play for such occasions as the Martinmas Annual Fair, when they perambulated the town and then retired to the Exchange, where one was 'elegantly entertained and dined as usual.' There were also concerts or performances of opera at the theatre or in such places as Ranelagh Gardens or in large rooms in inns or private houses, such as Mr Wrigley's Great Room or the Bucks Room where, in August 1762, the audience were privileged to hear the famous Italian singer Signor Tenducci. The public performance of good music was put on a more permanent basis with the opening in 1785 of the Music Hall in Bold Street. This had seating for 1,400 and was supported by 300 subscribers who paid two guineas each. Concerts were held every three weeks from February onwards and the arrangements were supervised by four stewards, one of whom in the late 1780s was Thomas Earle Jr, an active slave merchant but also a lover of music.[40]

There was no need to go to public places for amusement as Liverpool, like most other towns, had a strong tradition of entertainment of various kinds in private houses. Routs and balls were held by the wealthier inhabitants, while dining out in other people's homes or taking supper or tea or just visiting were a regular feature in the lives of those in polite society. In May 1787, Hannah Lightbody, aged 21 and soon to be married, confided to her diary the sort of hospitality which she hoped to provide in her own household:

> I should perhaps not keep what in Liverpool would be esteemed *an elegant table* [her italics] ... but tho' my style might have less shew I venture to hope it would not have less true taste than those which now pass for models in this gay town – hospitable plenty,

39 Broadbent, 1908; Ackroyd, 1996; Derrick, 1767, pp. 12–13.
40 Troughton, 1810, pp. 326–27; *WLA*, 12 November 1756, 2 August 1762, 12 January 1788.

neatness, simplicity, unaffected friendliness, rational conversation and tranquillity, I should ever be carefully solicitous to preserve.[41]

Gayness and elegance might well include good music in the house, as well as 'an elegant equipage', and there seems little doubt that the food and drink provided would be plentiful and impressive in its variety. 'The Liverpool merchants were hospitable, very friendly to strangers ... and their tables are plenteously furnished', wrote Samuel Derrick, 'they have plenty of the best and most luxurious foods at a cheap rate.' This was certainly true. Lancashire and Cheshire were famous for their excellent local food, while Liverpool as a great port could supply a vast range of foodstuffs and drink from America, the West Indies, France, Spain, Portugal and the Mediterranean, as well as such local delicacies as live fish from 'the fish-cisterns near the Dock gates.' Thomas Earle, John's second son, started his mercantile career in Livorno in Tuscany and was responsible for introducing the luxuries of Italy to his native town. There was no shortage of nice puddings either, as London confectioners set up shop in the Lancastrian port, selling sweets, cakes and 'ice creams, as soon as ice can be provided.'[42]

The people of Liverpool hungered for intellectual activity as well as copious quantities of food and drink. The Liverpool Library in Lord Street, 'a gentlemen's only library' supported by subscription, was founded in 1758 and in 1801 had 8,000 volumes, making it probably the largest subscription library in the country. There were also several private circulating libraries, often kept by women, such as Elizabeth Newman, whose library in Cleveland Square was listed in the Directory for 1777, or the perfume shop and circulating library kept by Margaret Burgess in Paradise Street listed in 1790. One also finds numerous references in the local paper to debating societies and discussion groups, as well as such institutions as the Society for the Protection and Encouragement of the Arts of Painting and Drawing in Liverpool, which was founded in 1769. This society also provided lessons in painting for those willing to pay for them.[43]

Judging by the advertisements in the *Liverpool Advertiser*, there was considerable demand in the town for the acquisition of new skills as well as general and practical schooling of various sorts. The local

41 Lightbody, 2008, 19 May 1787.
42 Derrick, 1767, p. 15; *WLA*, 2 July and 17 September 1787.
43 Flavell, 1985.

Free Grammar School, founded in 1610, was open to the children of all freemen and so became swamped as the town expanded, forcing the better off to educate their children elsewhere.[44] Two of the best-known schools in the country were nearby, Manchester Grammar School, where William Earle sent his sons, and Warrington Academy, most famous of the nonconformist academies which flourished in the eighteenth century. But entrepreneurs were quick to supply a suitable education for the better off in Liverpool itself. In 1773, the Rev. Mr Kitchen, late of Trinity College, Dublin, opened an academy near Clayton Square where young gentlemen could study 'living and dead languages, mathematics, philosophy, astronomy, geography, history etc. A guinea entrance and the same quarterly'. In the next year, the Rev. J. Shewell opened another academy in Temple Court: 'There will be an apartment for young ladies, so remote from that of the boys that there will be no possibility of any intercourse between them.'[45]

An emphasis on practical mercantile skills such as accounting can be seen in many advertisements, some of them offering evening tuition and clearly aimed at young men eager to improve themselves. James Whittle in Castle Street, for instance, was teaching in 1760 'at night as well as in the day ... writing, arithmetic, accounts, book-keeping etc.', while R. Shuttleworth in Williamson Square offered evening lessons in elocution.[46] There were also many advertisements for schools for girls but, sadly, none of these offered any more that reading, writing and needlework. Boys and girls together were offered tuition in painting and especially in learning to play various musical instruments, such as harpsichords, spinets, flutes, violins and cellos.

As can be seen, the local newspaper is a valuable source for understanding what was on offer in the town, but it has its limitations as it provides no information on who enjoyed such activities and how often. Unfortunately, Liverpool is not very well supplied with surviving diaries and domestic correspondence which might have helped to throw some light on such questions. There is, however, one diary which is very valuable in this respect. This was kept by Hannah Lightbody from the end of 1786, when she returned to Liverpool aged 20 after schooling in Stoke Newington in London. Hannah was a very religious

44 Touzeau, 1910, pp. 587, 631.
45 *WLA*, 28 May 1773, 1 April 1774.
46 *WLA*, 1 February 1760, 1 January 1762.

nonconformist, earnest, thoughtful and very well educated, but she had a lighter side which is well reflected in her diary. Her father, who died in 1778, had been a linen merchant and the family were fairly prosperous, renting a house in Dale Street and later moving to the smarter area of Bold Street, and they also had a country retreat at Wavertree, at that time a small village east of Toxteth Park. Despite her religion and a passionate interest in emancipation, Hannah and her family had strong ties with many of the Anglican slave-trading élite, including the Earle family, whom they visited on several occasions during the years of the diary, to dine, take tea, or simply to spend 'an agreeable half hour with Mrs Earle'.[47] It seems probable that the Earles also helped Hannah's widowed mother with financial advice. They certainly provided such services for her kinswoman Ann Hulton, who lived in Boston.[48]

Hannah was not always in Liverpool, visiting London, Manchester and the Lake District, amongst other places during the diary period, but when she was at home there was a clear pattern to her amusements. She was a very keen walker, especially when staying at Wavertree, from where she walked in Toxteth Park, in and around Otterspool ('a charming day and very happy, rambled about Otterspool, walked 13 miles') and best of all in Knott's Hole and the Dingle on the Mersey shore west of Otterspool, a picturesque bay much loved of painters. 'Went to [Toxteth] Park and walked in the Dingle, my favourite scene', she wrote on 25 March 1788: 'I sat on my beloved rocks.' Hannah also enjoyed walking in Liverpool itself, going up and down to look at the new buildings and those in the process of being built, though her favourite walk in town seems to have been the Parade, another name for the southern Ladies' Walk: 'Walked on the Parade which always elevates my spirits', she wrote, a nice tribute to the Corporation which had created it.[49]

Hannah was fond of the theatre, going three or four times a year during the Liverpool season and visiting theatres in London and Manchester when she was out of town. Theatre performances normally consisted of a play, often by Shakespeare or more recent dramatists such as Vanbrugh or Sheridan, followed by a farce and quite often incorporating dances, singing and other amusements. On Friday 22 August

47 Lightbody, 2008, 3 January 1787.
48 Lightbody, 2008, pp. 11–15; Hulton, 1927, pp. 53, 67, 80.
49 Lightbody, 2008, 22 May and 25 March 1788, 17 February 1787.

1788, for instance, Hannah saw Vanbrugh's play *The Provok'd Husband*, followed by a pantomime version of Robinson Crusoe 'with the original savage dance' and, after this, the audience were privileged to see Mr Banks, dressed as Mercury, 'take a flight (on a wire) from the lobby of the upper boxes to the further end of the stage, and go through a superb firework as he descended.' This description comes in fact from the *Liverpool Advertiser* of 18 August 1788. Hannah was generally a very laconic diarist and all she has to say about this remarkable series of spectacles was 'went to the play'. She did occasionally say that she 'was much pleased' with this or that actor's performance, but her most fulsome praise was reserved for Drury Lane in London, where on 15 December 1787 she saw Kemble and Mrs Siddons, 'the best acting I had ever seen.'

Hannah also enjoyed going to the concerts at the Music Hall, her greatest praise coming on 10 July 1787 when she was delighted to hear Miss Harwood singing 'Sweet Bird', accompanied by Charles Nicholson the Elder, the celebrated Liverpool flautist. These concert evenings were very social occasions, an opportunity to meet people, perhaps at supper during the interval, though it seems that conversation was not stopped by the music. On one occasion, Hannah had to admit to her diary that she had 'talked more than listened.'[50] Even more of a social occasion were the Assemblies, which Hannah attended on several occasions, in Liverpool itself but also elsewhere when she was out of town. She was keen on playing cards, mainly quadrille and picquet, but her main entertainment at Assemblies, apart from seeing people and being seen, was dancing. She often names her dancing partners and occasionally comments on the occasion, 'a very pleasant evening', 'very happy' or, in February 1788, 'danced an uncomfortable minuet.' She also went to balls in private houses, in April 1788 at 'Mr Kent's ball – very pleasant', for instance, and on 3 January 1789, her family reciprocated and 'had a pleasant little dance at home.' If this all sounds rather like Jane Austen, that should not be too surprising as Austen began to write her novels just a few years after Hannah wrote her diary.

Much of Hannah's time was taken up with chapel and serious religious discussion, but she still found plenty of opportunities to engage in the more social and trivial amusements mentioned above, as well as dining with relatives and friends (three evenings in a row in May 1787), going to art exhibitions in private houses, meetings of the debating

50 Lightbody, 2008, 22 February 1788.

society called the Octonian Club, music lessons, horse riding and such occasional amusements as 'the optical deceptions'. She also reports more gloomy occasions, such as the death at an advanced age in February 1788 of Joseph Brooks, a merchant and former business partner of Ralph Earle, 'passing bell very dismal'. Hannah, like others in Liverpool, was also much affected by the arrangements for the execution of Patrick Bourne and John Silvester Dowling, who were hung in front of the town gaol on 15 February 1788 before 20,000 spectators. They had been convicted at Lancaster but because the crime (a burglary) had been committed in Liverpool, 'the judges, thinking that the sight of a public execution might deter others, sent the prisoners to be hung at Liverpool'. This was the first execution in the town since 1715 and Hannah was duly affected when she 'went to view the scaffold' on the Saturday before the execution and she was 'much imprest' on the following day, when the convicts were prayed for in all the churches.[51] On a more joyful note, Hannah was happy to join in the celebrations on 26 March 1789 on the occasion of King George's sudden recovery from madness. The town was brilliantly illuminated and Hannah 'walked about till 12 o'clock in great admiration.'[52]

One's general impression, from Hannah Lightbody's diary, the local paper and the reminiscences and local histories which have been used in compiling this chapter, is that Liverpool in the late eighteenth century was an attractive place to live despite the close attention to business of its leading citizens, not to mention the nature of their most notorious trade. Such pleasantness was not to last long as further growth swamped the town and many of the town's amenities were lost to the demands of the builders but, in 1792, it is just possible to accept the eulogy of the town which Thomas Erskine, later Lord Chancellor, attributed to Liverpool's Member of Parliament, Bamber Gascoyne. 'All you see spread out beneath you', he declaimed from the eminence of a hill overlooking Liverpool:

> that immense city which stands like another Venice upon the waters, which is intersected by those numerous docks, which glitters with those cheerful habitations of well protected men, which is the busy seat of trade and the gay scene of elegant amusements growing

51 Lightbody, 2008, 30 March 1788; Baines, 1852, p. 483.
52 Lightbody, 2008, 26 March 1789. There were more celebrations in April, see Baines, 1852, p. 483; Brooke, 1803, pp. 278–82.

out of its prosperity ... where there are riches overflowing and everything which can delight a man who wishes to see the prosperity of a great community and a great Empire; all this has been created by the industry and well-disciplined management of a handful of men in a corner of this island since you were a boy.[53]

We will now examine in the next few chapters the activities of just three of this handful, the brothers Ralph, Thomas and William Earle, starting with William, who though the youngest, is the best documented of this energetic threesome.

53 Quoted by Stewart Brown, 1932, preface, p. v.

CHAPTER THREE

Slave Ship Captain

'The agreeable thoughts I have of some time spending my time with you, retired from this over busy noisey trade I am now in, raises my spirits beyond what you can imagine.'[1]

William Earle was 30 years old when he wrote this letter to the lady who two years later would become his wife. He was captain of the slave ship *Chesterfield* and had arrived in Old Calabar in the Bight of Biafra on 23 July 1751 after a two-month voyage from the Mersey. Like all ships' captains, he never missed a chance to send letters home and he was now taking advantage of the imminent departure of another Liverpool slave ship, the *Neptune*, to write home to the owners of his ship and his girlfriend, glad to be able to report that he enjoyed 'a perfect state of good health, thank God' and that his slaving activities were going well, having 'got more slaves than [I] did expect in the time.' This was William's last voyage as a slave ship captain, though he was to be busily involved in the Liverpool slave trade as part-owner, investor, administrator and supplier of trade goods until his death in 1788.

The historian of Liverpool shipping is fortunate in that two, really excellent, computerised datasets containing valuable information on the port's shipping have been created by dedicated researchers. The first of these is called 'Liverpool Trade and Shipping, 1744–1786', based on the port's ship registration books [Plantation Registers] and contains all known overseas voyages of Liverpool registered ships between those dates.[2] The information in the registers has been supplemented by relevant

1 Capt. William Earle to Mrs Ann Winstanley, Old Calabar, 30 August 1751. MMM D/EARLE/3/1.
2 UK Data Archive, University of Essex, #2923, compiled by D. Richardson, K. Beedham and M.M. Schofield, henceforth LTS.

sources in the National Archives and by material from the surviving newspapers of Liverpool and Manchester and the general shipping paper, *Lloyds List*. The data includes, where known, the ship's place and date of construction, dimensions and armament, owners, masters, crew numbers, voyages and subsequent fate. The second database is the 'Trans-Atlantic Slave Trade Database', published by Emory University in 2009. This amazing compilation is the culmination of many decades of independent and collaborative research in several countries and contains information on almost 35,000 slaving voyages between Africa and the Americas.[3] The data included are similar to those in the Liverpool database, with the very important addition of the number of slaves embarked and disembarked, the latter always lower as a result of the appallingly high mortality rates in the trade.

These two datasets enable us to outline William Earle's career as a ship's captain, which comprised five voyages in three different ships between 1747 and 1752. His first command was the *Lucy*, a 60-ton snow, a two-masted vessel similar to a brig. William was 26 years old when he took command in March 1747 for a non-slaving voyage from Liverpool to Jamaica and back to Liverpool, where he arrived in December, presumably with a cargo of sugar, indigo and the other products for which Jamaica was famous. Five or six months later, William set sail in the *Lucy* again, this time on a slaving voyage to an unknown destination in West Africa and then to St Kitts with a cargo of 240 slaves, of whom 197 survived the Middle Passage, the other 43 being 'buried', to use the slavers' euphemism, in other words found dead and thrown into the sea. William then sailed home to Liverpool where he arrived on 15 August 1749. He had no time to enjoy the pleasures of home for, just a week later, on 22 August, he set sail again in command of the 54-ton brig *Orrell*, for a voyage via Cork to Gibraltar and the Mediterranean, from where he no doubt brought back a cargo of wine, brandy, fruits and other specialities of the region to enhance the Christmas festivities in his home port. Whether this voyage took him to Leghorn, the Tuscan port where his older brother Thomas was beginning his own career as a merchant, is unknown, but William, like all the Earles, was later to show an interest in the Mediterranean which may well have been stimulated by this first visit.

3 Compiled under the direction of Stephen D. Behrendt, David Eltis and David Richardson, and accessible at www.slavevoyages.org. Henceforth TSTD.

William, then, engaged in general trading activities as well as one slaving voyage in his first three commands as a ship's master. This is worth noting, for the epithets 'slave merchant' or 'slave captain' can be a little misleading in respect to these Liverpool sea captains who were certainly efficient at trading for slaves and shipping them across the Atlantic, but usually had many other strings to their bows. Still, it was certainly as a slave ship captain that William finished off his career at sea. After spending the winter of 1749/50 at home, he set sail in March 1750 in a much larger ship called the *Chesterfield* owned by a syndicate which included most of the same merchants who owned the *Orrell*, most important of whom were William Whaley and William Davenport, both very prominent in the Liverpool slave trade and pioneers in the development of Old Calabar as a slaving station. William commanded the *Chesterfield* for two voyages, first to Africa and then St Kitts in 1750–51 and then, in his last voyage, to Old Calabar and Barbados in 1751–52. Command of the ship was then transferred to captain Patrick Black, who was to play an important part in William's career, and William himself set up as a merchant, activities which will be considered in the next chapter. William's career as a ship's captain was thus fairly short, some captains commanding ships sailing the slavers' triangle did the journey eight, nine and even ten times in their careers, a remarkable longevity given the very high mortality encountered by European sailors in African waters. But William's five voyages were certainly sufficient to ensure that he was familiar with the ways and potential of different ships, the routes sailed by Liverpool ships and, above all, the marketing problems to be encountered in those days without telegraphic or electronic communication. Later, as a merchant based at home in Liverpool, he had no problem understanding the difficulties faced by his captains as he had faced them all himself.

It seems unlikely that William was given a command in 1747 without having had several years of training and maritime experience. Nothing has been discovered of his apprenticeship, but one can assume that for maybe eight or ten years before this date William was learning his many varied trades. John Copeland, a slave ship captain who was to become William Earle's brother-in-law, was once asked by a merchant from the Isle of Man whether he could find a berth for his nephew who had 'an inclination to go to sea for three years.' Copeland thought that this was nowhere near long enough. 'He will find himself very deficient in his business at the expiration of that time.'[4] To be a ship's captain, a man needed to be able to sail a ship, to navigate and find his way about the ocean and, of course, he needed to be able to command and control his crew. This was never an easy task, but was particularly hard on slave ships, which provided employment for crews of varying sizes but usually around 30 or 35 men on the way out and much less on the way home, when there were no slaves to guard. Conditions for sailors on slave ships were worse than on any other sort of ship and discipline was accordingly difficult to enforce, the irons, the lash or the cane being employed more often than on any other sort of merchant ship except East Indiamen. Ships' captains also had to have many mercantile skills, since advice and instructions from owners and shippers were often several weeks or even months out of date, given the slowness of communications. Trading in West Africa was particularly difficult as the local African dealers who sold slaves to the ships' captains had a completely different value system to that current in Europe, so that some things seemed incredibly cheap and some very expensive to the newcomer. And finally, ships' captains had to have some diplomatic skills as they strove to deal with the often crass behaviour of the authorities in the various lands they visited.

Just two documents relating to William Earle's career as a slave ship captain have survived, the letter he wrote to Anne Winstanley from Old Calabar quoted above and the letter of instructions which he received from the owners of the *Chesterfield*. These instructions related to William's second voyage in the *Chesterfield* and are similar to other such instructions which have ended up in the archives. The letter starts by ordering him to sail to Douglas in the Isle of Man and there to load 'sundry goods as per list enclosed.' This list is unfortunately no longer enclosed, but stopping off at the 'Island' as they called it was a very common practice for Liverpool slavers. This semi-autonomous island in the Irish Sea played an important part in the slaving business of Liverpool, supplying far more than its fair share of captains, crews and ships for the trade and serving as a sort of offshore warehouse where captains could complete their cargoes. Goods shipped from Douglas tended to be those which would attract high duties on the mainland, such as brandy, or that were actually

4 Manx National Heritage Library, MS 09591, John Copeland to John Taubman, 29 June 1785.

illegal for an English ship to carry, such as French goods shipped in wartime.[5]

Liverpool slave ship cargoes were also often completed in various ports of Holland where suitable goods drawn from the East Indies, Germany, the Baltic and elsewhere were often much cheaper than in England or where the benefits of neutrality could conceal trading in goods in demand in Africa which had arrived in Holland from England's enemies. There is no evidence that William went to Holland in the *Chesterfield*, but the one slave ship whose logbook survives in the Earle Collection of documents, the *Unity*, shows that this ship certainly did. Captained by Robert Norris, the *Unity* set sail in July 1769 from Liverpool for Whydah (Ouidah), a very important source of slaves on the coast of modern Benin, and from there to Jamaica. She called in at Hellevoetsluis near Rotterdam, where they took in 'our cargo of cowries, iron etc, shipped five seamen, and lost Henry Moore who was drowned and Arthur Denley run away.'[6]

William Earle in the *Chesterfield* was ordered to proceed direct from the Isle of Man to Old Calabar, a slaving port some 60 miles up the Cross River in south-eastern Nigeria, where he was 'to barter our cargoe as per invoice annexed for slaves and elephants' teeth.' This invoice has not survived, but most cargoes sent out to West Africa were similar in general terms, though every slaving centre on the West African coast from the Gambia to the Congo required trade goods in different combinations and the local slave traders were very specific about the details of the goods they were prepared to accept as barter for slaves. Only 'Angola' guns could be shipped to Angola, every slave-trading community had different ideas of the correct colour and pattern of beads, some liked strong and some weak brandy, and so on. Nevertheless, the range of goods from which the particular combinations were made up was fairly consistent: iron and copper bars, rods and personal adornments such as bracelets and anklets, knives, guns and gunpowder, brandy, rum and gin, tobacco and pipes, brass

5   William's instructions are in D/EARLE/1/1. For another good, more detailed example, see Williams, 2004, pp. 486–88, instructions for Ambrose Lace, captain of *Marquis of Granby*, 14 April 1766. For Manx slave traders see Wilkins, 1999.

6   D/EARLE/1/1 – henceforth *Unity* log – 7 August 1769. Cowries were a type of shell which came mainly from the Maldive Islands and were in great demand in some parts of West Africa.

and copper pans and kettles, East Indian and Manchester textiles of various sorts, old sheets from Amsterdam, cheap linens from Silesia and huge numbers of beads of various sorts and cowries. African slave traders in the Cameroons wanted mainly beads, those in Angola mainly East Indian textiles, but they were all prepared to quote various combinations of these goods as the price of a man, woman or child shipped on board the European vessels. One could not learn how to do business in Africa in a few days, but there is no doubt that William Earle learned it very thoroughly during his apprenticeship and then during his three voyages as slave ship captain. The range of his knowledge of such matters as shown in his letter-book, written ten years later as a merchant in Liverpool, is pretty impressive, even if it was employed in such a brutal business.

Not many vessels were built specifically as slave ships, most of them being fast merchant ships which could be employed to carry slaves (often a remarkable number for their size) or other cargo as circumstances dictated. It was usually necessary then to convert the ship for a slave voyage and this would be done in the last week or so before they arrived in Africa or even after arrival as they made their way slowly along the coast. The carpenter, assisted by the crew, would prepare the slave rooms below deck, making bulkheads and gratings, and raising a platform to divide the slave quarters in two horizontally, thus enabling more slaves to be packed in. Separate 'rooms' would be built for men, women and child slaves – the women and children normally being freer to move about the ship than the men.

Preparations were also made against the dangers of attack, both from the slaves and from the free Africans ashore, who had a disconcerting habit of 'cutting off' weakly defended slave ships, murdering the crew, looting the cargo and often carrying off the slaves to sell once again to another ship. The gunner would get more guns up out of the hold, mount them and check their effectiveness. The carpenter would make the roundhouse in the stern into a potential stronghold and build a 'barricada', a strong partition ten feet high, running across the ship near the mainmast, behind which the crew could mass to deal with the common enough event of a slave uprising. And, finally, some effort would be made to make the ship more comfortable for both crew and slaves. Ships often spent several months on the African coast or up rivers accumulating their cargo and those aboard would be given some protection from the terrible African sun with awnings or a temporary house built on deck, while windsails and gratings would help to bring some air into the almost unbearable atmosphere of the slave rooms.[7]

Captain William Earle in the *Chesterfield* sailed into the Cross River and anchored at Old Calabar on 23 July 1751 after a passage of exactly two months. Most of the slaving stations in West Africa had no proper port, which meant that ships had to anchor out at sea and do all their business ashore in canoes manned by local boatmen. Old Calabar, however, had one of the best anchorages in West Africa, 60 miles up a river which was navigable by canoes far into the interior. Here the slave ships remained for the several months they spent slowly acquiring their human cargo. Old Calabar had only fairly recently become a major centre of the slave trade, but it had been developed rapidly since the 1740s, mainly by ships from Liverpool, and in William's time as a captain accounted for over a third of all Liverpool voyages to West Africa.

Later in the century, Old Calabar was replaced as the principal slave port in the Bight of Biafra by Bonny, about 100 miles further west, near modern Port Harcourt. Bonny was an unpleasant place, a 'horrid hole' in the midst of mangrove swamps, very hot, humid and infested with mosquitos, but it had the fastest turnaround of any slaving port visited by Liverpool ships, rising from just over three to five slaves loaded a day in the course of the second half of the eighteenth century, about twice the rate of Old Calabar. Such comparative speed obviously reduced costs and also reduced mortality of both slaves and crew. Slavers who specialised in trading to these two places and also New Calabar were referred to by William Earle and presumably by other slavers as 'Bite Men' (from Bight of Biafra) and were responsible for shipping almost 900,000 slaves to America from the 1740s to 1807, when the British slave trade was abolished. William was later to praise one of his captains, William Hindle, a former apprentice, who was 'so valuable a man as I have experienced him to be, for his knowledge in the Bite trade I put him in competition with any man

---

7   Here and elsewhere in this chapter, use has been made of surviving logbooks of slavers from Liverpool for the period when William Earle was a slave captain. The main ones used have been Martin and Spurrell, 1962 for Capt. John Newton's three slaving voyages in the *Duke of Argyle* (1750–51) and the *African* (1752–53 and 1753–54); HCA 15/55, log of *Blakeney*, Capt. Thomas Eaton, 1762–63; MMM, D/EARLE/1/4, log of *Unity*, Capt. Robert Norris, 1769–71 and HCA 16/59/18a, log of *Glory*, Capt. Robert Williams, 1770–71.

whatever.'[8] William Earle would have considered himself in the same class, these Bite Men being very well trained in local ways and just about the most efficient slave traders in the very efficient slave-trading port of Liverpool.[9]

All these Bight of Biafra ports engaged in what was known as ship trade, that is trade directly from the ships, rather than the castle trade employed elsewhere, in which the slave ships acquired their cargo from European and African middlemen who bought and deposited slaves in forts and castles, as was the custom for instance in Anomabu in the Gold Coast and Whydah in Benin. The captains and senior officers of slave ships in the Bight of Biafra had to be able to communicate and trade directly with the locals and over time they built up an interesting symbiotic relationship with members of the powerful African trading families who provided the political and commercial leadership in the region. Both parties, white and black, made efforts to accommodate themselves to their partners in trade. Many members of the African trading families could speak and sometimes read and write English and some sent their sons to school in Liverpool to learn the language and English ways. A witness in 1787 reported that 'about 50 mulatto and negro children, natives of Africa, are in this Town [i.e. Liverpool] and its vicinity, who have been sent there by their parents to receive the advantage of an European education', some of them put up in the homes of Liverpool slave merchants.[10]

The English traders, in turn, spent long enough in Africa during every slaving voyage to learn the customs of their African counterparts and to master the 'pidgin' or creole language which had been adopted for mutual convenience, as we can tell from a letter written in 1761 by William Earle to 'Duke Abashy', an Old Calabar worthy, two of whose sons had been abducted and sold as slaves by one of William's captains. William was embarrassed by this incident and was intent on displaying his loyalty to his African trading partners. 'You know very well I love all Calabar', he wrote, coupling this with greetings from his children and wife and an implied apology for not coming to Calabar in person

---

8 MMM D/EARLE/2/2, letter book of William Earle, 1760–61, henceforth WELB, 10 October 1760.

9 For Bonny see Lovejoy and Richardson, 2004; for an excellent contemporary description see Falconbridge, 1788.

10 Lovejoy and Richardson, 2001, p. 96.

as he had done when an active captain. 'My wife is well and sends you her Love & tho' I do not come to Calabar, I send ship there … give my service to [a long list of local worthies] and everybody you know that knows me and I remains Duke Abashys friend, Wm Earle.'[11]

Such 'love' was reinforced by the exchange of presents, such as the 'eight ruffled shirts made by his own daughter and marked with the African's name' sent by the merchant Robert Bostock to one of his trading partners. Brass basins and other goods might be personalised by having the African trader's name engraved on them when they were given as presents and the local traders reciprocated by sending slave children and ivory tusks to the Liverpool merchants and captains.[12] Dinner parties, hunting and fishing trips, and other entertainments were also shared by black and white, the Englishmen keen to flatter and impress their African counterparts, while the Africans paid the English the compliment of imitation, wearing European clothes to dinner parties aboard the slave ships, serving up European food and showing off such places as the two-storey Liverpool Hall, built with English bricks and 'fitted up in the English taste.'[13] Some of this friendship and bonhomie might have been genuine, though one suspects that most of it was just necessary lubrication to ensure commerce could be carried on effectively. The English might accept that these African traders were free men who should not be enslaved, but most of the merchants and captains were still racists who held all Africans, free or slave, in contempt. In order to be able to cope with the concept of slavery, Europeans sometimes 'reified' slaves, that is they treated them as a 'res' or thing, just another piece of the cargo. More often, they were in fact seen as animals rather than things, to be treated well enough so that not too many died, but still 'black cattle', to use one of many epithets. And as for the African slave traders, the free men or the 'Calabars' as William Earle called them, these were given what respect was necessary to do business, but were still regarded as lesser people, almost children, whose behaviour might be described as 'very sawsey', noisy, childishly argumentative and insolent, all expressions used by William Earle in his letter to Anne Winstanley.

11 WELB – the letter, 16 February 1761, is in Lovejoy and Richardson, 2001, p. 99.
12 Schwarz, 1995, p. 26; Radburn, 2009, p. 67.
13 Butterworth, 1822, p. 28.

Final proof of the indifference felt by English traders to the 'free' men with whom they did business can be seen in an appalling incident of 1767. A dispute between the Africans of Old Town and New Town, the two main settlements of Old Calabar, had led to much 'palaver' and a virtual stop to trade. This was resolved in the most brutal way by the crews of the six English ships in the river at the time, whose captains decided that the inhabitants of Old Town were most at fault. These Old Town men were invited aboard the ships with a proposal to mediate in the dispute and then, in what was seen as a terrible violation of hospitality even in Africa, were slaughtered or taken as slaves. Those who managed to get away from the English ships were killed by the eager New Town men waiting for them in their canoes. Most writers give a figure of 300 Old Town men either killed or carried away as slaves in this incident. Gomer Williams, the late nineteenth-century historian of the Liverpool slave trade, was not sure whether to applaud this method of bringing about an abrupt cessation of the interruption to the Old Calabar slave trade: 'The action of the captains has never been defended; but we must not forget that they were dealing with a shifty, greedy, and treacherous lot of rascals, who made a practice of selling their own countrymen into slavery.' No doubt the captains would have agreed with him.[14]

In more normal times, a lengthy courtship ritual would take place before trade began. Gifts, such as lengths of cloth, brandy and handkerchiefs, would be exchanged. The black 'gentlemen of the towns' would then entertain the white 'gentlemen of the river' and this would be reciprocated, often several times, with the utmost civility. A form of tribute known as 'comey' was paid and then at last negotiations could begin in earnest. These could be lengthy, but would eventually involve a promise by the Africans to deliver so many slaves at such and such a date for such and such a combination of goods and, once the terms of the deal had been settled, these goods would be unloaded and handed over to the African slave traders. Needless to say, there was little real trust between the parties and, in the absence of a strong central authority that could enforce repayment (as there was for instance at Whydah and Bonny), the credit was secured by placing human pawns or pledges aboard the English ships as security for the later delivery of the promised slaves.[15]

14 Williams, 2004, pp. 536–38.
15 On pawnship see Lovejoy and Richardson, 1999.

These pawns were often close relatives of the traders and, generally, these arrangements worked well enough, though there were inevitably many instances of dishonest captains shipping the freemen pawns as slaves, especially 'if their friends refuse or are not able to redeem them.' Pawnship was quite a common trading practice in West Africa, and not just for dealing in slaves, just one more local custom which the fledgling slave captain or merchant had to learn. The *Blakeney*, for instance, was trading for slaves on the coast of Sierra Leone in 1763, an area where many of the slaves were acquired by 'boat trade', whereby crew members went ashore in the ship's boats or in canoes hired or bought for the purpose and bargained for the slaves on land, a dangerous business since boats often overturned in the surf, small parties of white men ashore were vulnerable to attack and their very absence made security on the ship anchored out at sea more precarious. The ship's logbook frequently reports the arrival on board of pledges. 'Came off a canoe, trusted goods for five prime slaves, two freemen being left on board in pledge'; 'this day Mr Tucker's canoe brought off a freeman to be kept until he be redeemed.' It was not just the English who received pledges. Natives who had obligingly hauled ashore one of the ship's small boats after it had filled with water and sunk, refused to let the boatswain go 'untill they are paid for their trouble' and it was common practice for both parties to take hostages in the event of disputes.[16]

Acquiring slave cargoes in ones and twos and threes was very common, the main reason for the very long time that slavers spent on the unhealthy coasts, putting their own lives and those of the slaves already on board at risk. The *Blakeney*'s logbook, for example, reports the arrival on board of 133 slaves in 53 separate consignments between 1 January and 7 June 1763. Such small lots were also common at Old Calabar, but both here and even more so at Bonny much larger numbers were often delivered together. Both slaving centres benefited from access to extensive networks of navigable rivers which enabled them to trade long distances by water. Some of the slaves brought back to the coast were bought from fairs in the interior, but many were kidnapped from the region through which the black slavers travelled in huge canoes, some of them 80 feet long and carrying up to 120 people, including slave 'canoe boys' who provided the motive power, soldiers and traders. These fleets of canoes must have been truly frightening for those

16 HCA 15/55, 6, 20 January, 22 February 1763.

who watched their progress up river, only too aware of their purpose. Alexander Falconbridge, who wrote an excellent book in 1788 called *An Account of the Slave Trade on the Coast of Africa*, captured the terror and the magnificence of these expeditions:

> The preparations made at Bonny by the black traders, upon setting out for the fairs ... are very considerable. From 20 to 30 canoes, capable of containing 30 or 40 negroes each, are assembled for the purpose; and ... when their loading is completed, they commence their voyage, with colours flying and musick playing; in about ten or eleven days, they generally return to Bonny with full cargoes [of slaves].[17]

There has been much speculation about just who the slaves were who ended up on European ships to be carried off to the West Indies and America. Some were certainly unfortunates who had been sold into slavery to redeem a debt; others had been enslaved for some petty crime, for the profits to be made from the trade encouraged rulers to adopt slavery as the punishment for virtually everything, 'every trifling crime punished in the same manner.' Alexander Falconbridge thought that most of the enslaved blacks at Bonny and Calabar had been kidnapped by the armed men in the canoe crews and he was inclined to play down the importance of warfare as a source of slaves, since he had never seen 'negroes with recent wounds.'[18] This may have been true of the Bight of Biafra, the area he knew best, but elsewhere war was certainly important. Dahomey, which supplied the slaves shipped out of Whydah, 5,000 or 6,000 a year according to Captain Robert Norris, was a state organised to generate slaves, and hence income, by its terrifying king, the 'absolute master of the life, liberty and property of every person in his dominions.' His great army used to set out each year to expand the territory he ruled and to take captives to be sold to the Europeans in exchange for weapons. The Moslem warriors of the Fulani tribe in present-day northern Nigeria combined profit with the service of Allah in their practice of raiding their infidel neighbours, a policy of *jihad* which ensured a stream of slaves to be sold to Europeans. Further west, European slave merchants in the Gambia bought their cargoes mainly from the Mandingoes who marched their prisoners of war to the coast,

17 Falconbridge, 1788, p. 16.
18 Donnan, 1930–33, ii, p. 396; Falconbridge, 1788, pp. 16–20.

'tied by the neck with leather thongs ... with a bundle of corn or an elephant's tooth upon each of their heads.'[19]

This mention of elephants' teeth reminds us that slaves were not the only cargo shipped by Englishmen from West Africa. Gold dust, Guinea wood used in dyeing and the palm oil, which would later dominate the trade of the region, were all of some significance. But elephants' teeth or ivory was the most important, as can be seen from William Earle's instructions for his last voyage in the *Chesterfield.* This is only a short document, but the importance of shipping ivory is stressed three times. Other captains' instructions have the same emphasis and there are many references to the import of ivory in the Liverpool newspapers and customs records, so it is surprising in these green and eco-conscious times that more has not been written on the slaughter of elephants and the trade in their tusks which European demand for ivory brought about. We have not yet reached the great period of demand for ivory for piano keys in the nineteenth century, but there was already a wide range of products which benefited from the beauty, resilience and ease of working ivory, such as crucifixes, combs, cutlery handles, chess pieces and billiard balls, to name a few. All these end uses depended on the importation of ivory from Africa, which was much better for working than the tusks of Indian elephants, so much so that some of this African ivory was exported by the East India Company to Asia to be worked by Indian and Chinese artisans. Most of this ivory was carried from Africa in slave ships and so to the West Indies and then, eventually, to England, mainly of course to Liverpool as the most important slaving port. *Williamson's Liverpool Advertiser* reports the import into Liverpool of just under 25,000 teeth in the years 1773–76, the product of over 3,000 elephants a year. This hardly compares with the number of slaves imported in these years, but nevertheless it does seem too large a number of elephants to be ignored completely.[20]

In some slaving centres, ships' officers and crew members spent much time ashore, trading for slaves, as in Sierra Leone and other areas of 'boat trade', or paying respects or seeking assistance from local men of power. Captain Robert Norris, whose logbook for a voyage to Whydah is in the Earle Collection, spent three months in 1770 on a journey up

19 Norris, 1789, p. 157; Johnson, 1976, p. 28; Donnan, 1930–33, ii, pp. 393–96.
20 On the ivory trade see Feinberg and Johnson, 1982; Walker, 2009; Chalklin, 2010.

country to Abomey, the capital of Dahomey, 'to wait upon the King who sent for me in consequence of having my factory burned at Whydah.' This was a luxurious journey for a sailor, carried by the hammock men who 'jig on at their usual rate of about five miles per hour, relieving each other occasionally.' Norris carried with him 'a very handsome sedan chair and a chamber organ' as presents for the terrifying king who lived surrounded by the skulls of his enemies, but appeared civilised enough as he thanked the captain and asked after the health of his 'brother', King George of England.[21]

There were no such trips for William Earle and his men, who were largely confined to their ship with the occasional visit ashore for a meal or a fishing trip with the 'Gentlemen of the Town'. Old Calabar lay on the banks of a broad river and was backed by dense jungle. The explorer and journalist H.M. Stanley was there in 1884 and it is doubtful if its appearance had changed very much since the days of the slave trade. 'What struck me', he wrote, 'was its miniature reproduction of the Upper Congo … There were the same palms … the same density of forest, the same sweetly green verdure, the same rich reddish loam, the same kind of clearings, and the same architecture of huts.' Spending so long in such a place must have sometimes become tedious, but there is no sign of this in William's letter to his fiancée. There were five ships in the anchorage when he arrived, four from Liverpool and one from Bristol, all presumably in competition for the available slaves and in a hurry to get out of the river and start their journey home. But these ships were commanded and officered by men familiar to William, and indeed to Anne as well, and one gets an impression of camaraderie rather than cut-throat competition as they sat out their time in the unhealthy conditions of a West African river. William reported that he was 'very happy in my officers and sailors this voyage' and that there was also a 'good understanding amongst all the commanders.' Indeed, apart from the ever-present problem of maintaining good health – 'Mr Harding has had a Calabar seasoning, but in a very good way now' – everything seems to have been very jolly. One or other of the ships acted as host every evening for 'our general every night's meeting', where jokes and reminiscences of home would be shared and a pleasant time had by all. Such meetings might also have a more practical agenda, as is made clear by the instructions given to Captain

---

21 MMM EARLE/1/4, 10 February to 27 April 1770; see also Norris, 1789, pp. 68–123, in which he describes a repeat of this journey done in 1772.

Ambrose Lace in 1762: 'On your arrival at Old Calabar, if one or more ships be there, you will observe to make an agreement with the Master or Masters so as not to advance the Price on each other'. No sign here of restrictive trade practices legislation.[22]

Meanwhile, business continued and slaves began to accumulate aboard ship. But this was a very slow business, so that for many weeks, months indeed, conditions aboard did not remotely resemble one's impression of a tightly packed slave ship. The *Unity*, for example had only two slaves aboard for the first few weeks of her cruise along the coast and, even when she did set out to sea with 227 slaves five months later, was hardly crowded by slave ship standards as there was still room for another 200 to be transhipped from her sister ship *Society* on the Portuguese island of São Tomé, before setting out for the Middle Passage. As the ratio of slaves to sailors increased, it became necessary to tighten security. Captain John Newton of the *Duke of Argyll* noted on 18 December 1750 that 'having now 12 men slaves on board, began this day with chains and sentrys', while the captain of the *Blakeney* with five of his crew sick and others manning one of the ship's boats, felt it necessary to send the slaves below for reasons of security. These and similar logbook entries suggest that slaves were not fettered quite as much as sometimes suggested, at least in the early part of a slaving cruise.

Women and children were usually free to move about the ship, sometimes a sensible policy as helpful children warned friendly sailors of potential trouble, sometimes not so sensible as women were often agents in insurrections, collecting information, arms and tools for the men, while others used their comparative freedom to attempt suicide by jumping overboard. Crews were under no illusions; slaves did not want to be slaves and were quite prepared to face death in attempts to gain their freedom, so that most captains were 'always on … guard against insurrections', as demanded in their instructions. Such 'guard' involved members of the crew acting as watches and sentries, usually pretty effectively, while frequent searches were made of the slave rooms – 'secured the after bulkhead of the men's room, for they had started almost every stanchion'.

Despite such precautions, insurrection was a common enough event on slave ships. Eric Robert Taylor has identified over 400 cases of rebellion in the eighteenth century and there were probably many others

22 Stanley, 1885, ii, pp. 232–33; MMM D/EARLE/3/1; Williams, 2004, p. 486.

not sufficiently well documented to attract his attention. Other writers suggest that there was some form of uprising on ten per cent of all slave voyages.[23] And there were one or more insurrections on four of the six voyages whose logbooks have been used for this chapter. These occurred more often at night than in the daytime, but 'one unguarded hour, or minute, is sufficient', wrote Captain Newton. The *Unity*, for example, set sail from São Tomé for Jamaica on 31 May 1770 and the slaves aboard made repeated efforts to rise against the crew, on 4, 6, 26 and 27 June as reported in her logbook. None of these attempts met with much success, though they resulted in the loss of two female slaves overboard and one male slave condemned to death as a warning to the others. 'Their obstinacy put me under ye necessity of shooting ye Ringleader', noted Captain Norris, and this was effective in preventing further uprisings, though both men and women slaves continued to attempt to drown themselves.[24]

Trouble flared up on the *Blakeney* on 27 April 1763 at about nine in the evening: 'Our men slaves having broke down three stantions in their bulkhead, some part of 'em got upon deck and rose on us. Was oblidg'd to fire amongst 'em, kill'd two men and wounded three men and one boy more'. One of the wounded men later died. The worst rebellion faced by Captain Newton on the *African*, on 11 December 1752, was nipped in the bud by alert sailors:

> By the favour of Divine Providence made a timely discovery today that the slaves were forming a plot for an insurrection. Surprised two of them attempting to get off their irons, and upon farther search in their rooms, upon information of three of the slave boys, found some knives, stones, shot etc. and a cold chisel.

This cargo of slaves later underwent a sea change in acceptance of their fate, as Newton noted. 'From about the end of February, they have behaved more like children in one family than slaves in chains and irons, and are really upon all accounts more observant, obliging and considerate than our white people.'[25] Since this ship had almost as many attempted mutinies by the crew as attempted slave uprisings, one can understand Newton's pleasure at the behaviour of the slaves.

23 Taylor, 2006, pp. 3, 215.
24 *Unity* log, 27 June 1770.
25 Martin and Spurrell, 1962, pp. 71–72, 80.

Although there were a few occasions when slaves killed all the crew or captured the ship, these fairly trivial uprisings were the norm. It was inevitable that some slaves would attempt to escape their fate or at least test the watchfulness of the crew but, despite the huge disparity in numbers, always at least ten slaves to one crew member and sometimes nearer 20 to one, it was not very difficult for a reasonably alert crew to control them and put down any trouble. It is rare to find all the slaves united in aggressive opposition to their captors, most of them not taking any part in these uprisings. And some slaves do not seem to have been particularly hostile to the crew, accepting their fate and doing their best to make the voyage bearable.

It is interesting (indeed almost unbelievable) to find that quite often men slaves would actually fight for their captors in order to beat off attempted capture by privateers, a fact mentioned in many reports to owners. Captain Noble, commander of the *Brooks*, praised the valour of some of his slaves in a battle against an American privateer in 1777. 'I had 50 of our stoutest slaves armed, who fought with exceeding great spirit.' Captain Hugh Crow reports selecting 'several of the finest of the black men to be trained in shooting … They were, in a morning, eagerly employed in practising firing at empty bottles slung from the end of the yard arm.' All of which is a bit confusing; how did these captains dare to arm the slaves and how did they persuade them to fight?[26]

It is also worth noting here, before too many assumptions are made about crew and slaves, that many members of slave ship crews were black, some of them slaves themselves and some free men. There were Africans with maritime skills all along the coast from the Gambia to Angola and some were employed by the white slavers, not just locally in canoes but also upon the slave ships as sailors, pilots and interpreters. Most of these were free men, but slaves from the cargo were also pressed, willingly or unwillingly, into the ship's service as high mortality reduced the numbers of white crewmen below what was needed to operate efficiently. Such men might be given the worst tasks, such as manning the windlass or the pumps, but some at least learned so much that they could be said to be able seamen by the time they reached the West Indies and might be sold on to local shipowners as such.[27]

26 *WLA*, 25 February 1763; Williams, 2004, p. 561; Crow, 2007, p. 75.
27 For black sailors see Bolster, 1997, especially ch. 2, 'African roots of black seafaring'.

Most slaves neither worked the ship nor fought for it. They simply tried to survive the appalling experience of the Middle Passage. Much of the activity of the crew was designed to help them do this, from motives of profit if not humanity, since dead slaves had no value. Cleanliness, food, fresh air and exercise were seen to be the key factors in keeping slaves alive – 'serv'd the slaves with corn and beans at noon', 'the people buzy washing and dancing the slaves', 'scraping the slave rooms, smoking with tar, tobacco and brimstone for two hours, afterwards washed with vinegar'. Such unseamanlike activities punctuate the reports in logbooks of daily occupations for the sailors. Air and exercise on deck, the notorious 'dancing' of slaves, often with the aid of a whip, compulsory singing to exercise their lungs, washing and cleaning of slave rooms while their occupants were on deck, such activities probably did something to reduce mortality, but only rarely did slavers' logbooks not contain such entries as 'bury'd a boy slave No. 25', that is the twenty-fifth to die, and such entries sometimes came fast and furious if an epidemic took hold. In 1754, Captain Newton reported that on the return of his ship, the *African*:

> I had the pleasure of returning thanks, in all the churches of Liverpool, for an African voyage performed without any disaster, or the loss of a single man [neither slave nor crew] ... This was much noticed and spoken of in the town; and I believe it is the first instance of the kind.

But this was a short voyage and Newton carried only 90 slaves instead of the 220 originally intended. 'Had I remained there till I had completed my purchase, there is little doubt but I should have shared largely in the mortality so usual in vessels crowded with slaves.'[28]

We have no logbook or letters covering William Earle's last voyage in the *Chesterfield*, so we do not know whether he was beset by rebellious slaves or members of the crew. But we do know that he embarked 322 slaves in Old Calabar of whom only 263 were still alive when he arrived in Barbados on 27 February 1752. This, at nearly one in five dead, seems an appallingly high mortality rate, but it received no comment at the time. Captain Lace was told in his instructions what he already knew, that 'Calabar is remarkable for great mortality in slaves' and this was certainly true. Slaves and crew members alike died in large numbers,

---

28 Martin and Spurrell, 1962, p. 95.

Figure 4. Dancing
the Slaves (Dance
de Nègres) from
Amédée Grehan,
La France Maritime
(Paris, 1837) iii, 179

some while the ship was very slowly acquiring the desired number of slaves but many more during the Middle Passage. Many of the survivors looked more dead than alive and it was an important duty of the crew to improve their appearance before their arrival in a potential market. Greens and fruit were shipped aboard at the first landfall to bring a bit of freshness into the monotonous shipboard diet. The slaves were shaved and cleaned, sometimes being taken ashore in small parties to be washed in fresh water, their skins rubbed with palm oil and grey hair dyed with blacking.[29] Then they might be deemed fit to bear inspection by gentlemen who came aboard to view them and, even more when, after as short a time as possible, they were herded ashore for 'sale day'.

William Earle's instructions named Barbados, Antigua, St Kitts and the Dutch island of St Eustatia as potential markets, each listed with the name of a firm of slave factors to whom William should apply, though in fact his first caller, Mr Sam Carter of Barbados, was able to quote satisfactory prices and the business was given to him. Once terms had been agreed, the factor, who knew the island and the planters, would handle the actual sale and the captain's main jobs were, first, to agree a reasonable price per head and, second, to get the best deal possible for remitting the money back to Liverpool. There were four main ways of doing this, shipping the goods of the islands on behalf of the ships' owners, shipping such goods for others in return for a freight payment, accepting bills of exchange drawn on their London factors by the planters themselves or the slave factors and, simplest of all, selling the ship and returning home as a passenger with a big bag of bills in the captain's luggage. All four methods were used by Liverpool slavers, often in combination, though there was a tendency to remit more and more of the earnings of the slave trade by bill, as cargoes were slow to accumulate and prices could be volatile and difficult to predict. Bills had their own problems: would the London merchant who was named as guarantor or payee actually accept the planter's bill and pay out the money? Most did, but of course there were always exceptions. And then there was the question of the dates at which bills were due for payment. Ship's captains were always instructed to get the shortest bills possible, that is those which would be paid soonest. William Earle was instructed to remit 'in good bills at 30, 40 or 60 days sight, but if any offered

29 Butterworth, 1822, p. 132. For Lace's instructions see Williams, 2004, pp. 486–88.

above 90 days must object against them.' Such instructions were easier to write down than carry out, since planters and factors tended to have greater bargaining power, if only because they tended to be richer.

Once the slaves were sold or at least ashore, it was time to get the ship ready for the return voyage, which would be done quickly in the amazing peace and quiet of the slaveless ship. The vessel was cleaned and cleaned again to get rid of the filth and the terrible smell; and the alterations made on the African coast were taken down and removed. Sale day for the *Blakeney* at St Kitts was 2 August 1763; two days later the logbook reports the crew knocking down the bulkheads which had been erected to create the slave rooms, and the following days they were busy making and mending, caulking and careening, overhauling the rigging, mending leaks and generally getting the ship ready for her return voyage up through the Gulf of Florida or the Bahamas and then home across the Atlantic, while any cargo for the owners or freighters was loaded into the space now once more available. Voyages home were fraught with danger. In wartime, ships were at their most vulnerable in the West Indies or in the approaches to the English Channel, while the ships themselves were often in the most appalling condition after their long months under the African sun. However, Captain Earle in the *Chesterfield* seems to have had no serious problems and he arrived home safely in Liverpool on 10 July 1752. We can only hope that Mrs Anne Winstanley was there to welcome her commander as he came ashore from his last voyage, the man who had described himself in his letter from Old Calabar 'as allways Madam, your most affectionate and faithfull admirer William Earle.'[30]

30 MMM, D/EARLE/3/1.

CHAPTER FOUR

Slave Merchant

'The slave trade ... is accounted a genteel
employment and is usually very profitable.'[1]

William Earle's main business on his return to Liverpool in July 1752
was of a romantic nature, his courtship of Mrs Anne Winstanley, whom
he married a year later. Anne was a widow and, although no doubt
much loved by her 'faithfull admirer', it seems likely that her attractions
included a substantial dowry to add to what William had been able to
save from his five years as a ship's captain. These savings, too, would
probably have been substantial, as being captain of a slave ship was well
known as a path to comparative riches for a young man in Liverpool.

The pay of all ships' captains was reasonably good, from £5 to
£8 a month all found, but slave ship captains were able to accumulate
far more, some of this extra remuneration being spelled out in their
instructions. William was 'to have for your privilege five slaves', such
slaves being hand-picked by the captain, fed at the ship's expense and
often trained up by the captain or one of his crew to provide them skills
that would inflate their value on arrival in the West Indies. And it was
said that the captain's privilege slaves never died, being quietly replaced
by healthy ones if necessary. Captains also received a commission on
the cargo and many of them dabbled in private trade as well, shipping
gold dust or ivory on their own account. Such rewards and earnings
could add up to nearly £1,000 for a single voyage.[2]

---

1 Newton, 1764, p. 192.
2 MMM, D/EARLE/1/1 for William's instructions and cf. Williams, 2004,
  p. 486 for the instructions for Capt. Ambrose Lace, and pp. 605–07, for Capt.
  Robert Bostock of the *Bloom* in 1784, who accumulated £746, not counting
  private trade. Five privilege slaves was generous; Bostock, who operated on a
  fairly small scale, only granted his captains one; LRO 387 MD 55, letter to
  Samuel Gamble, 16 November 1790.

Such accumulation was obviously invaluable, indeed essential, for the next stage of William's career in the slave trade, as a merchant and shipowner. Nearly all slave merchants owned shares in ships and William's shipowning interests can be pieced together from the Slave Trade Database.[3] This shows that William Earle senior was either a captain or an investor in exactly 100 voyages. Three of these were the voyages already discussed, in which William had command but no share of ownership, leaving a total of 97 voyages between 1753 and 1787 in which William was a part-owner, making him the tenth most important slave merchant in Liverpool.[4] These 97 voyages were carried out in 41 different ships, the greatest continuity being the seven consecutive voyages undertaken by the *Chesterfield* (1750–59), the six by the *Polly* (1769–75) and the five voyages of the *Mars* (1770–76).

The number of owners of any one of these ships ranged from one (unusual) to 12 in these listings. However, there is no indication of the amount invested or the parts owned by each owner. Other sources, especially newspapers, quite often refer to a ship being owned by William Earle (or some other merchant) '& Company', which tells us who was in charge, but otherwise the only clue is the order in which the owners are listed, the assumption being that the most important owners are listed first. Such an assumption is generally accurate, judging by other sources, but caution is needed since some merchants quite low in these lists turn out to be major shareholders.

Bearing this in mind, there was a pattern in the utilisation of slave ships in which William had a major shareholding, i.e. was named first or second in the list of owners. From 1754, when he began his career as a slave merchant and shipowner, his activities focussed mainly on two ships, his former command the *Chesterfield*, which sailed from Liverpool, always to Calabar, in 1754, 1756, 1757 and 1759, and the *Grampus*, which was used to develop new sources of slaves, sailing to Gambia in 1753, the Windward Coast (between the Gold Coast and Sierra Leone) in 1755 and finally to an unknown West African destination in 1757, when she was captured by the French. Between them these two ships could carry over 600 slaves, 350–400+ on the *Chesterfield* and about 200 in the *Grampus*. In addition, William Earle was the most important owner of three other slave ships which sailed in the 1750s just once.

3 See above p. 46.
4 Calculated from the data in Pope, 2007, pp. 194–207.

No profit and loss accounts exist for these slaving ventures, but it is probable that the losses were considerable, for William Earle and partners suffered heavily from French privateers after the Seven Years' War broke out in the spring of 1756. Five ships in which William was a major investor were captured: four before the slaves were embarked, the *Grampus* in 1757, the *Chesterfield* and *Industry* in 1760 and the *Lyme* in 1761, and the *Calypso* in 1761 after the slaves had been disembarked. William was usually fully insured but, even so, so many lost ships must surely have reduced his profits to very little.

A desire to avenge such losses and the passion for privateering for which Liverpool was notorious probably accounts for William's interest in privateering ships in the late 1750s, declarations for letters of marque or privateering licences having been found for six ships in which he was one of the owners.[5] Some of these, including the *Chesterfield*, whose captain took out letters of marque in February 1759, were what contemporaries called 'marks', powerful trading ships carrying such a licence to act as a privateer just in case they should encounter an easy victim. But three of these vessels were true privateers, the *Adventure* (1757) and *Prince of Wales* (1758), both captained by William's brother-in-law John Copeland, and the *Liverpool* (1757), the most successful privateering ship with which William was associated.

The *Liverpool* was a powerful ship, 300 tons with 22 carriage guns, 18 of them twelve-pounders, and a crew which varied in size from 160 to 200 men. Witnesses who saw her under sail gave her 'a very great character, and say that she sails remarkably fast.' This emphasis on her speed was often repeated and she could move fast even when there was little or no wind, as she had been fitted with 11 oars on each side. Rowing in pursuit of 'the chase' was hard work, but very exciting and few men grumbled when ordered to take up the oars, especially when they got so close that their prey began to fire her stern chase guns, 'a sign of weakness and fear … which commonly gives joy to the chasing ship.'[6]

The captain of the *Liverpool* was William Hutchinson, perhaps the most famous privateer captain of the Seven Years' War, if only because he was the author of a much-quoted *Treatise on Practical Seamanship*. This was not only a manual of seamanship, it also had an interesting section on privateering. Hutchinson emphasised the need to deceive potential

5   HCA 26/6–10.
6   *WLA*, 5 August 1757; Hutchinson, 1979, pp. 182–84.

enemies. 'Trading ships ... to be made to look as big, powerful, and warlike as possible in order to intimidate; but privateers the contrary ... to conceal their power as much as possible.'[7] He also stressed the need for speed, first of all in the design of the ship, but also in the maintenance of a clean bottom. Hutchinson also placed much emphasis on discipline and frequent training of the crew in the use of the great guns and small arms and in working the ship.

The *Liverpool* was a new ship, built as a specialist privateer, and advance notice appeared in the *Liverpool Advertiser* of 22 April 1757 that she would be launched at the next spring tide 'and immediately fitted out and sent on a cruise against the French ... All gentlemen seamen and able-bodied landsmen, who are willing to try their fortunes, may apply to the Captain, or Mr Henry Hardwar', the managing partner of the syndicate who owned the ship. On 12 May, a letter of marque was issued for a six-month cruise and, on 3 June, the ship was reported to be 'in the river, ready for a cruise against the French.'[8] Hutchinson set sail for the sea area between south-west Ireland and the French coast, where he was to lie in wait for homeward-bound West Indiamen. He did not have to wait long. At dawn on Saturday 18 June, the masthead lookout cried out that he could see a sail due south of the *Liverpool*, 'some seven leagues [21 miles] ahead.'

All hands were summoned and the *Liverpool* gave chase 'with all sails set.' Her speed soon closed the gap between the two ships and, after six hours' pursuit, she was near enough to open fire. An hour or so later, between 11 and 12 in the morning, the French ship struck her colours. She proved to be *Le Grand Marquis de Tournay*, a 450-ton West Indiaman on the last stage of her journey from Santo Domingo to Bordeaux. It would have been shameful for such a big ship to surrender to a privateer without at least a token resistance. French witnesses stated that she exchanged fire with the *Liverpool* for about an hour and the French captain (but no one else) swore that it was in fact not him but the pilot 'who struck the colours without his consent.' But, to tell the truth, much of this was play-acting. No one was hurt, no important damage was done to either ship and, on 26 June, just over three weeks after she had sailed from the Mersey, the *Liverpool* was back home accompanied by her prize with its West Indian cargo of some 500 hogsheads of

---

7 Hutchinson, 1979, p. 160. There is a lot about Hutchinson in Williams, 2004.
8 *WLA*, 22 April, 3 June 1757; HCA 26/7 fol. 133, 18 May 1757.

sugar, together with coffee, indigo, logwood and hides – a cargo valued by knowledgeable observers at £20,000, some four or five times what it had cost to buy and fit out the privateer. Captain Hutchinson was much praised, both by his fellow townsmen and by his French captives, who 'gave him the best of characters, both as to conduct, courage and humanity.' They were particularly impressed with his ability to control his very excited crew:

> He would not permit the least article to be taken from any of the French prisoners, and to the honour of the whole crew, each man behaved well in his station. Some of the landsmen, who had not been at sea before, could scarcely be kept within bounds, they were so eager to come to action.[9]

Liverpool privateers were normally required by their orders to escort prizes worth over £10,000 back to their home port but, once this had been done, they were not expected to hang about for long. The *Liverpool* set sail again to continue her cruise on 6 July and she returned to the same cruising station between southern Ireland and western France. After three weeks, she captured or rather re-captured the *Sampson*, a 200-ton Bristol West Indiaman with a cargo of sugar, rum and ginger, which had been taken on her way home from Antigua by a French privateer. At the approach of the powerful English privateer, the French prize crew wisely launched the longboat and made their way with the ship's papers to the safety of the shore, leaving their prize to be recaptured without a shot being fired. Few privateers could afford to give the vessels they captured very big crews, so recaptures were common and could be profitable to the captors. The recaptured ship reverted to the original owners, but the cargo was available to pay salvage, the amount depending on the length of time the vessel had been in enemy hands. This varied from a payment of 1/8th of the value of the cargo if the ship had been recaptured within 24 hours to a maximum of one half if the period of captivity exceeded four days. In the case of the *Sampson*, the owners and crew of the *Liverpool* could expect to receive this maximum as the Bristol ship had been captured by the French on 20 July and recaptured on 26 July 1757.[10]

9   *WLA*, 1 July 1757; Williams, 2004, pp. 127–29; HCA 32/196 (1).
10 On the *Sampson* see Williams, 2004, p. 125; *WLA*, 5 August 1757; HCA 32/242. On the law regarding recaptures, see Starkey, 1990, p. 32.

Captain Hutchinson now reinforced the small number of Englishmen aboard the *Sampson* with some of his own crew and sent her back to Liverpool, while he continued his cruise south in company with a small Guernsey privateer called the *Fame*, whose captain was 'extremely well acquainted with the French coast.' The two captains made an agreement 'to cruise in consort and to share in proportion to their men and guns', a procedure frequently adopted in privateering by which the two predatory vessels could work together like a pair of hunting dogs. When the two privateers reached the mouth of the Gironde, the French-speaking crew of the Guernsey ship was able to give the impression that she was a French privateer with a prize – the *Liverpool* – in company and so lure three vessels into such a sense of security that they were easily taken by the two British ships and sent to Kinsale in Ireland, which they were using as a rendezvous. One of these vessels was wrecked off the Welsh coast on her way from Ireland to Liverpool, but the other two were brought back safely to the Mersey, where they were condemned and their cargoes sold at auction. The three captured vessels were all sailing from Bordeaux to Quebec, a city to be captured two years later by General Wolfe, and they were carrying a wide variety of foodstuffs, drink, small arms and clothing for the garrison, including 4,000 gold- and silver-laced hats and 3,000 pairs of shoes.[11]

So far, the six-month cruise of the *Liverpool* had been very successful, with five captures and a number of French ships either run aground or otherwise destroyed, all with no man lost in action. But their luck was to change somewhat on the way home from Kinsale, which they left on 11 September. Few potential prizes were sighted and those chased got away, while an unfortunate mistake led to the only serious damage incurred during this cruise. One night in early October, they hailed in French a large vessel which they took to be a French privateer, only to realise too late that the ship was in fact HMS *Antelope*, whose reaction was to fire a broadside, which did some serious damage to the *Liverpool* and wounded 28 of her men. The *Liverpool* had sailed into the middle of the British royal fleet and she kept in company with them for a few days before being ordered to make her own way as a result of an epidemic breaking out, which killed six of the crew and put over 100 on the sick list. It was then a rather sad ship that returned to the Mersey on 24 November, though not all that sad, as big profits had been made

11   Williams, 2004, pp. 129–31; *WLA*, 26 August 1757; HCA 32/249.

much easier and more quickly than would have been possible in the slave trade.[12]

The *Liverpool* went straight into dock for repairs and came out again on 2 January 1758, newly masted and ready to cruise once again against the enemies of Great Britain. A different cruising ground was ordered for this second cruise and the first we hear of the privateer is that she was outside Lisbon, waiting in vain for a French East Indiaman to come out of the port and then, on 26 May, the *Liverpool Advertiser* printed an extract of a letter from 'a merchant in Leghorn' dated 1 May 1758, which provided some more information. William's brother Tom was a merchant in Leghorn at this date and, since he was involved in privateering as an agent and dealer in prize cargoes, this letter was almost certainly written by him.[13]

The news it conveyed was good. The privateer had been cruising off the south coast of France and had captured and sent into Leghorn three of the ubiquitous French trading vessels called 'tartans' which were sailing from Marseilles. A little more information about these French prizes can be garnered in Leghorn itself. The city had a tax on goods sold at auction, and its registers provide an unique source for historians interested in the sale of prize goods since, at their best, they recorded the names of the agent selling the prize and of the buyer, the name and captain of the prize and the nature of the goods captured and what they sold for.[14] The registers have not all survived, but they do exist for several years of the Seven Years' War and do in fact include these three tartans. On 1 June 1758, the register notes the sale by Earle & Hodgson to a Tuscan sea captain of 'la tartana Gesù, Giuseppe e Maria, preda del corsale [i.e. privateer] *Leverpoole* inghilese', but this did not make the agents very rich as the tartan was knocked down for just 150 pieces of eight (about £37). The other two prizes were slightly more profitable, the *San Luigi* being sold for 525 pieces of eight and another *Gesù, Giuseppe e Maria* for 290. Various items from the cargoes were also sold, including cotton, sugar, 'caffè del Martinico', drugs, quicksilver and 525 pieces of eight in cash, but the total value was not very great, at least in comparison with other prize cargoes being sold to other English

---

12 *WLA*, 25 November 1757, extract from Hutchinson's journal, and 2 December, notice of arrival in Liverpool.

13 *WLA*, 28 April, 26 May 1758. For Thomas Earle see Chapter Six below.

14 ASL, *Asta Pubblica*, henceforward AP.

prize agents, such as the 15,000 pieces of eight paid for cotton from
Jerusalem and Acre captured aboard another ship.[15]

The movements of the *Liverpool* for the rest of her cruise are not very
well documented as prizes taken in the Mediterranean were normally
condemned in Gibraltar, whose vice-admiralty records have not survived.
News from the area was also infrequent and often inaccurate. In early
June, for instance, the investors in Liverpool must have been alarmed
to read in the shipping paper *Lloyds List* that their privateer had been
captured and taken into Toulon. But, just a couple of weeks later, letters
from Leghorn advised that this information 'appears to be a mistake'.
And a letter from Cagliari in Sardinia reported that, far from being a
captive himself, Captain Hutchinson had captured and 'sent into that
port a French privateer of 24 guns and 200 men, which was returning
from her cruise. We have the strongest reason to believe that she is
worth 50,000 dollars [c.£12,500], exclusive of head and gun money as
a privateer', such 'head money' being paid at the rate of £5 for each
man captured or killed in action, so another £1,000 in this case.[16] And
when the *Liverpool* herself returned to the Mersey at the end of July,
she did so in the company of another French privateer, *Le Roy Gaspard*,
350 tons and 22 guns, which she had captured on her way from Messina
to Marseilles. These two French privateers were both powerful ships
and their capture gives some idea of just how formidable an opponent
the *Liverpool* was.

The *Liverpool* was to sail as a privateer on one last cruise. The
advertisement in the local paper on 1 September, asking for volunteers
'willing to try their fortunes', described her as 'the fortunate ship
Liverpool privateer' and she certainly had been fortunate during her first
two cruises. This third cruise saw two Dutch ships carrying French
goods captured and sent into Irish ports, probably sufficient to cover
costs, but overall the cruise was not quite so fortunate as the first two,
maybe because Captain Hutchinson was no longer in command. He
had handed over the captaincy to his lieutenant John Ward, while he
stayed in Liverpool to develop his business supplying the local market
with live fish. The idea was to keep in the river a large vessel with a
well which would be supplied with live fish by the cod smacks as they

---

15   AP, vol. 26, 21 May, 1 June, 22 July 1758. For Earle & Hodgson doing rather
     better as prize agents see below pp. 128–30.
16   *WLA*, 23 June 1757; Starkey, 1990, p. 17.

came in, but the scheme was not very successful. Hutchinson abandoned both this business and privateering and devoted the rest of his long life to public office as water bailiff and dockmaster of Liverpool, the collection of observations on the tides, the weather and the winds, and the writing of numerous works on naval architecture, seamanship and related maritime topics.[17]

William Earle undoubtedly made a good investment in acquiring a share in the *Liverpool*, but whether his profits were sufficient to make up for his losses to French privateers is impossible to say for lack of evidence. We do not even know what share he had in the privateer, let alone what her many prizes fetched when they were sold though, since they included two large French privateers and several rich West Indiamen, this must have been substantial. Since 1708, the Crown had given up its claim to a share of prizes, which made privateering a more profitable activity. Most of the profits were now shared between the owners and the officers and crew, whose contracted rights improved considerably in the eighteenth century, from about one-third of the total in the 1690s to half or slightly less by the Seven Years' War.

What was left was available for distribution amongst the owners, though there were still deductions to be made. Selling prize goods cost money, for storage, porterage, auctioneers' fees and so on, while goods which were not sold in Liverpool itself would usually incur commissions paid to local prize agents. The costs of buying and fitting out the ship with arms, ammunition and victuals for 100 or so men for a six-month cruise were also considerable. Scattered evidence suggests that privateer ships normally cost about £3,000 and the fitting-out and victualling costs for each cruise were about the same, so that one decent capture would easily cover the total outlay of the syndicate, especially if the privateer ship was sold once its business had been done, as was the case with the *Liverpool*, which was sold at auction at the Merchants' Coffee House on 12 April 1759, just six weeks after her return from her third and final cruise.[18]

It seems reasonable to conclude that William's investments in privateer ships, especially the *Liverpool*, provided him with sufficient profits at least to balance what he lost to the French privateers. These

17 Williams, 2004, pp. 135–48.
18 For material on costs etc. see Williams, 2004, pp. 661–64; Radburn, 2009, p. 101.

losses continued into 1761, when his slave ships *Lyme* and *Calypso* were captured, but after that his luck was to turn. In the 1760s, 18 slave ships in which William had a major interest set sail, just under two a year. And from late 1762 a pattern similar to that of the 1750s emerges, with the repeated voyages of two ships dominating the slaving activity of this decade, though the total scale of William's slaving was much greater than in the 1750s. Most important was the *Dalrymple*, or rather *Dalrymple*s since two ships of this name sailed for William, a prize brigantine of some 120 tons capable of carrying just under 150 slaves and then a much larger French prize which could carry twice as many. These two *Dalrymple*s sailed in 1762, 1763, 1765, 1766 and 1769, always to Calabar, New Calabar or to an unspecified port in the Bight of Biafra and from there to the West Indies, where the slaves were sold in Antigua, St Kitts and Jamaica.

Similar voyages with some overlap were undertaken in 1763, 1765 and 1766 by the schooner *Friendship*, which also always sailed to Calabar or New Calabar and then the West Indies, twice to Barbados and once to Jamaica with 250–300 slaves aboard each time despite her small size. Three more ships, the *Jupiter* (1763), *Little Britain* (1766) and *Neptune* (1768), also sailed to Calabar so that 12 of the 18 ships in which William had a major investment in this decade were engaged in sailing the same route on which he had served his apprenticeship to the slave trade and his voyages as captain. The remaining six showed an interest in diversification on the part of the owners, with three sailing to Anomabu on the Gold Coast, one to the Île de Los in Sierra Leone (today off the coast of Guinea), one to Cape Mount on the Windward Coast and one to an unspecified port in the Bight of Benin. Only two of these 18 ships were captured by the French and none was wrecked, so one must assume that this was not just a busy but a profitable decade for William Earle and his partners. They were obviously prepared to experiment a bit, but the fact that two-thirds of their ships were despatched to the Bight of Biafra, including the two most important, a *Dalrymple* and the *Friendship*, suggests that he reckoned they had found a profitable formula.

Conditions, or William's mind, had changed by the next decade. These years were severely affected by the American War of Independence (1776–83), which led to a near cessation of Liverpool's maritime trade and especially the slaving activity, a fact which led both Liverpool generally and the Earles in particular to switch investment once again into privateering, a subject which will be considered in Chapter Eight, though we can note here that the Earles continued to be successful in their privateering ventures. William and his partners did virtually no slaving at all in the later 1770s, but the first five or six years of the decade were very busy with 20 ships in which William was a major investor being set out during this short period, about four a year. Most important were the *Apollo* and *Mars*, both of which sailed five times for William Earle and partners.

These too must have been profitable years, for all these ships completed their voyages as planned, with no captures and no shipwrecks. But the voyages themselves showed a remarkable change from the pattern established in the 1750s and 1760s. Just two of these 20 ships sailed to Calabar and only one to Bonny. These earlier destinations had been completely eclipsed by Cape Mount on the Windward Coast, which was the destination of ten ships, another two going to an unspecified destination on the Windward Coast, which may well also have been Cape Mount. Two of the other five ships went to Galinhas in Sierra Leone, one to Anomabu on the Gold Coast and one to the Cameroons east of Nigeria. Just why slaving destinations changed is difficult to say. Calabar was back in favour in the 1780s and was the destination of at least half of the slave ships owned by the Earles in the years 1784–92, so it does not seem that the place itself was responsible. Fluctuations in slave supply could normally be explained by the presence of warfare, plague or other disorder, either in the slave ports themselves or more commonly in the interior regions from which the African traders acquired their slaves. The most important source of slaves for the ports of the Bight of Biafra was the densely populated high plateau of West Cameroon known as the Grassfields and it was probably some change in conditions there that caused the Earles and other Liverpool slave merchants to seek other ports for their supply of slaves.[19]

Investment in a slaving ship was an activity which might be undertaken by just about anyone in Liverpool with some spare cash in the second half of the eighteenth century. This fairly casual involvement is reflected in an analysis of the 117 people who invested in slaving ventures with which William Earle was associated, 38 only investing once, 15 twice and 21 three times. There were, however, a few men who were true partners of William and played a very important role

19 For the 1780s and 1790s see below ch. 10, pp. 13–14; Law & Strickrodt, 1999, p. 6; Warnier, 1995; Richardson, 1989.

in his activities. Heading this list was William Davenport, a Londoner by birth and a major promoter of the Bight of Biafra as a slave-trading destination, who was a partner in 50 of William Earle's ventures (right through from the 1750s to the 1780s).[20] Next in importance were four men, all well-known former slaving captains, who invested in over 20 voyages each – Patrick Black (28), Nehemiah Holland (23), Robert Jennings (21) and Ambrose Lace (20) – and a further 12 men invested in between 10 and 19 ventures. Liverpool slaving syndicates, or at least those led by William Earle, knew what they were doing, and how to do it effectively and profitably.

The usual pattern of ownership was the same as that adopted for any other shipping activity. A syndicate would be formed to buy or have built a suitable ship for the trade and this grouping would usually hold together until that ship was deemed no longer fit for the task or had been captured or wrecked. The ships which have been identified above as William's main ventures, the *Chesterfield* and *Grampus* in the 1750s, the *Dispatch*, *Friendship* and *Dalrymple* in the 1760s, and the *Apollo*, *Mars* and *Dreadnought* in the 1770s, were all owned by such syndicates whose members either remained identical for the three, four, five or more successive voyages for which the ship served them or just changed marginally with one or two people dropping in or out as time passed.

A similar continuity can be observed amongst the captains. William himself was succeeded as captain of the *Chesterfield* for five voyages by Patrick Black, who would later become a major investor. John Ritchie captained the *Dispatch* for four successive voyages (1766–71) and Patrick Fairweather, who first visited Calabar in 1755 as a teenage apprentice, captained the *Dalrymple* for six successive voyages between 1769 and 1778. John Maddock, John Jones, Edward Fisher and Francis Holland were other captains who remained loyal to syndicates headed by William Earle. Stephen D. Behrendt has studied this continuity and the possibilities it created for the training of apprentices and mates to become captains in their turn and there seems little doubt that it was an important factor in the success of both William Earle and Liverpool as a whole. William seems to have had good relations with his captains, which was not of course always the case. After a major row with Stephen Bowers, one of his captains, the slave merchant Robert Bostock described

20 For Davenport see the thesis by Radburn, 2009.

the former as a 'damn'd scoundrel ... I think he may walk Liverpool streets some time before he gets another vessel or berth.'[21]

William Earle was still an owner of slave ships in the early 1780s, sometimes in conjunction with his elder son Thomas, but such activity was brought to a halt by illness and his death in April 1788. His slaving career had lasted almost 40 years from the sailing of the *Lucy* in June 1748 to the return to Liverpool of the *Maria* in May 1787. These pretty girls' names serve to camouflage the purpose of this activity. It seems probable that William Earle, as commander and part-owner of slave ships during these four decades, was at least partly responsible for the shipment of just under 30,000 slaves in 100 ships from West Africa, of whom about 5,000 died and 25,000 were actually delivered, nearly all to the islands of the Caribbean. We have no accounts for William Earle and so do not know what profits he made on his slaving activities, but two studies of William Davenport suggest that the average rate was about ten or 11 per cent per annum, a figure which Adam Smith believed to be normal in overseas trade. 'Double interest [i.e. twice five per cent, the maximum legal rate of interest] is in Great Britain reckoned what the merchants call a good, moderate, reasonable and usual profit.'[22]

We are fortunate that, in addition to the material which has enabled this broad outline of William Earle's slaving career to be established, there is another source which can be used as a sort of microscope to focus on his activities in much greater detail during one short period of his career. This is the letter book in the Earle Collection of the Merseyside Maritime Museum.[23] This covers 20 months, from 23 January 1760 to 23 September 1761, and contains copies of just under 500 letters to about 100 correspondents written by William Earle and his clerks during this period. These are business letters and provide virtually no information on William's private life, but they tell us a lot about his business. They are not always easy to understand since they portray only one side of a correspondence, but they provide insights into the business life of a Liverpool merchant which could hardly be gained from any other source.

21 Behrendt, 1991; LRO 387 MD 55, letter to James Cleveland, 20 January 1790. See also Hodson, 1953, p. 47.
22 Radburn, 2009, pp. 88–89; Adam Smith, 1961, p. 200.
23 MMM D/EARLE/2/2; references will be given to the date of the letter if this is not given in the text.

William was living in Water Street at the time of the earliest letter, but also had property in Red Cross Street on which he was planning to build. Both these streets were right in the commercial centre of Liverpool, running down to the Mersey, and so convenient for visiting ships in the river or the docks and doing business in the local inns and coffee houses. The counting house where William's clerks made up his accounts and wrote his letters was in his home, which thus doubled as office, a place where he might offer a merchant a bed for the night; 'make my house your home whilst in town', he wrote to the Jamaica merchant Robert Pooley.[24] William had a warehouse at the bottom of Strand Street, and he also had a shop where he sold goods wholesale and occasionally retail, so he was well equipped for his affairs.[25]

Judging by the dates of the letters, William was a conscientious attender at his counting house, though he was somewhat inclined to a 'pre-industrial' pattern of work with bursts of effort, when ten or more letters would be written in a day, interspersed with days when nothing or very little appears to have been done. He was also away from Liverpool occasionally, visiting friends and business contacts in the Isle of Man, on a week's journey 'in the country', and for two weeks in April and May 1760 on a journey to London to visit suppliers and business contacts, with similar visits made to people in Sheffield and Birmingham on the way home. William, a man of just under 40 at the time of the letter book, was also a sufferer from that most eighteenth century of ailments, gout, which confined him to his room for ten days or a fortnight at a time on three occasions during these 20 months. 'I have been laid up of the gout these ten days', he wrote on 18 April 1760 to Joseph Wimpey, his 'money man' in London, 'but my fits are generally smart and short. I am now very well.'[26]

The most important role that a partner could play in the operation of a slave ship was to act as ship's husband or managing partner. William acted as such for six ships during the period of the letter book, though he is only specifically described as ship's husband of the *Calypso*, 'a really fine ship' with 12 guns, a crew of 35 to 40 men and a letter of marque. She was commanded by William's brother-in-law John Copeland, who was also a part-owner, and she sailed for Bonny in the Bight of Biafra

24 15 September 1761.
25 For counting houses see Hancock, 1995, ch. 3.
26 For Wimpey see below pp. 94–95.

on 18 March 1760 with orders for Barbados, where she had sold her last cargo of slaves in the previous year, 'the best Bonny or Bite cargo of negroes imported for many years by the factor's own account.'[27]

William's main business as ship's husband involved buying the cargo and arranging for its delivery, and keeping in touch as far as possible with the captain and supplying him with information or revised orders. The first letters relating to the *Calypso* were mainly to do with items in her cargo, such as beads, cowries and Indian textiles but, once she had set sail, letter after letter was sent aboard outgoing slave ships to meet up with Copeland when he arrived in Africa. These refer to the changing markets in the West Indies and also to the ships making their way out to Africa that might give him trouble as competitors for the available slaves in Bonny. 'I hope this will meet you at Bonny', he wrote on 26 April, 'and so situated as not to be hurt by the later ships.' William, and presumably everyone else concerned in the slave trade, was always worried that delays in Africa would mean so long a stay on the coast that mortality rates rose to crisis levels. It was better to pay more and get the ship slaved fairly quickly, for 'it is notoriously known that slaves never will stand a long purchase'.[28]

On 12 October 1760, William Earle wrote to John Darbyshire, an ironmonger from Birmingham to whom he had sold a 1/16th share in the *Calypso*. He had good news. 'I have the pleasure to acquaint you the *Calypso* arrived on the coast on 19 April having had a passage of 27 days and beat off in her passage a French privateer of 24 guns.' William had earlier written to Copeland thanking him for risking his life in this fashion, something which many captains would not have done. 'I received yours this day from the Coast of 4 May and am very thankfull you cleared yourself so gallantly from a privateer of superior force, for which you and the crew have my particular thanks.'[29] These French privateers were a very real danger to the slavers, few of whom were strong or determined enough to resist as Copeland had. On 25 July 1760, the *Liverpool Advertiser* published a list of 142 Liverpool ships captured since the war began on 1 May 1756 and, on 16 April 1762, there was a report that a very successful French privateer, *L'Amethyst*, had sailed for the Portuguese island of São Tomé off the African coast with three

---

27 7 July 1760, letter to Messrs Turner, Hilton & Briscoe.
28 Letter to Capt. Francis Lowndes, 2 August 1761.
29 Letter to Copeland, 27 September.

Liverpool slavers and 1,200 slaves as prizes. Her captain was helped by a correspondent in England who sent him a regular notice of all the ships and their commanders that were trading on the African coast.[30]

These letters give a good idea of the communications problems involved in this 'triangular' trade. The vital news of the *Calypso's* safe arrival on the coast of Africa on 19 April did not reach Liverpool until late September, five and a half months later, and the letter had been conveyed to the Mersey aboard a ship from Virginia. Later in the century, there was a packet service from Falmouth to Dominica, the first landfall in the West Indies, but this invaluable aid was not available for William. On 27 January 1761, William wrote again to Darbyshire and also to Richard Rabone, another Birmingham ironmonger to whom he had sold a share in the *Calypso*. More good news! The *Calypso* had arrived in Barbados on 3 December with 'a very sufficient number of slaves', 370 in fact. 'This is a very fortunate event and will, I doubt not, be £200 in your pocket.' After much chopping and changing it had finally been decided to sell the slaves in Guadeloupe, conquered by the British in 1759, and arrangements were made for a factor to be appointed there and for fresh insurance to be negotiated for the voyage from Barbados. But it was the weather that finally determined on which island this cargo of slaves from Bonny would be sold. A gale drove the *Calypso* westward and she was 'obliged' to proceed to Jamaica, where the optimistic William had no doubt of 'her coming to a good market.' But he feared that the considerable delay would 'throw us behind hand for the next season.'[31]

Just now, however, affairs could hardly have been better for the ship's owners in Liverpool and Birmingham. 'Slaves sell very high in the West Indies', reported William, and Kenyon & Southwark, the Jamaican firm of slave factors entrusted with the sale, were therefore able to do very well for the ship's owners, selling the slaves for £16,000. 'The *Calypso* has sold very well and expect she will make a great voyage and will be very acceptable to everybody', wrote an enthusiastic William.[32] Meanwhile, Captain Copeland loaded 150 hogsheads of sugar and 20 butts of rum, negotiated 'a full remittance of bills at usual dates' and arranged to join the convoy sailing from Jamaica to England under naval escort on 20 April 1761.

30 *WLA*, 25 July 1760, 12 February and 16 April 1762.
31 14 March 1761, letter to Darbyshire.
32 Letter to John Humphreys, 21 March 1761.

Everything certainly seemed to be in good order and the success of the voyage made William confident that another voyage setting out that same year would also be successful. Two days after the *Calypso* sailed from Jamaica, William was making arrangements for cargo for a second voyage to be shipped from Holland to the Isle of Man and he also wrote to Kenyon & Southwark in Jamaica, congratulating them on their efforts on his behalf. 'He is resolved the *Calypso* will go to Bonny again this year and has already ordered a cargo for her and probably you will see her again by this time twelve month.'[33]

This must have seemed a reasonable assumption, but it was dangerous to assume too much about the slave trade in wartime, something William was well aware of. Everything seemed fine up to 1 July, when ships from the Jamaica fleet arriving in Liverpool reported that the *Calypso* had been with them and 'all well' up till 21 June, when they were in the approaches to the English Channel. But all did not seem so well on 3 July, when the *Calypso* had still not arrived and William decided to postpone her next voyage till the spring. By 6 July, he was certain she had been captured. 'The *Calypso* I have in my own mind given up as taken' and, in another letter written later the same day, he is sorry to report that his 'fears for her were but too grounded.' William, always one to look on the bright side, consoled himself with the thought that he was well insured 'and will be as near the value as possible'. In fact, financial problems in London rather than French privateers seemed more likely to bring losses to William and his partners. Mr Samuel Touchet, one of the big merchants in London on whom the bills to pay for the slaves had been drawn, had gone bankrupt and as a result '£5,023 of the ship's bills are protested for non-acceptance.'[34] This was not necessarily the end of the world, since neither the factors nor planters in Jamaica nor the London money men welcomed such bad publicity, but sorting matters out was likely to take several months and so cause the partners serious liquidity problems for their next voyage.

On 17 July 1761, William at last received a letter from his brother-in-law written on 29 June with information about his capture. Those who disliked Captain Copeland claimed that he had deliberately left the safety of the convoy, a common practice whose motive was to reach market ahead of the competition and also to avoid the press. Copeland

33 Letter to Kenyon & Southwark, 22 April 1761.
34 Letter to Copeland, 17 July 1761.

himself said that he had been separated from the fleet by foggy weather and William was inclined to believe him. 'I advise people to suspend condemnation until you appear to answer for your self.' His captor was a French privateer of 18 guns, *L'Amaranthe*, and Copeland did not make any resistance this time, probably because he had left most of his crew either dead or in Jamaica, as slavers never needed so many men on the voyage home with no slaves to guard. His ship was brought into the Breton port of Morlaix and Copeland himself was taken to be held prisoner on the Île de Ré.

William Earle set out to make the best of a bad thing. He wrote to his correspondents in neutral Rotterdam, Messrs William and Joseph Manson, asking them to send Copeland money if he should need it and to help him recover his freedom.[35] 'The Captain is my Brother-in-Law; if you have any friend you can influence for his being released by the first cartel you will much oblige', cartels being a sort of shuttle service by which French prisoners and an equivalent number of English prisoners were periodically sent home across the Channel. The efforts of the Mansons seem to have been effective, as news of Copeland being freed and arriving in London was reported in the Liverpool paper on 7 August, some three weeks later and less than seven weeks after his capture. Eighteenth-century wars were quite civilised, at least for the officers.[36] William also asked the Mansons to see if they could purchase the *Calypso* cheaply from her French captors and have her sent 'in the name of a neutral person' to Dublin or the Isle of Man, and he tried to get hold of the captured rum cheaply as well. Nothing seems to have come of these enterprising ventures, but he was more successful in pressing ahead with the necessary business of getting a copy of the ship's condemnation so that he could prove her loss to the insurers.

William wrote an unusually cross letter to his brother-in-law on this subject, as Copeland had 'omitted to send copy of the condemnation. The loss will not be signed off till it comes. This is a very material thing to people who want their money and besides our underwriters may crack [i.e. go bankrupt] which hath been the case with one already.' Even with the condemnation, William was not too sanguine about getting paid quickly, given the number of English ships in French hands. 'The custom is to be paid in a month after signing off but our underwriters are at

35 Letter to Mansons, 17 July 1761.
36 *WLA*, 7 August 1761.

present much burdened with losses.'[37] While William concerned himself with important but no doubt boring paperwork, Captain Copeland was in London engaged in the more congenial task of finding himself a new ship. 'If you do incline to go to sea again', wrote William on 4 August, 'and any thing you see in the river pleases you, that is British built and from 150 to 200 tons send her dimensions and wait our answer.' And, in virtually the last letter in the letter book, we learn that Copeland's quest had been successful. The syndicate had acquired a Liverpool-built ship of the right tonnage called the *Mentor* to replace the *Calypso* and William was busy arranging a cargo for her. She had 14 guns, a crew of 30 men, and she sailed for Whydah under Copeland's command on 12 November 1761 on what turned out to be his last voyage as a slave ship commander.[38]

William was not described as ship's husband of any ship other that the *Calypso*, but he did in fact act as such for this new ship and also for two others in the period covered by the letter book, the *Industry* and the *Prince Vada*, while he shared the duties with another co-owner for two more, the *Minerva* and the *Sea Horse*. To be entrusted with such a responsibility for so many ships would suggest that William was pretty competent at the job and this is certainly the impression given by the correspondence. This was a very difficult period for Liverpool ships, but none of the problems encountered were of William's making and he coped admirably with each contretemps in turn.

He seems to have been most upset by the fate of the *Industry*, an American-built schooner commanded by his former apprentice and friend William Hindle. She sailed from Liverpool for the Cameroons in November 1759 and we first hear of her on 30 January 1760, when a letter was sent instructing Hindle to proceed to South Carolina. On the same day notice was sent to Messrs Austen, Lawrence & Co. of Charleston, instructing them to make preparations to welcome the *Industry* and her small cargo of 100 young slaves. 'We expect they will be early at market and doubt not their selling at a good price.' News of Indian wars and smallpox in South Carolina caused William to change his mind and, in early April, he wrote to Hindle to make for Norfolk, Virginia, and to deal there with the firm of Sparling & Bolden. The owners had plans to provide Hindle with a bigger ship and William suggested he try to

37 Letters to Richard Rabone, 23 July, and Copeland, 24 July.
38 Letter to Copeland, 4 August 1761, to W. & J. Manson, 22 September 1761.

sell the schooner in Virginia if he could get a reasonable price and, if not, to load her with lumber 'or a freight of tobacco' and to 'proceed home north about [i.e. round the north of Ireland], as the privateers are numerous in the Channel'.[39]

But, sadly, privateers were also numerous off the American coast, as William reported to his friend John Joseph Bacon, a merchant from the Isle of Man. 'She was got within nine miles of her port in Virginia with 112 slaves when cut out by a French privateer ... They reckoned themselves in the greatest security, for no privateer has ever dared to sail so far up the bay [i.e. Chesapeake Bay].' 'It was really very unfortunate the *Industry* being taken', he wrote to the factors Sparling & Bolden. 'She would have made a good voyage.'[40] It was also very unfortunate for Duke Abashy, the African prince whom we met in the last chapter, for it was on the *Industry* that his two sons had been abducted from the island of São Tomé. When William wrote to him on 16 February 1761, he said that he had as yet received no news as to which French island the privateers had taken their prize. William's claim of ignorance was almost certainly a lie. He had made exertions to get Hindle freed and find him another ship, and these had been successful. William Hindle sailed from the Mersey in command of the slaver *Tyrrell* on 3 February 1761, two weeks before William Earle wrote to Duke Abashy. It seems certain that the two Williams would have met before the ship set sail.

William had many business contacts on the Isle of Man and in the summer and autumn of 1760 was busy looking for a suitable ship to carry Manx trading capital on a slaving venture. He selected for the voyage a brig called the *Mercury* whose name was changed to *Prince Vada* and shares were acquired by three wealthy Manx merchants, William Quayle, Hugh Cosnahan and John Joseph Bacon, who was William's particular friend and would handle most of the business on the Isle of Man. 'I shall take upon myself the direction of the vessel', William wrote to Bacon, and it was decided to send the brig to Angola for a cargo of 350 negroes.[41]

The conversion of the *Prince Vada* and her acquisition of a trading cargo were done at great speed by the standards of the day. Suppliers were

---

39   Letter to Austen, Lawrence & Co., 30 January 1760; to Hindle, 3 April; and to Sparling & Bolden, 8 April, 1760.
40   Letter to Sparling & Bolden, 27 November 1760.
41   20 October 1760. On Manx participation in the slave trade see Wilkins, 1999.

urged to make certain they could supply the goods by the due date and 'to advise by return of post' if unable to do so. William was pleased with the prompt response of his correspondents. 'I think we are very lucky in collecting our cargo so speedy', he wrote to Bacon, who was responsible for organising matters on the Isle of Man, where the ship was to remain while she was fitted out and loaded and then to sail directly to Africa. Much of the cargo came from Holland – beads, Indian textiles, silesias (coarse linens) and knives – and this was to be sent 'by ye first opportunity [i.e. ship] bound for ye Isle of Man'. Other goods came from London, another source of Indian textiles, and from the various manufacturing areas, more knives from Sheffield, ironmongery from Birmingham, guns (heavy Angolas) and cutlasses also from Birmingham, cloth from Halifax, 'deep blue Colchester bays. They are for Angola. I doubt not you know the sort that will do.' An order for provisions was sent to William's correspondent in Belfast, David Gibell, 'ten tierces beef, let it be well cured … twelve firkins butter', and then, shortly before the *Prince Vada* set sail under the command of Captain John Clifton on 22 December, 'sundries' from John Joseph Bacon's own store on the island – brandy, wine, vinegar, tea, soap and a 'sow in pigg.'[42]

William and his clerks and suppliers could now rest for a few days, but not for long as new worries soon appeared. The greatest was the absence of any news of or from Captain Clifton. However, no news might well be good news, as the route to Africa was swarming with French privateers and nowhere more so than in the mouth of the English Channel. William had still heard nothing by 12 February and his letter of that date to Bacon is brimful of his usual confidence:

> I make no doubt he is gone clear … We have heard of many vessels being taken since he went and he has passed the privateers in the mouth of the Channel. If he misses the enemy he is extremely well set up for a voyage which would give me infinite pleasure … I have great expectations which I hope I shall not be disappointed in. I return you my best thanks for the fine codfish and claret and will send you as soon as ready some ale of my own brewing.

There is no real news of Clifton in the rest of the letter book and the remaining letters relating to the voyage of the *Prince Vada* all concern

---

42 Letters to James Wetherhead, 1 November; Thomas Jordan, 8 November; J.J. Bacon, 18 December 1760.

payment of various outstanding bills for the cargo, arrangements for insurance from Angola to the West Indies and the usual contradictory and confusing flurry of letters to Clifton himself and to the various slave factors in the West Indies and Virginia as to where he should seek his market. William was nervous about the possibility of peace, which seemed imminent in the early summer of 1761 and would almost certainly have led to a collapse of prices. Clifton was therefore told 'wherever you sell take no produce upon our account except cotton, nor stay long for a freight.' The British government, however, had little interest in peace, since every year the war continued more French colonies fell into their hands. With this in mind, they deliberately provoked the French by sending an expedition to invade and seize Belle Isle off the Breton coast, 'an intolerable humiliation to Louis XV and, as Pitt intended, a major obstacle to peace.'[43] And so the war continued until February 1763 and in fact increased in scope, as Spain joined in on the French side early in 1762, which enabled the British to add Manila and Havana to their haul of colonies in addition to large numbers of Spanish merchant ships. Meanwhile, the *Prince Vada* loaded just 203 slaves in Angola, a long way short of the 350 planned. The 180 who survived the Middle Passage were sold in Barbados and St Kitts, no doubt at the high prices prevailing, and the brig was back at the Isle of Man to unload a cargo of sugar on 16 April 1762. Just two weeks later we learn that she was to be sold by auction, 'a remarkable fast sailing vessel and well found … fit for the Africa trade', though presumably not fit and fast enough to be used on a second voyage by William and his Manx partners.[44]

There are letters in the letter book relating to three ships in which William Earle was a part-owner but played no part in the management. All three caused William difficulty and losses. On 10 July 1761, he wrote in a letter to John Joseph Bacon that not only was the *Calypso* missing and almost certainly taken but 'we have also had the mortification to hear of our good ship the *Lyme* being taken by five privateers. She had 350 slaves alive out of 514 and two tons of ivory.' The fate of the *Francis* was rather different. William owned a thirty-second part of this 200-ton slaver, which sailed for Africa with Thomas Onslow as commander on 22 February 1760. She was a new ship with 16 six-pounder guns and

43 Letter to Clifton, 18 May 1761; Rodger, 2004, p. 284.
44 *WLA*, 12 April 1762.

a crew of 55 or 60 men and 'promise[d] to do well.'[45] This promise was not fulfilled. On 3 June, William wrote to Mr John Humphreys, to whom he had sold another thirty-second share in the ship. He had terrible news. 'I have the most shocking disagreeable account of the ship *Francis* being lost on the island of Fuertaventura, one of the Canary Islands, and 23 men drowned, 21st of last month in the night.' He enclosed Captain Onslow's

> most melancholy account by which at the conclusion you see the ship was lost by neglect of the second mate keeping no look out, at a time they knew they must be near the land and by which he and his son lost their lives and many more. I am heartily sorry for all concerned.

And that was that. There are no more letters relating to the *Francis*, except a rather protracted correspondence with the underwriters, who were very slow in paying out what was due. Poor watch-keeping in the Canaries had sunk many good English ships and there was nothing much that William could do about it.[46]

William had also sold Humphreys a 1/16th share in the *Baltimore*, a powerful ship with a letter of marque, 18 guns and a crew of 60 in which he had a 1/16th share himself. Captain Francis Lowndes was her commander and she sailed from Liverpool on 25 June 1760 to Malembo in Angola with plans to sell the slaves acquired there in Guadeloupe. 'A great prospect', William wrote to Humphreys, 'which I pray God send that it may reinstate you the loss of the *Francis*.'[47] The voyage of the *Baltimore* was slow but otherwise uneventful and she was back in Liverpool on 27 January 1762, having delivered 287 slaves to Guadeloupe. The main interest in the Earle letter book relates, however, to the *Baltimore*'s previous non-slaving voyage to Maryland in 1758–59 to pick up a cargo of tobacco. In the course of this voyage, on 26 September 1758 she captured a Dutch ship called the *Resolute* sailing from Curaçao to Amsterdam with a cargo of sugar, coffee, indigo, tobacco, hides and other colonial goods. The *Resolute* and her cargo were then declared good prize in the Vice-Admiralty Court of Maryland on

45 Letter to Bacon 10 July 1760; letter to Butler & Mauger, 22 February 1760.
46 Letter to Humphreys, 3 June 1760; notice in *WLA*, 6 June 1760, with a copy of a letter from Mr Nathan Dickinson, chief mate, dated Tenerife, 17 April.
47 Letter to Humphreys, 2 July 1760.

the basis of what reads like very dishonest evidence from members of her crew and, especially, from the mate, who seems to have been offered command of the prize if his evidence should condemn her.[48]

The syndicate that owned the *Baltimore* may or may not have believed that the *Resolute* was justly condemned, but they were certainly pleased to get this windfall addition to their working capital. An auction 'of the entire cargo of the snow *Resolute*' was held at the Merchants Coffee House in Liverpool on 5 February 1760 and the proceeds of the sale of the ship and her cargo, estimated at £8,000, was to be used to fit out the *Baltimore* for her slaving voyage to Angola. William approved of this plan and advised John Humphreys to keep his 1/16th share and remain in the syndicate. 'I have 1/16th myself and reckon it a good prospect and you have no reason to dispute my judgment.'[49] William's judgment was normally sound enough, but not on this occasion. Over a year later, on 6 July 1761, he reported to Humphreys that the former owners of the Dutch prize had appealed her condemnation in the High Court of Admiralty in London and had won their case, the Maryland Court being judged 'too much favouring the party of the said Francis Lowndes [Captain of the *Baltimore*] ... and not in the least regarding the requisites and forms in law ... and had condemned the said ship ... against right and justice.' William apologised effusively to Humphreys for this contretemps. 'I am sorry to acquaint you restitution is ordered to be made to the applicants in the *Baltimore*'s prize', a decision that would ensure a very substantial loss on her last cruise and little likelihood of profit in the current one. 'Never was anything so unlucky as you knowing me, to be drawn into the *Francis* and *Baltimore* ... I can say I never in all my foreign trade lost £20 of a voyage before.'

A few weeks later he was writing to Captain Lowndes to let him know

> the worst concerning your voyage to Maryland. The *Resolute* is ordered by the Lords of the Admiralty to be restored to the Appellants ... Pray, God bless you and send you luck. Mine is very bad. I have lost the *Lyme* and *Calypso* both taken, the latter homeward

48 Evidence for both the original case in Maryland and the appeal can be found in TNA HCA 42/91.
49 Auction notice in *WLA*, 4 January 1760; letter to John Humphreys, 23 April 1760.

bound had made a good voyage. I wish you your health and success, Mrs Earle joining me in best respects.

This is the lowest point in the letter book, but such despair did not last long and William was soon once again his usual sanguine self. On 30 July he wrote to Bacon in answer to a letter in which the Manx merchant had offered to lend him money to get him through his bad patch. 'I am very much obliged to you as also your very kind offer to serve me, which I must acknowledge as a very particular favour and confidence put in me.' However, William assured Bacon that his affairs were in good order despite all. 'Things will soon come round, and I am not at all pinched.'⁵⁰ Things did come round, but they were not quite as rosy as he reported since he was forced to borrow money from his sister Sarah, Captain Copeland's wife, and he also borrowed on the money market. 'I have been so pushed for money that I have taken £450 on bond', he wrote, these being the only two occasions in the letter book when he mentions borrowing money, though he like everybody else did most of his business on credit. Borrowing on bond, at or just below the legal maximum rate of interest of five per cent, was certainly common in the Liverpool merchant community, so William may have been unusual in avoiding this additional expense. He was certainly careful with his money and borrowing was not generally seen to be a very good idea, 'a possible first step toward financial and moral bankruptcy', as David Hancock puts it.⁵¹

It must be obvious from the past few pages that marine insurance played a big part in William's business life. By this date it was usual to insure both ship and cargo (though not everybody did) and, since the 1730s, it had become customary for the underwriters to pay out virtually the full value of a loss if they were satisfied that the claim was an honest one, instead of as little as three-quarters as had previously been normal. Shares in slave ships were insured by the individual owners, so that there were rarely policies covering the whole of a ship and its cargo. One regularly recurring risk against which owners could not insure themselves was the death of slaves by what were considered natural causes. 'The insurance takes upon him the risques of the loss, capture, and death of slaves', we are told in a contemporary manual, 'but

50 Letters to Humphreys, 6 July; to Lowndes, 2 August; to Bacon, 30 July 1761.
51 Letter to Copeland, 17 July 1761; to Carter, n.d. but early July; Hancock, 1995, p. 247.

natural death is always understood to be excepted – by natural death is meant, not only when it happens by disease or sickness, but also when the captive destroys himself through despair, which often happens,' thus providing a compelling motive to keep the slaves alive.[52] William did not underwrite insurance himself, but he was seen by his contemporaries as knowledgeable in such matters and many letters in the letter book concern policies he had arranged for himself, co-owners and other individuals who sought his expertise. Since the letter book covers just about the worst period of the Seven Years' War, it comes as no surprise that premiums were very high. The *Calypso*, for instance, was insured at 12 guineas per £100 for the voyage out to Africa and then 'at and from the coast of Africa to her first port or ports of discharge in British America ... at 8 guineas per cent.' Such figures should be compared with the standard rate in the peaceful early 1770s for the whole voyage from Liverpool to America via Africa, which was seven or eight guineas per cent.[53] Given the fact of high premiums, merchants and ships' captains had various options. They could simply shoulder the risk themselves and sail with no insurance, and many apparently did, while others reduced the size of the premium somewhat by sailing 'short insured'. William Earle did not like to do this, though he sometimes had no choice. He was an adventurous and sometimes innovative merchant, but he was also prudent and his ideal policy embodied the advice that he gave to a business partner in Barcelona. 'Run no risques', he wrote, by which he meant insure our ship and its cargo to the full amount. 'Pray God she arrives', he wrote of a ship sailing for the Mediterranean, 'but if not, she is full insured at a moderate premium', an ideal situation which enabled everyone concerned to sleep soundly.[54]

Insuring to the full amount did not mean foolishness and William took great pains to get premiums reduced. Risk assessment was not yet a science and there was plenty of scope for negotiation. But, first of all, it was important to choose the brokers carefully. 'Good' and 'safe' were the adjectives usually used, by which he meant honest and able to pay, sound

52 John Weskett quoted in Oldham, 2007, p. 303.
53 TNA C107/11, underwriting books of Abraham Clibbon, 1768–75.
54 Letter to James Crisp, 4 June 1761; to Earle & Hodgson in Leghorn, 20 May 1761. There is much useful material on insurance in LRO 387 MD 59, the letter book of Thomas Leyland, 1786–88. He claimed (pp. 101, 105) that Liverpool premiums in the slave trade were lower than those quoted at London, one of many ways in which Liverpool slavers undercut their rivals in other ports.

men whose resources could cover any contingency. 'Your underwriters', he wrote to Richard Rabone, who had invested in the *Calypso*, 'are both looked upon as very safe men.' William's letters show no great loyalty to any particular broker. His normal habit was to shop around till he found the best deal. In January 1761 he was trying to arrange insurance for Mr James Littley, a relative of his wife, but the premium asked was so high that he advised him 'to get it done in Dublin.' Bargaining could also be effective; for one voyage he got the premium halved from ten to five per cent.[55] Merchants and brokers alike depended on an efficient information service to calculate risks and William was well organised in this respect. Private information that a French frigate was just about to sail from Bayonne for Africa prompted him to get insurance at the low rate of six per cent on the *Prince Vada* very quickly before the insurers found out the dangers that she would be running. 'By this you will be much short insured on both ship and cargo', he noted, 'but you have time to add sufficient to cover your interest if you choose', though as it turned out it proved impossible to get full cover, so great was the danger from privateers at that time. 'I couldn't get any more insurance', he complained to John Joseph Bacon, though 'I make no doubt he [i.e. Captain Clifton in the *Prince Vada*] is gone clear.' Nevertheless, he often did top up the insurance on his ships, sometimes after they had sailed and sometimes so much that underwriters became suspicious that he had insured the vessel and her cargo for more than they were worth. Messrs Butler & Mauger, for instance, the underwriters who insured the *Francis*, were not satisfied until William had produced an affidavit made under oath before the local Member of Parliament that the insurance made with them 'was all the insurance he made on the said ship.'[56]

The months covered by the letter book were exceptionally difficult for both merchants and insurers; indeed, they were probably the worst in the whole of William's career as a slave merchant. Premiums shot up as insurers panicked, from ten to 25 per cent for instance on voyages to South Carolina after a ship had been captured. Sometimes insurers simply refused to quote when times seemed particularly hard. 'There is a vessel taken by the French worth £30,000', William wrote to his friend

---

55 Letters to Rabone, 23 July; to Littley, 26 January; and to Carter, 10 August 1761.

56 Letters to Bacon, 31 October 1760, 12 February 1761; to Butler & Mauger, 19 June 1760.

John Darbyshire, who was asking him to fix up some insurance. 'The underwriters don't care to underwrite any vessel further at present and I would advise you to let it alone for a while.' Such a situation required careful thought by a man who preferred to 'run no risques'. He could wait a bit until the panic died down or he could just go ahead without insurance if he thought 'the voyage will bear it'. And even when he could get insured there was the problem of the snail-like speed with which insurers settled claims in difficult times. They were slow to agree a claim and slow to pay and sometimes they paid in very long-dated bills. But none of this was very surprising, given the hard times, and most Liverpool merchants would probably have agreed with William Earle that 'our underwriters are good and so we shall be little in the losing'.[57] The times may have been hard but they were still making money.

William Earle's ability to make this money depended very heavily on the business skills and trustworthiness of a wealthy London merchant, Joseph Wimpey of Newgate Street, to whom about ten per cent of all the letters in the letter book were directed. Wimpey's role in William's affairs was never given a particular label, but he was in fact his money man, his banker and acceptance house, and a very necessary part of his business life. Very little in English commerce was done for cash, and there was as a result a stream of paper in the form of bills, drafts and promissory notes coming into William's hands to be paid out by him or to him at various due dates in the future. It was the function of Wimpey to act as a banker for William, receiving bills owing to him and paying bills drawn by him when they were due, at the same time keeping a careful balance of William's account.

A typical letter from William to Joseph Wimpey would warn the Londoner that he had drawn on him one or more bills, mainly to be paid to suppliers, and would enclose bills due to William Earle himself which would sooner or later cover this outlay. For instance, on 14 June 1760, he wrote: 'I have taken the liberty to draw upon you the sundry bills as under and enclosed you have two bills, value £85, and you may be sure before the rest become due, you shall be in cash.' Listed below were five short-dated bills payable by William, total value £275, with dates for payment a few weeks in the future. On other occasions, William sent Wimpey bills drawn in his or his partners' favour and asked him

---

57 Letters to Darbyshire, 28 March 1761; to Buddicomb & Woodhouse, 19 June 1761; and Isaac Dove, 1 August 1761.

to get them accepted by some acknowledged 'name' and then either pay them into his account or return them to Liverpool. Here, such accepted bills, suitably discounted, circulated as money. In this way, a bill drawn on his London correspondents by a slave factor in the West Indies to pay for a cargo of slaves could be brought back to Liverpool in the slave ship that had conveyed them. And then, by return of post, this bill could be converted into a negotiable piece of paper which could be used to pay for export goods or fitting out costs some months or years before the bill was due for payment. In other words, much of Liverpool's slave-trading business was financed by the wealthy West India merchant community in London, a fact well known to William Earle and the slave ship captains and merchants in Liverpool, who were not heard to complain that the Londoners grew rich even quicker than they did. They just hoped that these Londoners would stay solvent and meet their claims on them. This did not of course always happen. We have seen above that Samuel Touchet, guarantor of most of the bills to pay for the slaves aboard the *Calypso*, was unable to honour his guarantees and, in June 1772, there was an even greater disaster when Joseph Wimpey, banker to many other Liverpool merchants besides William, 'stopt payment and afterwards became a Bankrupt.'[58] Trading in slaves was profitable but, like all branches of trade, it had its problems.

58 For the bill system see Checkland, 1958; Anderson, 1977; Price, 1991. On Wimpey's bankruptcy see TNA B4/21/52 and Radburn, 2009, p. 105.

CHAPTER FIVE

Jack of All Trades

> 'To be sold, a parcel of fine dryed lyng, … and
> cod fish in barrels, also a quantity of fine cod
> train oil of the best kind. Apply to Mr William
> Earle in Water Street.'[1]

This advertisement in the *Liverpool Advertiser* may not be quite what
one might expect a major slave merchant to insert in the local paper,
but it is in fact a fair reflection of the wide range of activities, other
than slave trading, in which William Earle participated. Some of
these were quite closely related to the slave trade, but others had
nothing whatever to do with it. William was described as 'merchant
and ironmonger' in 1766 in the first local Directory and, although
this was still short of the whole truth, it is a lot more accurate than
simply labelling him 'slave merchant'.

A good idea of the range of his non-slaving merchant activities can
be gained by an analysis of the ships owned or part-owned by him in
the Liverpool shipping database.[2] This confirms that William was an
important slave merchant, with a share in the ownership of 41 ships,
which made between them 97 voyages. But it also shows that he was
part-owner of another eight non-slaving ships, which made between
them 30 voyages. Two brigs accounted for over half of these, the 70-ton
Neptune, which was sent out on four voyages from 1764 to 1767, and
the 100-ton *Stanley*, bought new in 1765, which made 12 voyages in
the years to 1776. Both ships had exactly the same ownership, William
Earle, John Woodhouse and Joseph Carter, who was master for 12 of
the 16 voyages made by the two ships. Neither of William's partners
had anything to do with slaving, but they both played a prominent part

1 *WLA*, 27 August 1756.
2 LTS.

in the fishing voyages, which are well documented in the letter book and will be discussed later. Woodhouse was one of William's closest business associates and the partnership of Earle & Woodhouse often appears in the shipping news reported in the local paper, nearly always as importers of fish from the North Fishery or the Isle of Man, or of butter from Belfast.

Woodhouse & Earle did not use their own ships for these short voyages, reserving them for longer expeditions. The first two of the four undertaken by the *Neptune* were from Liverpool to Portugal, Cadiz, Leghorn (Livorno) and back; and from Liverpool to Quebec and then to Malaga, presumably with fish, and then back home with wine. The other two voyages were both to Barbados, stopping at an Irish port for a cargo of provisions, and then back to Liverpool with colonial staples. Most of the voyages of the *Stanley* were similar to the first voyage of the *Neptune* in 1764–65, no less than ten of them from 1766 to 1776 involving a visit to the Mediterranean, sometimes via an Irish port and nearly always via Gibraltar or Cadiz, and then mainly to the wine ports in eastern and south-eastern Spain, such as Denia and Malaga, but sometimes much further, to Port Mahon in Minorca (an English naval base), Leghorn, Zante (the modern Zakinthos, famous for its currants), Venice and, on the last of these voyages in the summer of 1776, to Smyrna in Anatolia via Leghorn. One suspects that William's elder brother Thomas who, in partnership with Thomas Hodgson, owned a merchant house in Leghorn, played some part in these Mediterranean voyages, but he does not appear in the list of owners of the two ships. The *Stanley* made just two voyages which differed from this pattern, one to New York, Philadelphia and then to Hamburg and back home, and the other to Hamburg and then Riga and back to Liverpool.

The same syndicate, with the addition of Thomas Hodgson, a partner in many Earle enterprises, and Peter Holme, a Liverpool brandy merchant, were owners of a 100-ton French prize called the *Providential Friend*, which made four voyages between 1758 and 1764. Three of these were from Liverpool to St Petersburg and back, a trading route which, we shall see later, was more the preserve of the eldest brother Ralph Earle than of William. Ralph was not listed as a co-owner of the *Providential Friend*, but he was for the 90-ton *Polly*, a vessel which traded to the Mediterranean in 1762 and Barbados in 1763 and had the distinction of being co-owned by all three brothers, William, Thomas and Ralph, together once again with Thomas Hodgson and Peter Holme. The *Venus*, a 150-ton brig built in North Carolina, was entirely owned by the brothers Thomas and William. She traded to Charleston in 1771–72 and to Philadelphia, Jamaica and Honduras in 1772–73.[3]

The product of this last voyage can be seen in *Williamson's Liverpool Advertiser* for 14 May 1773:

> To be sold at auction Monday the 7th of June next, at Mr Ralph Earle's timber yard, a cargo of mahogany (in lots suitable to the purchaser) now landing from over board the ship *Venus*, from the Bay of Honduras; the logs are large and the quality supposed to be the best of any cargo arrived here of a long time. Any person desirous of viewing the same may apply to Mr Thomas Earle.

So the ship was owned by Thomas and William, the sale was held in Ralph's timber yard, and those interested should apply to Thomas, truly a family venture though the amount of active interest of each brother is not stated. Both Thomas and Ralph took shares as sleeping partners in William's slaving ventures from time to time, and the *Polly* may reflect similar investment by William in a ship managed mainly in Thomas's interests, as he appears elsewhere as an importer of mahogany, an expensive wood in the height of fashion.

The remaining three non-slaving ships in which William Earle had a share were the 80-ton *Jupiter*, which made three voyages from Liverpool to the West Indies and back in 1762–64, the 330-ton 'mark' *Baltimore*, which we encountered in the last chapter, undertaking one voyage to Maryland and back in 1759 with a prize, which was restored to her Dutch owners on appeal, and another slaving voyage to Angola and Guadeloupe, and finally the 70-ton snow *Thomas & Mary*. This last ship, probably named after Thomas and his wife Mary, made two voyages under Earle ownership, one to Leghorn and the other to Ireland, Newfoundland and then to the Mediterranean with a cargo of fish.

These 30 voyages show that William was much more than a slave merchant; indeed, one might call him a general merchant, since they encompass the whole range of Liverpool's trading empire, from Smyrna and Venice to Newfoundland, from Riga and St Petersburg to the West Indies, and of course as a slaver to Africa as well. And these are just

---

3 For Ralph Earle, see pp. 181–92.

the voyages in which William had a share of the vessel. Much of his trade was conducted in vessels belonging to others, as can be seen from notices of incoming ships and auctions in the local paper, where we can see him importing and selling goods from the Shetlands, the North Fishery and many ports in Ireland, as well as places mentioned above, such as the Mediterranean and the West Indies.

The only one of these Earle-owned ships to appear in William's letter book was the snow *Thomas & Mary* which, like the slave ships discussed in the last chapter, had a fairly chequered experience under Earle ownership. The dataset names the owners as William Earle, John Brooks (a wealthy merchant and an associate of his brother Ralph), Peter Holme the brandy merchant and Thomas Hodgson. The letter book, however, shows that half the ship was owned by the firm of Earle & Hodgson in Leghorn and, in the only letter in the letter book between the two brothers, we learn that she had taken a cargo of fish to the Tuscan port. The only other information about this voyage is in the Liverpool paper, which reported that the *Thomas & Mary* had been captured by the French and ransomed for £1,000.[4] Ransom was an alternative to the captured vessel being taken to a French port and there sold after being condemned by a suitable court of admiralty. The normal procedure was for the two captains to negotiate a figure for the ransom, usually 'no more than a third part of the intrinsect value of ship and goodes.' Two of the prisoners would then be taken to France or a French colony as hostages for the payment of this sum, while the captured ship was free to continue her voyage with a pass to protect her from recapture by another privateer, such passes normally allowing 'sixty days grace'.[5]

There is much more information about the next voyage of the *Thomas & Mary*, her last under Earle ownership. This begins with a letter written on 16 February 1761 to James Moore, a merchant in Waterford in south-east Ireland. 'I have a vessel about 120 tons burthen that intend [I] for Newfoundland if you can give any encouragement for passengers from your place ... She is a fast sailor, has two decks and a good cabin, has eight guns and every way compleat for her size.' William was about to enter the emigrant business. Waterford, and south-east Ireland generally, were prominent in the cod fishery and the

---

4 WELB, Letter to Earle & Hodgson, 21 May 1761; *WLA*, 13 February 1761.
5 *WLA*, 13 February 1761; Earle, 1998, p. 123.

Irish trade with Newfoundland and the region was also the main source
of Irish emigrants to the 'Land'. These were Catholics and should not be
confused with the Protestant emigrants from Ulster, the Scots-Irish who
were to play such a prominent part in American history. The carriage
of emigrants from Waterford was a new business for Liverpool shipping,
but there was no denying the attraction of a cargo who walked on board
and paid in advance for the privilege of being carried across the Atlantic.[6]

This was William's first venture into this business and his letters
suggest he did not know much about it. 'Should be glad', he wrote to
Moore on 16 February, 'if you could advise me as soon as possible
the possibility of getting 100 passengers and what they pay and what
privilidge of luggage each person has, and whether if no possibility of
passengers whether a freight ...' A month later, he wrote again. 'I find we
are already too late for passengers so have dropt that part of the scheme.'
However, he had second thoughts on this and felt they could probably
get 30 or 40 passengers, but meanwhile he asked Moore to gather a
cargo of pork, beef, butter and oatmeal for him. The *Thomas & Mary*,
commanded by William Buddicomb, eventually sailed from Waterford
on 1 May 1761 with this cargo of foodstuffs, and 44 passengers, 'and
has a good prospect ... Please God she arrives, if not she is full insured
at a moderate premium.'[7]

Once again, William's usual policy of covering himself fully with
insurance turned out to be a wise one. For God did not oblige and just
two weeks later, the snow was again captured, this time by a privateer
from Nantes, and these captors also agreed to negotiate a ransom rather
than take her into port. This was agreed at 450 guineas and the captain's
brother-in-law was taken to St Malo as hostage for payment. Directly
he got the news, William ordered a credit of £10 to be paid to him
to cover the hostage's expenses in France, while he got down to the
business of adjusting matters with the underwriters 'so as to get the
money [and then] I will get him discharged and order him to London.'
Meanwhile, Captain Buddicomb continued his voyage to Newfoundland,
where he had orders to sell his cargo and then load dried and pickled
fish and oil and 'all the passengers you can stow for Ireland', many of

6 Mannion, 1977, introduction; Lockhart, 1976, ch. 7.
7 Letters to Moore, 16 February, 16 March 1761; to Earle & Hodgson, 21 May
   1761.

these Irishmen just working their summers in Newfoundland rather than settling there permanently.[8]

William did not despair at the misfortune of having the same ship captured and ransomed twice. He was instead determined to make the best of a bad thing, making the passengers contribute a pound or more each towards the ransom and arranging for the ransom bill to be paid promptly by the due date of 10 September. He was not too pleased with Captain Buddicomb or his friend and partner John Woodhouse who had travelled with the ship. They had been guilty of the heinous crime of not keeping him fully informed, no letters when they sailed from Ireland, no account of the number of passengers, no details of the capture and the amount of plunder seized by their French captors, no copy of the ransom bill sent in order to speed up the settlement. Worst of all, they had given in to their captors too quickly and so had agreed to too high a ransom. 'The underwriters think if you had had a little patience you might have ransomed much easier.' Still, all in all, things were not too bad, as he wrote to Joseph Carter. 'The passengers out and home will pay all the expenses of the voyage. I am greatly in advance for that concern', a comment which explains why he was tempted into the emigrant business. It paid well. And, sure enough, in the final pages of the letter book, William is arranging for another voyage from Waterford to Newfoundland with passengers and provisions.[9]

The main purpose of these voyages to Newfoundland was to acquire a cargo of fish, and fish, from Scottish waters as well as from 'the Land', played an important part in the business life of William Earle, who was prominent on the Liverpool waterfront as a fish merchant as well as a slave merchant. This interest was apparent in the very first year of *Williamson's Liverpool Advertiser*. Here can be found an advertisement, on 27 August 1756, for the sale of 'fine dryed lyng, ... and cod fish in barrels, also a quantity of fine cod train oil of the best kind, lately imported in the *Adventure* from the North Sea Fishery. Apply to Mr William Earle in Water Street.' The *Adventure* was described in the following year, in an application for a Letter of Marque, as a vessel of 80 tons, eight guns and 25 men, and she was owned by the old team of William Earle, John Woodhouse and Joseph Carter.[10]

8 *LL*, 9 June 1761; WELB, letter to Mrs Buddicom, 12 June 1761.
9 Letter to Joseph Carter, 6 July 1761.
10 HCA 26/8, 19 October 1757.

Similar advertisements for the sale of fish – ling, cod, herrings, mainly from the 'North Fishery' and the Shetlands – can be found in succeeding years and some of these notices mention other Scottish goods for sale, such as whale and fish oil, hides, tallow, calfskins, stockings and slates. Most of this fish was 'well-cured in tight barrels', that is split open, salted, dried and tight-packed in layers of salt, but the business was not entirely wholesale. There were 'small quantities for house-keepers.' For larger quantities there were two main markets, Liverpool itself for the provisioning of ships, especially slavers and West Indiamen, and Spain, Portugal and the Mediterranean, where cargoes of cured fish were always welcome.[11]

The key man in this business was John Woodhouse, a merchant of Liverpool. William often referred to him, and Joseph Carter, as the 'young men', an epithet which probably meant they were former apprentices. Woodhouse was an imaginative and innovative merchant, just the sort of man to appeal to William Earle. In 1773, we learn that he sought safety from a storm in the harbour of Marsala in north-western Sicily. Woodhouse enjoyed the local wine so much that he decided to add brandy to it and market it as an alternative to the very popular Madeira, sending 8,000 gallons to Liverpool on trial. The new product, named 'Marsala', was a mixture of 100 litres of the Sicilian wine and two litres of spirits. It enjoyed a boom in Britain and especially in the navy, where its ability to survive long voyages as well as its taste and strength found great favour. Nelson described the wine in 1798 as 'so good that any gentleman's table might receive it, and it will be of real use to our seamen', while the museum in Marsala displays a letter from the Admiral to Woodhouse, with an order to furnish the Royal Navy with 40,000 gallons of this wonderful fortified wine.[12]

In 1755, Woodhouse was granted a lease of Isle Martin,[13] one of the beautiful Summer Islands off the north-west coast of Scotland, where he set up a business curing herrings which he bought from the local fishermen and shipped to Hull, London, Liverpool and the Mediterranean. Judging by Woodhouse's other activities in the 1750s and 1760s, he was probably in partnership with William Earle for this

---

11 *WLA*, 27 August 1756, 11 and 16 February 1757, 10 February 1758, 11 January 1760.

12 Trevelyan, 1972, pp. 15–17; http://www.wine-searcher.com/regions-marsala.

13 www.islemartin.co.uk/history.

enterprise and it is more than likely that some of the fish from the 'Northern Fishery' sold at William's warehouse in Liverpool was in fact from Isle Martin. The fishing expeditions covered by letters in the letter book were, however, further north, partly on the Isle of Lewis with Stornaway as a base but mainly in the Shetlands. Although the locals did some fishing, most of the fish sold until the mid-eighteenth century was caught by the Dutch, much to the disgust of mercantilist English and Scots. A tract was published in 1750 by a John Campbell who had spent five years in the islands, 'to awaken you my countrymen out of your deep lethargy.' Campbell claimed, presumably with some exaggeration, that each year 'ten or eleven hundred [Dutch] sail ... enter fishing upon this coast the beginning of June and continue till the beginning of September.' They were said to employ 20,000 hands and to make a profit of a million pounds sterling a year. He suggested that the Dutch could be outmanoeuvred by English and Scots fishermen arriving shortly before them, 'about the latter end of May, and then you will have the start of the Dutch who will be very much displeased to see English ships upon the coast of Shetland.'[14]

This and other publicity did awaken the writer's countrymen, but attempts to set up a company to compete with the Dutch were not very successful. William Earle and his partners, from Liverpool, London, the Isle of Man, and from as far away as Italy and Spain, were to fare rather better. Just when he started to exploit the vast fish stocks of Shetland is not clear, but he was certainly importing fish from these northern islands by 1757. What this involved can be seen from a mass of letters in his letter book that concern an expedition which set out for the Shetlands early in 1760. William was associated in this project with his two 'young men', Joseph Carter and John Woodhouse. These two were friends as well as partners, judging by the fact that he signed a letter to them in June, 'yours very affectionately', something he did not do for anyone else. In the winter of 1759/60, Carter had been in Stornoway and Woodhouse in Liverpool, where his presence is marked by an advertisement offering for sale in William's warehouse 'a parcel of Scotch white herrings just imported.'[15] 'White' refers to the method of curing, sometimes known as 'Dutch white', in which the fish once caught were opened and gutted on board the fishing boat, then salted

14 Campbell, 1750.
15 *WLA*, 8 February 1760.

by rubbing their inside with salt and packed into barrels with more salt between the fish. This, considered the 'most esteemed' method of curing the fish, should be contrasted with 'red herrings', which were soaked in brine for 24 hours, then taken out, spitted and hung in a chimney above a very smoky brushwood fire for at least ten days.

The plan was for Carter and Woodhouse to sail for the Shetlands at the beginning of April 1760 and to spend the whole spring and summer there, buying cured fish, mainly ling, from the local fishermen until 'all August', by which time it was considered that enough fish would have been cured to fill a vessel of 80 to 90 tons. If all went well, this should be a very profitable enterprise, since cured ling fetched £17 to £20 per ton and outgoings were very small, compared for instance with those necessary for a slaving expedition. There was also money to be made exploiting government schemes to promote fishing by offering bounties for boats built for the trade and tax breaks on the salt needed to cure the fish. In order to ensure that Carter and Woodhouse would have enough money, William arranged a line of credit with the bankers William Hogg & Son in Glasgow, who were also to oblige with other favours such as accepting bills and forwarding mail.[16]

Once he had seen his associates off to the Shetland Isles, William settled down to business, writing letter after letter to reduce any risks associated with this expedition. William was a prudent merchant who never liked to have 100 per cent of anything, so his first task was to bring in men with money as partners and so reduce the commitments of Earle, Woodhouse and Carter. This did not prove too difficult as most people were optimistic about the prospects of the voyage. It was decided that the main market for the fish should be Barcelona (with Leghorn as a possible second choice), so he was pleased to acquire a partner familiar not just with Barcelona but also with the Shetland fishing industry. Joseph Crisp, a London merchant with a large share in a merchant house in Barcelona, agreed to become his main partner, taking 62 tons of the fish cargo and so leaving 28 tons to William.[17] He reduced his commitment still further by disposing of some of his own share to John Finch and John Joseph Bacon, two Manx merchants who were old friends. If all this sounds a bit too cautious, one should

16 The story is pieced together from several letters in the letter book, mainly written to J.J. Bacon, James Crisp and Carter & Woodhouse.
17 On Crisp's trading activities see Colley, 2007, ch. 3.

remember that this expedition was being planned in the middle of the Seven Years' War.

The next task was to find a suitable vessel to carry the fish from the Shetlands to Barcelona. Given William's unfortunate recent experiences with privateers, it is not surprising that his plan was to charter a neutral ship and fake its papers so that it would seem that the fish was the property of neutrals. This was easy enough as it was standard procedure for Liverpool merchants to ship in neutral ships with false papers, and the choice fell on a Dutch brig, *Susanna & Cordelia*, commanded by Captain Berond de Boer. William sent to the Shetlands a charter-party with blanks for the fake foreign names of the shippers and consignees and detailed instructions on how to fill it all up. 'This trip will determine our pursueing or dropping this trade', he wrote to Carter and Woodhouse. 'This is a great undertaking. I pray God it answers.'[18]

Everything went very well, at least at the Scottish end of the voyage. On 30 July, he wrote to his 'young men' in a generally optimistic tone. 'Since my last the weather has been very favourable, in hopes you will have a good summer to make your fish. I think there will be a deal of money to be made from fish arriving before Lent.' News did not travel very fast from either the Shetlands or Barcelona, but early in September he was able to report to John Joseph Bacon on the Isle of Man that Captain de Boer had arrived in the Shetlands on 14 August. 'The fish was all bought and only waited a few good days [i.e. calm days for loading]'. And on 29 October he wrote to James Crisp in London, informing him of

> the departure of *Susannah & Cornelia* on 16 September with a fine wind ... and I hope you will soon hear an account of her arrival at Barcelona and a good market. 65 tons shipt for your account. As to the quality of the fish ... the young man who shipt it says it is the best cargo they ever saw.

William arranged for Joseph Carter to sail with De Boer to Barcelona, where he was to spy out the market, as he had little faith in James Crisp and his associates. Patience was now needed by William in Liverpool as 'the letters from Barcelona seldom come under six weeks.' But at last, in a postscript to a letter written to Bacon on Christmas Day 1760, he was able to tell him that the *Susanna & Cordelia* had

18 Letters to Carter & Woodhouse, 24 June and 7 July 1760.

arrived safely at Barcelona on 11 November, having been stopped three times on the way and boarded 'by two French privateers, an English man-of-war and a Turk [i.e. Moslem corsair].' All that trouble getting a neutral Dutch carrier had been worthwhile. The fish had sold easily and well and in a few days the brig would be sailing along the coast to Sette (Sète) to take on her return cargo, French brandy cunningly disguised as Spanish.

The *Susanna & Cordelia* now set sail back to the Isle of Man, her final destination in this roundabout voyage. In addition to the brandy, she carried wine, lemons and 63 dozen silk handkerchiefs, a product for which Barcelona was famous. There were no stops and searches on this return voyage, but there were plenty of other problems. The various owners in the Isle of Man, London and Liverpool were in dispute over just how much cargo belonged to each of them, this getting sufficiently heated as to cause William to swear he would never do business with Crisp again. Coming from the Mediterranean, the ship was forced to do quarantine either in England or Ireland when she arrived at the Isle of Man on 4 February 1761. The quarantine station at Highlake (Hoylake) on the Wirral was chosen and eventually reached, despite the local pilot somehow managing to put the ship aground on Hoyle Sand. William was now confident that his local knowledge would enable him to shorten the quarantine. But he reckoned without the local collector, a petty bureaucrat 'who sticks up literally to his instructions' and kept the brig in quarantine not just for the 40 days that the name implies, but for another 14 days on top of that 'to air his goods'. So it was not until 28 March, 54 days after his arrival, that De Boer was able to sail into the harbour at Douglas and begin to unload the cargo. And even then there were problems in shifting the brandy. But such things are sent to try the patience of merchants and, by March 1761, William was becoming more interested in his new scheme, the emigrant business from Ireland to Newfoundland discussed above.[19]

William Earle clearly enjoyed novelty and there is a freshness and enthusiasm in the correspondence relating to the fishing expedition and the emigrant trade which make his letters on these subjects enjoyable to read. But he must have been well aware that his greatest skills were those acquired in his years of apprenticeship and training in the slave trade. And it seems probable that of all the skills necessary for

19 See above, pp. 100–2.

this trade, William's greatest pride was in his impressive knowledge of exactly what goods were in demand in the various slaving centres on the African coast. He could and did employ this expertise as ship's husband, and there are many letters in the letter book referring to his acquisition of goods such as beads and Indian textiles for ships in which he had a managing interest.[20] But his activities in providing cargoes or parts of cargoes went further than this. William owned warehouses and a shop and these provided a store from which slave merchants could buy a range of goods in demand in the slave trade. Much of this could be described as 'ironmongery', thus justifying his description as 'merchant and ironmonger'.

The most important class of iron (and sometimes copper or brass) goods were the bracelets and armlets known as manillas or maneloes, which were used in West Africa for personal adornment and sometimes as a medium of exchange. William ordered these from two main manufacturers, Messrs Joseph Percival & Co. of Bristol and John Darbyshire of Birmingham. Sometimes the maneloes would be ordered for a specific ship, such as the basket containing 300 arm maneloes and the five baskets with 1,000 leg maneloes ordered from Darbyshire to be delivered to the owners of the *Pitt*, a London ship. Both Darbyshire and Percival also supplied iron, copper and brass rods, such as those ordered from Percival for the *African*, another London ship owned by Messrs Hutchinson & Mure. 'You may depend on them being down in London at the limited time [i.e. within the time limits agreed]', wrote William. 'You may be assured of every thing being good in their kind and charged the lowest price.'[21]

In addition to these specific orders, William kept in his shop an assortment of similar goods from which slavers could make their purchases. On 27 February 1760, for instance, he wrote to Darbyshire ordering maneloes for his shop. 'When it suits, you may send me 1,000 leg, 100 arm and 30 long leg for stock.' And, in October, he added a postscript to an order of 1,400 maneloes for the ship *Hammond*. 'As the Calabar ships will be going out in the spring, I think about 2,000 leg, 500 arm and 80 long leg exclusive of this order will be needed.'

20 William and other Earles were later to be involved in a bead exporting company; see below pp. 150–51.
21 Letter to Hutchinson & Mure, 3 July 1761. See Johnson, 1976 for information on maneloes and similar products.

In December, it is clear that he had had another stock check. 'We have not many brass maneloes by us, a few will not be amiss for an assortment.' Joseph Percival was also approached to keep stocks up. 'We make a poor figure in the retail copper business for want of assortment', William wrote on 7 February 1761. Carriage from Birmingham was by canal but from Bristol it was by sea and, although not very far, this could be a tricky voyage in wartime. 'Please forward some rods soon', William wrote on 18 October 1760. 'We shall want I suppose about 100 boxes [125 rods in each] very soon after Christmas. The passages are so uncertain from Bristol that I doubt unless sent soon we may be disappointed.' Although maneloes and rods were the main items in this ironmongery business, Darbyshire and Percival supplied William with many other goods, not all of them for the slave trade – hoes for work on plantations, smoothing irons, tea kettles, locks and a host of other things. William also supplied ironwork for ships, such as the swivel hooks and marline spikes for which he billed the owners of the ship *Brew* on 31 December 1760.[22] The word 'manelo' is so close to 'manacle' that it is something of a surprise to find that William does not seem to have dealt in manacles, chains, irons, neck collars, thumbscrews and the rest of the obscene paraphernalia used by slavers to restrain their cargo. There is an advertisement in the *Liverpool Advertiser* for 27 May 1757 for a parcel of shackles, handcuffs, chains and neck-collars to be sold at auction, but it does not tell those interested to apply to Mr William Earle in Water Street to view them.

There were, however, three other sorts of metal goods, quite specifically for the slave trade, in which William dealt. These were guns and cutlasses, both made by gunsmiths, and knives. The firearms trade to Africa grew fast in the eighteenth century and improvements in the weapons demanded and exported, such as longer barrels, flintlocks instead of matchlocks and more attention to proofing, made the guns supplied to the African traders much more effective in 'slave gathering', a process which required guns that stopped men rather than killed them. 'In West Africa', writes W.A. Richards, 'guns raised man-theft by war to a new level of productivity.' J.E. Inikori has estimated the average gun cargo of British slaving ships in the second half of the eighteenth century at 610 guns, most supplied from Birmingham though the Dutch provided

---

22 Letters dated 5 and 18 October, 7 and 31 December 1760 and 7 February 1761.

some serious competition.[23] These guns were of many different sorts. Samuel Galton of the famous Birmingham firm of Farmer & Galton listed 14 types in 1757 with prices from six shillings and eightpence for 'Catch Trading guns (got up in the common way without proof)' to 18 shillings for the best sort of swivel blunderbusses, with a division between 'cheap' and 'better quality' at about 10 shillings, the price of 'plain birding guns.'[24]

Virtually all of the guns sold by William Earle were bought from one gunsmith, Thomas Jordan. These were mostly ordered for specific ships. On 9 October 1760, for example, William acknowledged the arrival of a previous order, 'your guns, viz. 72 guns, are all come in' and then went on to give orders for the guns for two other ships, the *Brew*, in which he had no personal interest, and the *Prince Vada* of which he was a part-owner and ship's husband. 'The 25th September I got an order for 350 Danish guns [i.e. copies made in Birmingham of a Danish type of musket] and 50 plain birding guns, to be here in six weeks but I think you may take two months', an unusual concession, for William was normally insistent on deadlines being met exactly. These were both described as 'better quality guns' in Galton's list, especially the Danish guns, which were valued at 12 shillings and sixpence each. Jordan was also asked to supply 400 'heavy Angolas', a cheap musket, and 400 'crooked cutlasses', these being similar to machetes and available in 'straight' and 'crooked' form. Orders for other ships appear from time to time, often with urgent demands to deliver the weapons promptly. 'It causes much trouble to us when the orders we apply for are not regularly provided and disables us from asking for more orders from those persons we disappoint.' Most of the shipowners were familiar with the quality of Jordan's guns and simply left the business of getting the correct order to Liverpool to William, but new customers might demand rather more. Thomas Rumbold, managing partner of the Liverpool ship *Rumbold*, which was fitting out for Angola, asked his captain, John Sacheverell, who was travelling to London with his wife, to call on Jordan in Birmingham on the way south 'to look at his heavy Angola muskets.' William, writing to Sacheverell to make the arrangements for this visit, assured him that 'when I saw them hitherto,

---

23   Richards, 1980, p. 57 and *passim*; Inikori, 1977.

24   Quoted in Richards, 1980, p. 53. Galton's later opened up a branch nearer to their Liverpool customers. See Samuel Galton & Son's gun warehouse at 53 Old Dock in the Liverpool Directory of 1790.

they have been esteemed the best.' But then he would, wouldn't he? William also kept guns in stock in his warehouse, though not on the same scale as in his ironmongery business. In an afterthought to an order sent in March 1761 for 'a quantity of long, heavy Angolas' and 1,600 cutlasses, he asked Jordan to 'lay in an assortment of other guns as Mr Parr [one of William's employees] will acquaint you with the sorts most likely to be wanted.'[25]

Most of William's knives were supplied by Joseph & Benjamin Broomhead of Sheffield, 'factors and manufacturers of cutlery wares', who supplied forks, scissors and a few other things in addition to knives. The knives were of many sorts, penknives, spring knives and so on, some no doubt for domestic use but most specifically described as 'Guinea knives' and intended to make part of a slaving cargo. These were cheap knives with handles and other appurtenances made for the most part from cheap substances such as pressed wood, pressed horn and 'sham stag', though ebony was also used and ivory too, so much so that the custom had grown up of the Liverpool merchants bartering ivory, mainly the cheap sort called scriveloes, for knives. 'Some people pay for all their Guinea knives in ivory, but I expect no such thing', he wrote on 7 April 1760, though William certainly made part of his payments in this way.[26]

Occasionally, William refers to the purchase of knives for the cargo of a specific ship, usually because the ship was going to take on most of its cargo on the Isle of Man, in which case the knives were likely to be of Dutch manufacture and supplied with other goods by the Rotterdam firm of William & James Manson. On 8 October 1760, for instance, he sent an order to Manson's for '20 gross wood knives [i.e. 2,880 knives] without sheaths' to be consigned to John Joseph Bacon in Douglas and then loaded on the *Prince Vada* for her voyage to Angola. An exception to this general rule was the *African*, a London ship owned by Messrs Hutchinson, Mure & Co., who were newcomers to the trade. On 23 July 1761, he wrote informing them that he had sent a puncheon containing 40 gross of pressed horn Guinea knives suitable for Bonny to be delivered by carrier at the Axe in Aldermanbury by 5 August. But then, on 6 September, we find him writing again to the London

25 Letters to Jordan, 9 October 1760, 28 March, 19 August 1761; to Sacheverell, 1 April 1761.
26 Letter to J. & B. Broomhead, 7 April 1760.

merchants saying how sorry he was that 'the knives are not the sort expected', rather an ironic apology one suspects and one accompanied by a flood of resentment that anyone should doubt his competence

> I do declare upon my honour I never sold any larger sort for Bonny than those sold you ... I am myself largely concerned in the African trade and for some years past sheaths have been omitted as an extravagance. I sell many of these knives in a year and the ships I am concerned in take no other. Whoever advises you to take larger are not friends to the trade. It is not in my power to replace them, but if you please to take them and they are not as good as any sent from this town, I will be liable to your censure.[27]

William sold a few other things in his shop, looking glasses for instance, but this splendid statement of his complete faith in his own competence seems a good place to finish this section. But we can hardly pretend to have exhausted the range of business activities in which he dabbled. This chapter is titled 'Jack of All Trades' and, if he was not in fact involved in all trades, he certainly engaged in a fair number. What, for instance, was this slave and fish merchant doing selling 'sundry anchor-smith's materials, wrought iron etc at the Anchor Smithy, facing the Dock Gates, lately belonging to William Earle, ironmonger' in November 1757? A year later we learn a little more. 'All persons who have any demands on Mr William Earle, for and on account of the anchor smithy, are desired to bring in their accounts ... he having some time ago dropped that concern.'[28] A few years later, there is a petition in the Liverpool Customs Letter Books from Messrs Atherton & Earle, Liverpool merchants, relating to the import from the Isle of Man of 19,964 gallons of brandy. Atherton is a common Liverpool name, but no other Earle document mentions a partnership with an Atherton in the brandy trade.[29] These and other puzzles must remain unresolved and we can but conclude that William seems to have been a man who found it very difficult to resist a new challenge or a profitable sounding invitation to invest.

However, by the 1780s, he was slowing down. Fewer and fewer shares in slave ships were registered in his name and he no longer had shares in non-slaving ships. He dissolved his partnership with John Woodhouse

---

27 Letter to Hutchinson, Mure, 6 September 1761.
28 *WLA*, 4 November 1757, 8 December 1758.
29 Jarvis, 1954, p. 247.

Figure 5. William Earle of West Derby (1721-1788),
portrait n.d., attributed to Wright of Derby

as 'importers and sellers of fish' in 1777[30] and in 1783 he withdrew from
a partnership with his two sons, William Jr and Thomas Jr, and the
merchant Edmund Molyneux 'in the trade and business of an ironmonger
in Liverpool'. As these assets were realised he, like most merchants,
invested more and more of his money in financial securities. His partner
and friend William Davenport retired from business in 1786 and he
shifted his assets into government consols at three per cent, bank deposits
at four per cent and £14,000 lent to a friend on bond at five per cent.[31]
William Earle almost certainly behaved in a similar way. There were

30 MMM D/EARLE/4/3, 26 December 1777; D/EARLE/4/4.
31 D/EARLE/4/6-7.

definite signs of gentrification as the now fairly elderly merchant moved into his seventh decade and out of the commercial centre of the port into a much grander house set in farmland in West Derby to the north-east of Liverpool.

Here, on 10 October 1782, aged 61, William Earle of West Derby (as he now styled himself) made his will.[32] An income for life was provided for his widow Anne, the capital reverting to the estate at her death. Thomas was given the option of inheriting the 'house and estates at [West] Derby', while the younger son William was offered 'my house in town … and the seat or pew in the Church of Our Lady of St Nicholas in Liverpool' where William the Elder was to be buried All that remained was bequeathed 'share and share alike' to his two sons and his daughter Mary, who had married the merchant and banker Richard Heywood in the previous year.

The rare survival of a family letter tells us that both William and his wife Anne had been 'much indisposed this past winter … though approaching spring will, I hope, set you up again.'[33] Maybe it did, but not for very long, as William died on 28 April 1788 and his wife two years later. His will was proved in the Consistory Court at Chester in 1790 and his personal estate was assessed at £5,000 for the purpose of the recently introduced Stamp or Probate Duty. This figure places William about halfway down the list of 94 leading Liverpool slave merchants whose assessments for this duty have been analysed by David Pope.[34] But such figures should surely be taken with a pinch of salt. Five thousand pounds would hardly cover William's legacies and one must assume that the merchant sons and banker son-in-law of a wily old merchant would know how to conceal assets when necessary. It seems safe to state that William Earle of West Derby, merchant and ironmonger, had done pretty well for the son of a bankrupt, but not anything like as well as his sons were to do. William Earle, as Nicholas Radburn has observed, 'turned the slave trade into a family business, with his sons taking over the helm of the company when the patriarch retired.'[35] In fact, as we shall see, the slave trade was only one part of this family business which, like the business built up by their father, covered a very wide range of activities.

32 There is a copy in MMM D/EARLE/10/3.
33 D/EARLE/7/9a, Lady Jane Stanley to William Earle.
34 Pope, 2007, pp. 208–15.
35 Radburn, 2009, p. 113.

CHAPTER SIX

Thomas Earle of Leghorn

> 'A man who has not been to Italy is always
> conscious of an inferiority, from his not having
> seen what it is expected a man should see.'[1]

The life of Thomas Earle is not nearly so well documented as that of his
younger brother William. But what has survived suggests that it was an
interesting life. This was divided between the Italian port of Livorno,
known to the English as Leghorn, where he lived and brought up his
family from the late 1740s till 1766, and Liverpool, where he lived from
then until his death in 1781. Thomas was one of the first Liverpool men
to make a career in Leghorn, hence the title 'Thomas Earle of Leghorn'
by which he was often known.

Leghorn was founded in the late sixteenth century and had
prospered thanks to the liberal policies of successive Medici Grand
Dukes of Tuscany, who decreed it a free port in 1593, and adopted
a policy of neutrality in the numerous wars of the seventeenth and
eighteenth centuries. The trade of the port also benefited from the
permission given to Jews to settle there and freely practice their religion
and, from the 1670s, the decision of English merchants to make the
Tuscan port their main *entrepôt* in the Mediterranean, a marketplace
where the goods of North Africa and the Levant were traded for
cargoes brought in from the north and west. Leghorn reached its peak
in the early eighteenth century and, by our period, was beginning to
decline a little in the face of competition from other Italian ports,
such as Ancona and Civitavecchia, which were also free ports. But,
in the years around 1750, when Thomas Earle settled there, Leghorn
was still an important place with a population between 30,000 and
40,000, of whom some ten per cent were Jews. Leghorn was therefore

---

1 Boswell, 1965, p. 742.

Figure 6. Thomas
Earle of Leghorn
(1719-1781), portrait
1761, school of
Pompeo Batoni

considerably larger than Liverpool in 1750, though the positions had
been reversed by 1800.[2]

Livorno must have been an attractive place in the years that Thomas
was resident there, still small enough to be entirely contained within
the massive walls of the fortifications so that one passed immediately
into the Tuscan countryside as one left the city on the landward side.
The moats or *fossi* at the foot of the walls had been extended to create
a system of canals criss-crossing the city, so that goods could be

2 Population figures in Trivellato, 2009, pp. 54–56. For the impact of the English
   after 1670 see Pagano de Divitiis, 1990 and 1993 and, in general, see Filippini,
   1998 and Guarnieri, 1962.

transported on barges or *navicelli* (small boats) from the seagoing ships in the harbour to the warehouses and shops of the merchants. *Navicelli* were also used to transfer goods along narrow waterways to the River Arno and so to Pisa and Florence, avoiding the dangerous passage by sea to the mouth of the river. The canals might have been designed for commerce, but they were also available for recreation, as can be seen in the entertaining journal kept by Captain Augustus Hervey, a fine sailor but also a fun-loving 'naval Casanova'. He visited Leghorn often in the middle years of the eighteenth century and he always offered the town a good time while he was there, the best perhaps being the entertainment laid on for the governor of the city in 1748:

> I had a very fine concert of music on board, and in the evening when dark all the bridges upon the many various canals in that town were illuminated by my orders ... we all went about the night with our boats and music too, with thousands of spectators who accompanied us along the streets of the canals and all the people at their windows made it a delightful show.[3]

The area of the city around the canals was known as *La Venezia Nuova*, but it was more like Amsterdam than Venice with busy waterways crossed by elegant bridges and lined with the houses of merchants with shops or warehouses beneath the three- or four-storied buildings. A tour of the canals is still the best way to see Livorno and to appreciate what it meant to be a merchant there, even if few of the houses now are those built in the eighteenth century. But there are some reminders of the busy and prosperous past, such as the occasional ground-floor warehouse roofed with arches supporting the house above and with access to the canal at one side and to the streets of the city at the other. Today, such spaces are likely to be garages, but it is not difficult to imagine them full of bales of wool and cotton and the other goods traded in the town.

The years following the end of the Seven Years' War in 1763 were 'the golden age of the British Grand Tour', as streams of upper- and middle-class travellers came south to admire (and purchase) the glories of classical and renaissance Italy.[4] Since a short voyage in a *felucca* from Genoa or Marseilles to Leghorn was one of the main ways for British

---

3   Erskine, 1953, pp. 64, 67.
4   Bignamini, 1996, p. 33.

tourists to arrive in Italy, there are plenty of comments on the Tuscan port. No one could pretend that it was a really old city or that its buildings could match those of Florence or Pisa, but there was still much to admire. Alexander Drummond, for instance, on his way to take up his post as British Consul in Aleppo, described Leghorn as 'an agreeable place, and disposed in a very commodious manner, with canals and a fine mole ... for the conveniency of trade: the houses are neat and the streets very clean'. But what was convenient for trade and money-making did not please some of the more aristocratic and artistic visitors to the port. Robert Adam, the famous Scottish architect, found the place 'depressingly mercantile and sadly lacking in *bon ton*', but was later more enthusiastic when he discovered that several clever and amusing Scots had settled there. The poet and essayist Leigh Hunt was blunter: 'Leghorn is a polite Wapping, with a square and a theatre', 'Wapping' being upper-class short-hand for a dirty, vulgar place full of sailors.[5]

Most visitors, however, were kinder. They praised the buildings and structures that should be praised, the mole or breakwater which protected the harbour from the sea and the system of canals that gave the port the look of a little Venice, the cathedral, the theatre, the 'extraordinary good opera-house' and, perhaps above all, the Jewish synagogue, a splendid building which was visited by a surprising number of Christian tourists. But what really attracted visitors was the exotic character of the place, 'the richness of the shops ... the motley crowd of all nations.' 'You may see every day on the Exchange merchants from Tangiers and all along the coast of Africa to the top of the Mediterranean, and also those from Turkey, Greece etc all dressed in the habits of their country which makes an appearance like a masquerade.' Livorno must have been the most cosmopolitan place in Europe.[6]

Livorno was also, despite its free trade and its freedom, a place just as permeated by slavery as was Liverpool, more so in a concrete sense since most of the fine buildings, fortifications and port facilities had been built by slaves. But the slaves of Livorno were not black men and women from West Africa. They were Turks and Moors from North Africa and the Levant who had been captured by Christian naval ships and corsairs and sold into slavery in Livorno. The heyday of the Christian corsairs

5 Drummond, 1754, p. 33; Fleming, 1962, pp. 125–26; Hunt, 1850, iii, p. 11.
6 Starke, 1815, i, p. 155; Brooke, 1798, pp. 210–11.

was the late seventeenth century, when the galley fleets of Spain, France and many Italian states provided a market for Muslim slaves who could be employed as oarsmen or used for building work and other duties when the galleys were in port. A magnificent slave prison, known as the *bagno*, was built in Livorno to house the slaves and within its walls could be found sleeping accommodation, hospitals, shops run by slaves and no less than three mosques. The *bagno* could hold up to 3,000 captives, more than the entire population of the town when it was first built.[7]

By the time Thomas Earle arrived in Leghorn in the middle of the eighteenth century, this whole system was in decline. The number of corsairs, both Christian and Muslim, was now quite small and so there were far fewer captives than in the past. Mediterranean navies were now nearly all abandoning galleys in favour of sailing ships so that there was a much smaller demand for slaves. France, once the biggest purchaser of slaves in Leghorn, abandoned her galley fleet in 1748, and two years later the Grand Duke of Tuscany followed suit and made plans to convert the *bagno* into apartments and warehouses, the 300 slaves still in residence being sent to Pisa to work on the roads, nearly half of whom escaped and dispersed through the countryside to the alarm of the authorities.[8] Nevertheless, there were still plenty of slaves to be seen in Leghorn. When Alexander Drummond was in the city in the early 1750s the flagship galley of the King of Sardinia was in port, crewed by 75 sailors and 363 slave oarsmen, 'seven men to an oar abaft the mainmast and six to each forwards ... Three times a week the slaves are shifted, and wash each other every morning; so that every thing is so sweet and clean ... that there was not the least offensive smell.' When the prison reformer John Howard was in Leghorn in 1778, he saw 47 slaves building a new *lazzaretto* or quarantine station and he also inspected the slave prison, which he found well ordered and humane in its treatment of the inmates, so it seems that the order of 1750 to convert the *bagno* into apartments had been abandoned or ignored. Indeed, right up to the French conquest of the city in 1796, Muslims were being employed as forced labour on the docks and in the streets or as unpaid domestic servants. This sad history of slavery in Leghorn is dramatically symbolised by a sculpture facing the port, the upper part of which is a statue of the Grand Duke Ferdinand I while, at the base, four North African slaves in chains peer

7 Earle, 1970. For the Livorno *bagno* see Frattarelli Fischer, 2000.
8 TNA SP 98/57, 23 January, 4 December 1750.

out proudly at visitors today, as they have done since they were created in 1626 by the sculptor Pietro Tacco.[9]

It was then quite an exotic city in which Thomas Earle came to make his living in the late 1740s. He first appears in surviving documents in June 1748, when he was described by the British Consul as 'Mr Thomas Earle, Captain Fortunatus Wright's agent.'[10] Thomas was 29 years old at this date and such a job was likely to have been remunerative, but also difficult to carry out, for the splendidly named Fortunatus Wright was not an easy man to represent. He was a Liverpool man who in 1744, after the declaration of war by Britain against France, transformed himself into 'the most famous British privateer commander of his time, and Liverpool's favourite hero'. He operated exclusively in the Mediterranean and, by December 1746, it was reported in the *Gentlemen's Magazine* that he and his ship the *Fame* had already 'by his uncommon vigilance and valour' taken 16 French ships worth £400,000, two of which were brought into Messina and the others sent into Leghorn for sale.[11]

No papers relating to Thomas Earle's years as agent to Wright have survived, but it is clear from other material what such a position involved. Leghorn was in Tuscany and thus neutral in wars between England and France but, as the busiest port in the central Mediterranean, it was an excellent place to dispose of prizes and their cargoes. Leghorn was also a good place to fit out, repair and provision ships and to find crews, and so was used as a base by both privateers and naval ships. This placed the neutral citizens of Livorno in an ambiguous situation and many felt obliged to support either England or France, for their own hope of profit or simply out of affection for the belligerent of their choice. The French 'party' was usually the larger or at least the more vociferous and the more active amongst them would be busy lobbying the Tuscan government to get the laws changed or interpreted in ways favourable to French interests. At a lower level, this rivalry was manifested in a variety of ways, such as insulting the Royal Navy in the Corpus Christi procession by parading 'a pirate's ensign with an English pendant on each side of it', or sneering at the English humiliation following Admiral Byng's loss of the island of

9   Drummond, 1754, pp. 33–34; Howard, 1791, pp. 7, 57; Trivellato, 2009, p. 70.
10 SP 98/55, 10 June NS 1748.
11 On Wright see Williams, 2004, pp. 40–67 and Roberts, 1936.

Figure 7. View of Livorno harbour with statue of The Four Moors (i quattro mori)

Minorca in July 1756. Such English defeats were rare, but it was still 'very mortifying to see a rabble (though of boys) go about for several nights with white cockades, crying Viva Francia, Burn the English.'[12] One place where representatives of both belligerent nations were likely to be present (and possibly a little inebriated) was the theatre, whose patrons were divided into French and English factions supporting different actresses. Catcalls could quickly lead to insults and, on at least two occasions, to swords being drawn in the theatre.[13]

All this was fairly trivial and quickly forgotten in the pursuit of profit. And there were plenty of opportunities for that as Leghorn merchants acted as agents for British privateers and Royal Navy ships in the wars of the eighteenth century. Selling naval prizes could be particularly profitable, as most naval captains were not very businesslike and would not wait, like a merchant would, to get a good bargain, wanting their money in cash up front and as quick as possible. The same conditions encouraged French privateers to use the Tuscan port and an elaborate set of rules had been established to attempt to ensure that ships of the two warring nations did not disregard the port's neutrality, the main rule being that ships of either nation leaving the port should have 24 hours' grace before being chased or attacked by privateers of the other nation. Such rules were often disobeyed, but never so much as to prevent the use of the port by privateers completely.[14]

Thomas Earle was probably chosen as agent by Fortunatus Wright simply because he, like the privateer, was a Liverpool man, such local connections being an important feature of mercantile and shipping networks in the eighteenth century. Thomas may also have had a share in the ownership of the *Fame*. Either way, he was likely to have done well out of Fortunatus Wright's success, since prizes and prize goods were sold by the agents on commission (normally three per cent) and Fortunatus took many prizes. Such rewards had a price, however, as Wright was not a man who obeyed the rules of privateering as a matter of course. In December 1746, for instance, he was in trouble for capturing

12 Reported in a letter from Leghorn in *WLA*, 24 September 1756.
13 SP 98/63, 25 June 1756; SP 98/52, 16, 21 February 1747; SP 98/59, 2 March 1753.
14 Hervey, 2004, *passim* for naval use of Leghorn; for the Articles of Neutrality for Leghorn, 22 April 1744, see ADM 1/3828 fols 649–50; see also SP 98/63, 14 May 1756, for the rules at the beginning of the Seven Years' War.

and bringing into Leghorn a French ship which had a pass from his 'Sacred Majesty, King George the Second [of England].' Early in 1747, he was in trouble again for seizing Turkish property being carried on the French ship *Hermione*. Great Britain was not at war with the Ottoman Empire and Wright's action caused consternation amongst the merchants of the Levant Company who, alone among Englishmen, were allowed to trade in the eastern Mediterranean and would bear the brunt of Turkish reprisals for Wright's action. Representations by the British government caused Wright to be arrested and clapped into prison in Leghorn in December 1747, prior to being sent home for trial in England. It was in connection with this affair that the consul in Leghorn referred to Thomas in his letter of June 1748. Wright's young agent was obviously competent, for he secured a mandate from the High Court of Admiralty ordering the privateer's release.[15]

The War of the Austrian Succession ended in 1748, but Thomas Earle's connections with privateers and shipping generally were to continue a little longer. In December 1748, the British Admiralty decided that four of its ships should be sold to reduce expenses and, after a survey of those available, chose the *Lowestoff*. This ship, a frigate of 500 tons and 24 guns, had often been at Leghorn during the war, but was now at Deptford on the Thames, where she was sold on 2 February 1749 for just £605.[16] Her buyers are not named in the Admiralty papers, but it seems probable that they were a syndicate headed by Thomas Earle, who was now beginning to establish himself in a mercantile career in Leghorn.

The database of Liverpool shipping[17] shows that in 1753 the *Lowestoff* was registered at Liverpool and was owned by Thomas Earle, Thomas Hodgson, his partner in Leghorn, and William Hutchinson, second only to Wright as a famous Liverpool privateer of this period. The *Lowestoff* was employed at Leghorn as a merchant ship with voyages between England, the Mediterranean and the West Indies from 1751 to July 1753, her last appearance in this database. The former English warship then became once again a fighting machine, though it was not for the English that she was to fight. At this date, the Pope was still an important secular ruler and his officials maintained a small navy based at Civitavecchia, the port of Rome. These ships engaged in various fairly

15 Williams, 2004, pp. 46–49; SP 98/55, 10 June NS. 1748.
16 ADM 106/2/84, pp. 283, 347; ADM 180/3 f. 379; Lyon, 1993, p. 51.
17 LTS, 1744–1786.

pacific functions – ensuring the provisioning of Rome, carrying great men in state to their destinations and so on – but their most dramatic activity was to seek out and fight against the ships of the Muslim Barbary corsairs. Such warfare was known as the 'guerra eterna', the eternal war against the enemies of the faith, the Christian equivalent of *jihad*. In 1754, the naval authorities of the Papal States decided to buy two frigates, each carrying 30 guns. They bought the *Lowestoff* and ordered another identical ship to be built. The price of both ships was the same, £4,700 sterling, a vast sum compared with the £605 paid for the *Lowestoff* at the Admiralty sale in February 1749, even allowing for the costs of repairs and fitting out. But the Pope and his officials were happy with their acquisition. They re-named the *Lowestoff* and her consort *San Pietro* and *San Paolo* and these two frigates were in fact to have some successes against the corsairs in the next few years.[18]

Thomas Earle and his partner Thomas Hodgson, another Liverpool man and family friend, were now well supplied with trading capital, which they used to set themselves up as merchants in Leghorn. There were about 15 British merchant houses in Leghorn at this time and, between them, they conducted about a third of the trade of the port. They were banded together in what was known as the 'British Factory' and came under the general authority of the Consul. Such Factories existed in most places where there were several British merchants in residence, such as Aleppo, Lisbon or St Petersburg and, although the merchants or merchant houses were in competition with each other, there seems to have been little real economic rivalry. The merchants were more aware of their common heritage and their common problems, and dinner parties or evenings at the theatre were more their style than cut-throat competition. The first we know that Thomas Earle and Thomas Hodgson had joined this co-fraternity is that in February 1755 they were both among 'the Gentlemen of the Factory' who signed a letter written in support of John Dick, the incoming British consul.[19]

The trade conducted by British merchants in Leghorn followed a fairly unchanging pattern, the same sorts of things being imported and exported each year, though most of the merchants specialised in just a few of the many different goods traded in the city. The general picture was summarised in a report prepared in July 1765 in response

18 Guglielmotti, 1884, pp. 163–64; SP 98/59, 16 March 1754.
19 Hayward, 1980; SP 98/60, 28 February 1755.

to a demand from home for more information than was currently available. The chief imports 'from his Majesty's dominions' were fish from Newfoundland and elsewhere; various sorts of woollen cloth; re-exported colonial goods such as sugar and especially tobacco; tin, lead, hides, leather and some re-exports from India, especially pepper. Other imports not appearing in this list were goods from the Levant brought in by Tuscan, Greek and other non-British ships in order to circumvent the monopoly of the Levant Company and, in wartime, prize goods, especially those carried by French ships on their way to Marseilles from ports in the Levant.[20]

Earle & Hodgson (as their house was styled) did not meddle with such goods as woollen cloth, tin and re-exported India goods, which were mainly handled by the London-based houses, these being the great majority of the merchant houses in the Factory. The imports in which Liverpool merchants had a comparative advantage were salt, fish, sugar, tobacco and a group of products not mentioned in the report which came under the general heading of an 'Irish cargo', that is butter, cheese, salt meat, tallow, hides and linen. The most important import for the Liverpool men was Newfoundland salt cod and the safe arrival of the 'baccalà boats', hopefully in time for Lent, was always eagerly awaited. One last import should be mentioned. Italy was fairly densely populated and each poor harvest was likely to lead to dearth. This in turn meant high prices for imported grain, an invitation to speculative trading which could be very profitable, but often led to far too much grain being sent to Italy and the return of low prices and even lower profits.

The exports by British merchants from Leghorn were much more heterogeneous and can best be examined through the export listings for individual ships prepared by officials in the port and often included in merchants' letters home.[21] These show that the great majority of English ships carried as ballast between ten and 100 tons each of three heavy products, brimstone or sulphur (mainly from Sicily), marble from nearby Carrara, and boxwood, the wood of the box tree, much used by turners and engravers. Most ships also carried oil, fine quality salad oil from

---

20 SP 98/70, pp. 90–98, Leghorn, 11 July 1765. For an earlier account of English trade with Italy see Gee, 1729, ch. 3.

21 The examples below are from letters written from Leghorn to Messrs Nightingale & Scott of London and their successors, TNA, C 109/1–14, 1759–1765.

Lucca and Florence and cheaper oil in bulk, used in cloth manufacture and other industrial processes, mainly from Calabria and Apulia, which was shipped to Leghorn in vast quantities by the Neapolitan merchants who controlled the industry.[22] Other important food and drink items included wine, juniper berries, often in very large quantities and destined to flavour English gin, capers and anchovies, which were loaded on most outgoing ships and formed a substantial part of the cargo of some of them, such as the *Duke of Savoy* and the *Crown Galley*, which in 1765 carried over 6,000 barrels of anchovies between them. There was also much fruit shipped, especially figs and raisins, most of the latter being the product of the Lipari Islands north of Sicily and the Greek islands of Zante (Zakinthos) and Cephalonia in the Aegean.

Another important group of exports comprised textile raw materials and finished cloth and clothing items. Most important in this category was silk, raw or twisted into organzine thread (using the famous Italian invention of water-driven throwing machines), which came mainly from Sicily, Calabria, Lombardy and Piedmont, and silk fabrics, mainly from Bologna and Florence. Also to be found on the great majority of outgoing ships were two types of straw hat, the fashionable 'Leghorn' hats made from wheat straw and the cheaper 'chip hats', which were plaited from woody fibres split into thin strips. Another fibre, used for coarse clothing and cordage, was hemp, which came mainly from Ancona on the Adriatic. Other raw textile materials came from further east, including goats' and camels' hair, cotton wool and cotton thread, mainly from Egypt, Cyprus and Anatolia, and (though hardly raw textile materials) the skins of various animals, especially kids and lambs. One other product found in nearly every cargo was coral, which was fished or dived for by poor men and women in many places along the North African coast and on the west coast of Italy and the offshore islands. This industry was under the control of the Jews of Livorno, who shipped the worked coral to London and from there in East India Company ships to the sub-continent, where it was much in demand for traditional jewellery. Here, Jews living in India traded the coral for diamonds, which, with other jewels, were exempt from the Company's ban on trading by private merchants. It was a very specialised and profitable trade.[23]

22 Chorley, 1965.
23 Trivellato, 2009 and see pp. 226–29 for coral fishing in the Mediterranean.

In later years, Thomas Earle certainly imported marble and many Italian foodstuffs into Liverpool, but we do not have the evidence to state with any confidence the range of products in which he traded in the years he actually lived in the Tuscan port, with the exception of the cargo of the snow *Polly*, which sailed from Leghorn to Liverpool on 8 March 1762. This ship was jointly owned by Earle and Hodgson, the first ship they had purchased since the sale of the *Lowestoff* in 1754, and she carried to Liverpool a fairly standard cargo, Levantine cotton, olive oil, Corsican and Florentine wine, brimstone, boxwood and anchovies, all of Italian origin except the cotton.[24]

The description of Livorno's trade above is based mainly on English sources, necessarily so since not much has survived in Italian sources which could illuminate the English role in the trade of the port. The best source would have been the records of the *dogana* or customs office, which recorded the ships coming into and going out of the port. But, sadly, these records no longer exist, having fallen victim to the Italian government's passion for pulping historical documents in the 1930s. Potentially more useful are the registers of the *sicurtà*, a tax on marine insurance policies contracted in Livorno, whose receipts were intended to provide a fund for the relief of the needy. This certainly sounds promising and one can imagine how pleased economic historians of Britain would be if all marine insurance contracts were recorded in a register.[25]

The surviving records start in 1763 and are packed with interesting material which gives a vivid insight into the trade of the port and reminds one that Livorno was truly cosmopolitan, with ships insured not just from everywhere in the Mediterranean, but also from the countries of the North Sea and the Baltic, from the West Indies, the American colonies, Newfoundland and as far away as the 'costa di Coromandel' in India and Callao in Peru. Here one can find what goods were traded, the shipping used, the routes followed and the rates at which insurance could be attained. More generally, one can learn things not immediately apparent from English sources, such as the leading role of the Jews in Livorno, and the great importance of Greek and Italian shipping (especially that from Livorno itself) and that of the Croatian republic of Ragusa (now Dubrovnik), a very successful specialist centre

---

24 TNA C 109/8/1, cargo list letter to W. & M. Nightingale, 26 March 1762.
25 For the *sicurtà* see Addobbati, 1996; the records are in ASL.

in shipbuilding, shipowning and the employment of shipping since the middle ages.

But, valuable though all this is, it is rather misleading as a guide to the trade of the port, for there are only a few records of insurance policies taken out by French, Dutch and, above all, English ships. The reason is obvious; when English merchants wanted to insure their ships and the goods they were carrying, they looked to their own well-established market in London and not to the one in Livorno, which, by contrast, was much in use by the Jewish merchants, who very often insured with brokers of their own faith resident in the city. So, the *sicurtà* records are invaluable as a source for the general study of Mediterranean trade, but are not much use for a study of Earle & Hodgson, who appear only very occasionally, such as in the policy taken out on 28 November 1763 on a shipment of hides from Livorno to Naples, or the time contract registered on 18 December 1763 for three months on the hull and fittings of their snow, *Polly*, at 1.25 per cent per month.[26]

A much better Livornese source for one important part of Thomas Earle's business life is the *Asta Pubblica*, the tax on goods sold at public auction discussed briefly above.[27] The records are fairly complete for the Seven Years' War (1756–63) and most of what follows is drawn from the three volumes covering the years 1756–59.[28] Fifty vessels and a few rowboats were brought in as prizes and sold at auction in these years. However, these successes were by no means evenly distributed in time; over two-thirds of them occurring in two periods of much greater activity, August–December 1757 and May–July 1758, while the whole of 1759 saw practically no prizes sold at all. This lull was caused by the rulers of Livorno enforcing too strictly the rules governing privateering, a result of French pressure, a policy which simply caused English privateers to take their prizes to other ports. Naturally, local merchants as well as the English complained of this, 'as so considerable an advantage arises from the prizes that used to be brought hither.'[29]

The vessels sold in 1757–59 reflected those used in Mediterranean trade at this time, especially trade in the Tyrrhenian Sea and the Levant, where most were captured. The great majority were either three-masted

26 ASL, *Sicurtà*, ii, pp. 86, 100.
27 See above pp. 73–74.
28 ASL, *Sicurtà*, vols 24–26.
29 TNA SP 98/66, 23 June 1759.

polacres (*polaccas*) or the much smaller tartans (*tartanas*), two-masted vessels with lateen sails, used for fishing as well as carrying cargo. The average sale price at auction of the polacres was just over 1,000 pieces of eight (say, £250), the commonest currency in use at this time not just in Livorno but throughout the world, while the tartans went for about half this sum. Just nine bigger ships were sold, described as *naves* (i.e. ships), pinks or snows and worth about twice as much as a polacre. Such prices, however, need to be treated with caution for there is plentiful evidence that most of the auctions were rigged to reduce liability for the tax, the buyers being simply mediators who resold the ships and their cargoes at higher prices in later private auctions.[30]

These were all French vessels captured by British warships or privateers, but there were also some other vessels which showed Livorno's role as a general prize market and not just a British one. The change in war alliances in 1756 which brought Prussia in on the British side and Austria on the French side meant that there were Prussian as well as British privateers at sea and this was reflected in the capture of an Austrian *polacca* from Trieste by the Prussian ship *Aquila* and her sale in Livorno in February 1761. One suspects that this 'Prussian' privateer was in truth British, but it would have been unwise to capture an Austrian ship while flying the British flag, for Austria was ruled by the Emperor, who in turn was the ruler of Leghorn and 'our important trade with Leghorn depended on keeping on good terms with the Emperor.' Such were the complexities of eighteenth-century international relations.[31] The Barbary Corsairs may have been a shadow of their former strength, but Algiers, Tunis and Tripoli still sent out fleets to hunt down the shipping of those nations deemed their enemies. Most of the prizes captured went back to North Africa, but a few were sold elsewhere and so we find two prizes sold in Leghorn at the end of 1755, one from Genoa and one from Naples, by the Tunisian corsair Rais (i.e. Captain) Amett Salami, who also arranged for the sale of two wooden statues of St Benedict and Christ Resurgent.[32]

The most important non-British source of prizes was, inevitably, France. French warships and especially privateers (i.e. *corsaires*) did at

---

30 Lo Basso, 2008, pp. 159–60.
31 Corbett, 1907, i, p. 267.
32 AP, 9 October, 24 November 1755, 10 February 1761 and cf. the sale of a Neapolitan prize by Rais Mahamett bin Abdal of Algiers on 30 June 1761.

least as well and probably better than their British counterparts, but they sold most of their prizes in France or sometimes Malta, which was officially neutral but operated as a sort of unofficial French naval base just as Livorno did for the British. Captain Hervey described the island as 'in fact a French arsenal in time of war, neither more or less.'[33] The French also sold some prizes in Leghorn, the most impressive sale during the period studied being conducted on 19 January 1759, when the French Consul arranged the sale of 13 *baccalà* ships and their escort from Newfoundland, a ship called *San Guglielmo* of Livorno itself, which had been captured by a French privateer from La Ciotat, a port between Marseilles and Toulon. The prizes, together with their cargoes of salt cod, sold for a total of 21,304 pieces of eight, most being bought by local Italian shipowners.[34]

There were 12 merchant houses named as the agents who sold the ships captured by British warships and privateers, but most of these only handled one or two sales, leaving the bulk of the business to just four merchant houses: James Howe, who was agent to Captain Hervey amongst others; Francis Jermy, a long-established house; the newcomers Earle & Hodgson, who sold nine of these 50 prizes; and John Dick (later Sir John when he inherited a baronetcy), who was Consul at Leghorn from 1754 to 1776 and dominated the prize business, being named as seller of 22 of the 50 vessels sold. Sir John was described as 'a clever little man', a collector of paintings and marble statuary who lived in great elegance and splendour, much of which was no doubt financed by his activities in the prize market which continued even when England was not at war, it being reported that he 'cleared no less than £50,000' as agent for the Russian fleet during the Russo-Turkish wars of 1770–75.[35]

Ships did not fetch much money at auction and the prize agents' most profitable business was selling captured cargoes. This cannot be analysed quite as easily as the sale of the ships, for cargoes were normally sold separately and the clerks did not usually assign them to specific ships. Nevertheless, it is clear that these cargoes were often worth several times the value of the ships on which they were being carried, the most valuable being woollen cloth in passage from Marseilles to the Levant,

33 Erskine, 1953, p. 187.
34 AP, 19 January 1759. For other prizes sold by the French see 26 September 1758 and 13 February, and 3 and 31 May 1758.
35 Ingamells, 1997, pp. 298–99.

which was often sold for sums ranging from 30,000 to 60,000 pieces of eight and, in the other direction, cotton from Cyprus, Egypt, Palestine or from Smyrna, the great *entrepôt* of the eastern Mediterranean just as Leghorn was for the sea as a whole.

Overall, the great majority of captured cargoes were being carried along these routes, wine, colonial goods and a variety of luxuries being shipped from Marseilles in addition to woollen cloth, and cotton, wool, silk, wax, hides, drugs and so on being shipped from the Levant. Other more pedestrian prize cargoes were also sold, such as grain from North Africa, and there were one or two really exciting items, such as the three gold clocks, with quadrants 'alla Turca' being shipped to the east in the *Santa Teresa* and, most interesting of all, a consignment of over 300 books captured on their way to the Levant in 1758 and sold by Earle & Hodgson on 21 November.[36] Most of the titles are listed and they include bibles, korans and other religious books, Arabic–Latin and other dictionaries, books of entertainment such as the three copies of 'curiosità di Parigi' (dirty books?) and a wide selection of historical, geographical, mathematical and philosophical works, including four copies of 'lo spirito delli leggi' which is presumably Montesquieu's *De l'esprit des lois*, first published just ten years earlier, in 1748. Earle & Hodgson can be found in these records as both buyers and sellers. They bought, for instance, four dictionaries from the book auction and, from another cargo, '164 pieces of porcelain of diverse quality', as well as large quantities of cotton, which was their main interest when buying at these auctions. Earle & Hodgson were thus involved in every aspect of the prize business and, in wartime, this must have taken up much of their time, though the scale of the activity was in fact far smaller than it was to be during the American War of Independence (1776–83).[37]

Twelve of the French prizes in 1758–59 had been captured by warships, not privateers, and the proportion was to be even greater later in the war. This predatory activity by the royal ships is quite easy to research, since the official letters home of the captains and their logbooks have for the most part survived. To illustrate what such 'cruising' involved, we can look at the voyages made in 1761 and 1762 by HMS *Pallas* and *Vestal*, two English frigates whose prizes appear prominently in the Leghorn registers of the *Asta Pubblica*. Admiral Sir

36 AP vol. 26, fols 139–41.
37 See below pp. 176–80.

Charles Saunders commanding in the Mediterranean had two main tasks in these years, keeping an eye on the size, state of preparation and movements of the French fleet in Toulon and employing his frigates to destroy French trade with the Levant. He usually had six frigates engaged in the latter activity; in December 1760, for instance, there were two frigates cruising between Leghorn and Naples, one between Leghorn and Villafranca, a port near Nice, which belonged to the King of Savoy, two off the south end of Sardinia and one off Malta, which was regularly visited by British warships despite its Francophile reputation.[38]

Being assigned to such cruises in the rich waters of the Mediterranean was every naval captain's dream, since the rules were incredibly generous, the captain of a successful ship receiving three-eighths of the proceeds of the sale of prizes made under his command, plenty of money even if the auctions were rigged. This being so, the historian has to be a little suspicious of the motives of Samuel Hood, captain of the *Vestal*, who wrote to the Secretary of the Admiralty from Spithead on 30 April 1760, 'humbly entreating' that his ship be 'one of the squadron going to the Mediterranean', as he had found that southern climates provided relief from a bilious disorder which afflicted him. And maybe they did; they were certainly likely to provide relief from poverty for young officers.[39]

These frigates were very powerful compared with the French privateers and merchant ships on which they preyed. HMS *Vestal*, for instance, carried 32 guns and 220 men and the *Pallas* was slightly bigger with 36 guns and 240 men. Their job was to cruise in the sea area assigned to them and chase, bring to or 'speak' every ship they met or saw to ascertain whether they were French or carrying French goods. Most ships they encountered were of course neutrals, Dutch, Danish, Greek, Italian, Ragusan, Turkish and so on, but every now and then they would discover and capture a French vessel, from which they would take aboard most of the crew and passengers as prisoners and provide a prize crew in their place. Sometimes these prizes would sail in company with the frigate, sometimes sail directly for Leghorn and quite often they would be sent to some intermediate port, such as Cagliari in Sardinia, to be put in storage till it was time to return to Leghorn. Cagliari was also useful for buying food, wine, water, wood

38 Saunders' letters, orders etc. are in ADM 1/384/5.
39 Erskine, 1953, pp. xviii–xix; ADM 1/1895/16, Hood to Admiralty, 30 April 1760; an endorsement reads 'Let him know it is done.'

and equipment, as were other ports in or near the cruising area, such as Tunis, Malta, Villafranca and Milos in the southern Aegean.[40]

It is clear from the naval logbooks that these prizes did not go to Gibraltar, the only place housing a British Vice-Admiralty court in the Mediterranean after the loss of Minorca to the French in 1756. How, then, was it possible to prove that the ships and cargoes that they captured were 'good prizes'? The answer has recently been discovered by the Genoese historian Luca Lo Basso, who has drawn on the despatches of the Genoese Consul in Livorno, Giovanni Antonio Gavi, a man described by a contemporary as an 'occhio indiscreto' ('inquisitive eye'), whose letters are a mine of information on the Tuscan port. The High Court of Admiralty in London, no doubt at the entreaty of the English Factory in Leghorn, had decided to delegate its powers to two local commissioners, who were to be the Consul and one of the principal English merchants, in order to speed up the process of selling the booty. Such decisions could be appealed, but it was obvious that the decisions of the commissioners were likely to favour the claims of British warships and privateers.[41]

Neither of these two naval frigates lost a single man in action, though there was occasionally quite a fight. Samuel Hood, captain of the *Vestal* and already famous in naval circles for winning a single-ship action against a French frigate in 1759, was later to become an admiral and a viscount. He kept an informative logbook and recorded these encounters in some detail, such as that with the *Marquis de Pilles*, a French letter of marque sailing from Scanderoon (Iskenderun), the port of Aleppo, to Marseilles. Hood took six hours on Sunday 21 December 1760 to catch and capture her after first sighting the Frenchman at daybreak. About ten weeks later the prize was sold at auction in Leghorn and Earle & Hodgson bid successfully for some of the cargo. Altogether, 12 French ships captured by these two warships were sold in Leghorn in 1761 and they were not the only frigates 'cruising', so it is no surprise to discover that 'the diligence of Admiral Saunders was such ... that the enemy's trade was reduced to a state of stagnation.'[42]

Most of these 'royal' prizes were consigned to John Dick and

40 Description of cruises etc. from the ships' logbooks, ADM 51/4000/4&5 (*Vestal*) and ADM 51/666/3&4 (*Pallas*).
41 Lo Basso, 2008, pp. 162–63.
42 Quoted in Corbett, 1907, ii, p. 92.

this was very much a perk of being Consul. The Consul also often acted as agent for the warships, arranging for refitting, repairs and careening, supplying equipment, drink and victuals, and the profits and commissions from this activity were likely to be much more valuable than simply selling the prize ships that they brought in. The Consul was also likely to get the valuable orders for the provision of salt meat, bread, flour and other necessaries for the fleet. On 21 February 1756, for instance, Dick received orders to supply 1,000 barrels of salt meat to provide provisions for the soon to be doomed garrison at Port Mahon in Minorca. He replied that he would buy the cattle from local farmers and have them salted, both activities being likely to earn him profits.[43]

There is evidence of Earle & Hodgson's involvement in two types of trade not yet mentioned. Nearly every ship's cargo list contained the item 'sundry parcels', sometimes just a few but often several hundred. Such a description could of course cover virtually anything. Nevertheless, there was one Italian export only rarely listed in ships' cargoes which certainly filled many 'sundry parcels'. This was art, in the form of books, prints and pictures, and statues, many of them classical artefacts (and some faked up to look like classical artefacts). Some was shipped legally with export licences from local authorities in Tuscany, Rome and elsewhere, and much was shipped clandestinely, but it was all destined to embellish the country houses of the English aristocracy and gentry.[44]

The accidental survival of an account book kept in Rome during the years 1747–54 throws some light on this business and the role Earle & Hodgson played in it. This account book belonged to Matthew Brettingham, son of the architect of the same name, who built Holkham Hall, the magnificent seat of the Earls of Leicester in north Norfolk. Matthew the younger, aged 22, was sent to Rome in 1747 to study architecture and the account book makes it clear that he was expected to pay his way by buying 'ancient sculptures', plaster figures and paintings for the Earl of Leicester and other members of the acquisitive aristocracy,

43 TNA SP 98/63, 21 February 1756.
44 On the papal licences for exports from Rome and permission to excavate see Brewer, 2012, pp. 57–60; for the edict of 4 January 1755 banning export from Tuscany of works of art without permission see SP 98/62. On 'the traffick of new antiques' see BM TY 7/416, Thomas Jenkins to Charles Townley, 2 November 1782.

as well as for his architect father. These were shipped from Civitavecchia to Leghorn and then re-shipped aboard larger vessels for the long sea journey to London. Several Leghorn merchant houses were involved in this business and amongst them we find old friends, such as Fortunatus Wright, now a merchant shipping plaster figures and paintings in 1753 and 1754, and also Earle & Hodgson. In February 1754, for instance, they received from Mr Gilly of Civitavecchia two cases of antique busts, which they shipped aboard the *Anna Maria* under Captain Elias Hampton, for London. A couple of months later, they handled the shipment of seven cases containing tables of 'antique mosaick' and also some marble tables for the Earl of Leicester. Such work was fairly pedestrian, arranging shipment, 'charges at Leghorn', getting payment and so on, but it all earned commissions and was a useful way of getting oneself known to the gentry and aristocracy. The general impression one gets of Thomas Earle is of a man of considerable taste who was unlikely to make a fool of himself in the presence of the great and the good, and this was obviously an asset when dealing with such people. A few years later, when Earle & Hodgson were doing similar business for Jonathan Skelton, by his own account 'the best landscape painter in Rome', they had moved on from the simple shipment of artistic treasures to arranging loans for travellers, and had built up a useful little information service. 'If it should import you', they wrote to friends of Skelton in England desirous to know the details of the artist's sudden death, 'we will inform our selves from our friends in Rome.'[45] Later still, after Thomas Earle and his family had returned to Liverpool, the house of Earle & Hodgson was to engage in such business on a much bigger scale and this will be discussed in the next chapter.

This sort of work was probably only a small part of most Leghorn merchants' business, though some of Thomas's colleagues in the Factory were quite well known as collectors themselves, as well as acquiring *objets* of various sorts for aristocratic clients. Sir John Dick and John Udny, both consuls at Leghorn, were collectors of marble statuary and paintings, and the merchant George Jackson was 'well known as a bibliophile' and built up a famous library.[46] It seems probable that Thomas collected a few nice things for himself, though we have no evidence of this except for his purchase of 'three medals' in an auction held in Livorno in February

45 Kenworthy-Browne, 1983; Ford, 1960.
46 Ingamells, 1997, pp. 298–99, 547, 595–96, 961–63.

1757.[47] Apart from this, just a few mentions in Matthew Brettingham's account book and a letter or two are all that survive to document his role in the export of art while he was actually in Italy.

There is, however, in the National Archives at Kew a large collection of letters throwing light on the activities of Earle & Hodgson in another branch of Leghorn trade. These were written by a London mercantile house called Nightingale & Scott and later William & Miles Nightingale. These merchants were drysalters, not a word much used today, but their speciality filled an important niche in international trade in the eighteenth century. They dealt in 'chemical products used in the arts, drugs, dye-stuffs, gums etc. and sometimes also in oils, sauces, pickles etc.', to quote the *Oxford English Dictionary*. The Nightingales were international middlemen in such products and their warehouses in London contained an exotic treasure house of materials from all over the world, from India and the Americas as well as throughout Europe, and their surviving letters were written to correspondents in every major port from St Petersburg to the Levant.[48]

Leghorn, as the most important *entrepôt* in the Mediterranean, had a central part to play in this worldwide business. On the general basis of 'divide and rule', the Nightingales corresponded with two merchant houses in the English Factory in Leghorn, Wills & Reynolds as well as Earle & Hodgson, and both houses were sometimes jealous of the business given to the other. Dealing in the products demanded by the Nightingales required very specialised knowledge which the merchants had to acquire on the job, since they had not of course benefited from an apprenticeship in drysaltery. It must have been fairly easy for local specialists to cheat them and it is hardly surprising that they received several letters from London complaining about the quality of what had been supplied. There was also a problem of vocabulary. The names given by the Nightingales to some products such as 'black chalk' or 'Turkey berries' were unknown in the Mediterranean. 'We have made the best inquiry we can about the black chalk ... but cannot find anybody here that comprehends what sort of commodity it is.' Even the Jews, who knew most things, could not tell them.[49] 'Turkey yellow berries' posed similar problems, though the consensus of opinion was that the

---

47 AP vol. 25, 12 February 1757.
48 C 109/1–14. For the business of the Nightingales see John, 1965.
49 C 109/9, 20 May 1768.

Nightingales must be referring to a product known as 'grain jaune', which was only available in Marseilles.

The product most frequently purchased for the Nightingales was safflower. This is defined as the 'dried petals of the *Carthamus tinctorius*, also the red dye produced from these petals, used in the preparation of rouge,' so no doubt essential for the make up of English ladies. Safflower came from Alexandria in Egypt, most of it in a few ships sailing together, and each year there was speculation as to when the new *raccolta* (harvest) would arrive, its quality and at what price it would be sold. Earle & Hodgson had to compete with other houses acting for rivals of the Nightingales in London and also with the correspondents of Dutch and Italian companies. The Nightingales obviously wanted safflower of the very best quality at the very lowest prices, but so did everybody else. The easiest way to operate would have been to trust Earle & Hodgson to do their best, but this the Londoners were reluctant to do and so often demanded that Earle & Hodgson send them samples by post before committing themselves. But these took at least two weeks to arrive in London and by the time a firm order had been despatched and received back in Leghorn, there might well be no good quality material left to be bought. 'You will have to wait for another year', wrote the Leghorn firm with a certain glee, as they were keen to have the choice of purchases in their own hands.

The business of choosing good quality or good enough quality safflower, bargaining for it, storing it until shipping was available and then insuring and shipping it to London was very drawn out, typically taking about three months from the first appearance of the new *raccolta* in the late autumn. Buying and selling anything took a long time, but this was stretched out by the need for all goods from the plague-ridden eastern Mediterranean to go through quarantine. Deals could be settled on goods while they were still in quarantine, but there was no way of circumventing the inevitable delays. In the first few years of the surviving correspondence, there were further delays due to the need to wait for a Royal Naval ship to convoy the outgoing fleet of merchantmen through the hordes of French privateers waiting for them. Merchants did not have to use the convoys but those who employed the 'runners', as the free spirits were known, had to pay much higher freight and insurance rates which might well wipe out the advantage of being the first to market.

As the years went by, Earle & Hodgson got better at dealing in safflower, and in the vast number of other goods traded in Leghorn. They were less likely to be tricked by the importers from Egypt and could state with some confidence that much of the safflower imported in 1764 was adulterated. As their knowledge grew, they were happy to make investments in the dyestuff themselves, offering to go shares in a consignment and, in 1765, buying up 30 bales of the best quality material while it was still in quarantine. They felt certain they would be able to sell them to advantage. 'We believe we shall have orders to forward them to London so soon as we have prattick [i.e. clearance from quarantine].' Safflower was of course just a very small part of the business transacted at Leghorn, minute compared with oil or silk for instance. But merchants, especially comparative newcomers, had to take what they could get. A typical year's supply to the port would be from 300 to 500 bales, of which the Nightingales would normally take less than ten, but getting these ten gave Earle & Hodgson a lot of work and of course earned them a nice commission, not to mention the profits earned on safflower bought for their own interest.

Several other products from the Levant were bought in Leghorn for the Nightingales by Thomas Earle's house, including various sorts of gum, such as mastic from the island of Chios and gum dragon from Persia, galls and vallonea, both products of oak trees used in dyeing and tanning, and Turkish alum imported from Smyrna and used as a mordant to fix the dyes in woollen cloth manufacture. From Italy the most important products demanded by the drysalters were Roman alum and red and white argol (cream of tartar), a by-product of winemaking which came from Florence, Bologna and Sicily and was used in medicine as a laxative. 'There are few medicines more commonly employed', we are told in the *Edinburgh New Dispensatory*.[50] There was also a high quality soap from Leghorn itself. This last gave Earle & Hodgson much satisfaction, for they were responsible for the creation of a manufactory in Leghorn producing 'genuine marbled soap' in imitation of the product of Marseilles, funding the manufacture themselves, and importing the raw materials, good quality olive oil available locally and barilla (an alkali derived from seaweed) imported from Spain. Marseilles, incidentally, was a major source of many other quality goods sold on the Leghorn market and, in wartime, Earle & Hodgson and the other English merchants had no compunction in importing such goods on Genoese or other neutral

50 *Edinburgh*, 1797, p. 254.

vessels with papers stating they were consigned to a neutral, such as their cashier Rigoli.

During the Seven Years' War, the Nightingales, like many other English merchants, invested some of their capital in privateer ships and used Leghorn as their base. Their first venture was in partnership with another London merchant house with interests in both Leghorn and Naples, Messrs Anthony Merry. They bought a 100-ton vessel, the *Fame*, which received its letters of marque in February 1759 under the command of Captain John Patrick, and Wills & Reynolds were chosen to act as agents in Leghorn. In the previous summer, Captain Patrick had been in command of another privateer, the *Leopard*, and had captured the *San Giovanni Evangelista*, a 300-ton ship which was sold in Leghorn by Earle & Hodgson to an Italian shipowner for 3,355 pieces of eight, and he would continue to be successful.[51] He went on three cruises for the Nightingales and their partners and took prizes on each of them, especially on his third cruise from September to November 1760, on which he captured a whole string of French shipping in the Levant, earning substantial profits for his owners and commissions for his agents, who received three per cent on prize goods sold in Leghorn and one per cent on those shipped back to London. Captain Patrick 'was a terror wherever he went' and he was also an efficient and well-organised privateer who usually sailed in consort with a *felucca* which 'could be manned with 50 hands for rowing and boarding'.[52]

Captain Patrick, like that former commander of another *Fame*, Fortunatus Wright, was unable to behave himself and respect the rules and, after 'outrageously breaking quarantine at Leghorn', had his commission revoked by the High Court of Admiralty in London. Nevertheless, he and the Nightingales had done well for themselves, a fact which must have frustrated Earle & Hodgson, who, in April 1762, got their chance to manage a new privateer acquired by the Nightingales, the 220-ton *Brilliant*, commanded by Captain Creighton. But this vessel was first of all slow in getting out to the Mediterranean. 'Tis a pitty

---

51   HCA 26/11, 22 February 1759; AP, 1 July 1758 and see 16 June and 21 August 1759 for the sales by Wills & Reynolds of two tartans captured by the *Leopard*.

52   Letters relating to these privateering ventures are scattered through the collection. See C 109/6/2, Capt. Patrick to Nightingales, Messina, 16 November 1760, for details relating to his third cruise. See also Harriott, 1808, chapter called 'Anecdotes of Captain Patrick'.

your *Brilliant* privateer should be so long detained. French shipping is very active', their Leghorn agents wrote on 11 June. And when the ship did arrive, it took no prizes at all, so that the Nightingales had to console themselves with sending her home at the end of the war in March 1763 with a normal Leghorn cargo – silk, coral, straw hats, oil, wine, fruit, 200 sacks of juniper berries and 20 casks of argol. No French goods there, though maybe Earle & Hodgson were pleased to be 'congratulated on their management of the cargo.'[53]

No doubt Earle & Hodgson traded in many other goods besides those mentioned above on which we have evidence. And all this meant a lot of work, hundreds of letters to be written, in Italian and French as well as English, goods to be inspected in warehouses and in the *lazzaretto*, visits to be made to Italian suppliers, deals to be made with wily foreign merchants, cargo space to be found and freights and insurance negotiated. But, despite all this, there seems no doubt that Leghorn also encouraged vices of the sort so often associated with the lazy sun-soaked south. Many years later, there are some interesting comments on the Tuscan port in a travel diary kept by Thomas Hodgson's younger brother. Young Hodgson really enjoyed himself, going to the opera and the theatre, chatting up the ladies, making visits and return visits to 'several gentlemen of the Factory', cards, ice cream, lemonade. 'I now begin to think', he wrote at the end of his stay in Leghorn, 'that the inhabitants of this place live in a superior style of elligence to any I ever saw. The forenoons are appropriated to business, the afternoons totally to pleasure ... I begin to be in love with this country, particularly the English factory are remarkably sociable.'[54]

Thomas Earle, or Tom as he was to his friends, was himself a sociable man, especially after his marriage in June 1754 to Mary Mort, the only daughter and heiress of Adam Mort of Wharton Hall in Lancashire, a wealthy country gentleman, a further injection of country money to finance Liverpool merchants and their trade. They were married in England but soon returned to Leghorn, where they made their home in 'a great rambling house'. Here a son, Adam, was born but died in childhood. Mary was more fortunate with her two daughters,

53 TNA C 109/8/1, 11 June 1762, 13 May 1763. Earle & Hodgson did not themselves invest in privateers during the Seven Years' War, though several other merchants in the British Factory did.
54 MMM D/EARLE/8/3.

Maria, born 16 August 1761, and Elizabeth Jane, born on 14 February 1764, both of whom survived and lived well into the nineteenth century. Some scraps of information about their lifestyle can be gleaned from the letters and journals of visitors. Sir William Farington, a Lancashire gentleman, dined with the Earles and their business partners twice in June 1765. He was much impressed by Mary, 'a very agreeable woman', and also by the music laid on by Thomas, which included a recital by Pietro Nardini, a native of Livorno and the most famous violinist in Italy. Nardini was a friend of Thomas's clerk William Hempson, who lived with the Earle family and 'played the flute to admiration', while the Earles themselves owned a harpsichord, though who played it we do not know.[55]

More bits and pieces about this musical household can be gleaned from two collections of letters written by the entertaining Joseph Denham. He was a charming and witty Irish adventurer whose letters reveal that he had deserted his young wife Sukey and fled England to avoid being imprisoned for debt. He was an excellent linguist and certainly possessed the gift of the gab. After very brief service in both the English and Portuguese armies, he arrived in Italy in 1763. He managed to get a post in Genoa writing Italian and French letters in the counting house of an English merchant and, while there, began a correspondence with Mary Earle in Leghorn, whom he had met on his arrival in Italy. He was 21 and she was in her thirties and his jokey flirtation by letter with her was typical of relations in Italy at this time, where it was a social convention for young single men to become a *cicisbeo* or gallant (not quite a gigolo) to a married woman. Some of this flirtation seems pretty risqué by modern conventions, but it was really quite harmless, Mary's husband clearly as amused by the letters as she was. Tom and Mary Earle were indeed the stars in Joseph Denham's firmament, Mary being not just beautiful but 'the cleverest woman I ever met with', while 'Mr Earle … has been my father, my brother, my guardian angel, I had almost said my Deity!'[56] Denham's letters to Mary Earle (and occasionally to her husband) were paralleled by a correspondence in a rather different tone to Sukey, his estranged wife, who eked out a living as a domestic in the houses of various members of the English aristocracy while Joseph gallivanted in Italy. The letters

55 Ingamells, 1997, pp. 327–28.
56 D/EARLE/3/3/15, Denham to Sukey, 29 April 1771.

are still amusing but they reveal a less pleasant side to his character. He repeatedly declares his love for Sukey and longs for her to join him in Italy, or so he says, but in truth it is clear that he is quite happy without her.[57]

Denham's letters to Mary show a mutual interest in food, nostalgia for such English favourites as venison pasties and mince pies, which Mary makes, as well as delight in a lavish meal in the English style produced to put some tiresome Francophile guests in their place, 'a very elegant dinner, ham and fowls, ducks, boiled beef, plumb tarts and pudding, roast venison ... a dish of sweetbreads etc.' But they also had an interest in Italian food and Denham encouraged Mary to learn how to cook the local dishes, especially ravioli, so that when she returned to Liverpool she would be able 'to teach her neighbours how to cook their victuals and make soup *all'Italiana*.' There are also many references to dinner guests and to visits to the opera. In June 1764, for instance, he writes from Genoa to say that he is 'glad to hear such good accounts of your opera. I wish we had some chance to get the same company here.' And, like most English visitors to Italy, they both found the summers too hot and the winters too cold, Denham complaining on one occasion of the 'large windows, doors that will not shut ... it only serves to put me in mind of Lapland.'[58] He also refers quite often to Mary's two little girls, especially when Mary was on a tour of places of interest in Italy and Denham was living in the Earle house in Leghorn. He tells her that a guest, the wife of another English merchant, had praised 'your little ones up to the skies for their good behaviour Saturday at dinner.' He reports that they are very well and notes that 'the little one ... walks alone all over the house as well as I can [at 18 months].'[59]

But punctuating this seemingly carefree life, there are signs that Mary is not really happy. She is homesick and wants to return home to her friends and relations in Liverpool. She may also have been alarmed at a perceived threat to her daughters from militant Catholics eager to seduce innocent English girls into their faith. In 1762, Phoebe Lefroy,

57 The letters are in MMM, D/EARLE/3/3/1–16, mainly to Sukey; ibid., /3/2/1–31, mainly to Mary Earle. For some comment on the letters see Goodwin, 1999, pp. 85–89.
58 MMM D/EARLE/3/2/17, 17 July 1765; ibid., /3/2/24, 1 February 1768; ibid., 3/2/6, 2 June 1764.
59 D/EARLE/3/2/17, 17 July 1765; ibid., /3/2/24, 1 February 1768; ibid., 3/2/6, 2 June 1764.

daughter of the merchant Anthony Lefroy, disguised herself in men's clothes and with the help of a servant ran away to Florence, where she was accepted into the Convent of Santa Agata. Though this behaviour was much condemned by the other English merchants in Livorno, it was to turn out very favourably for both Phoebe and her father. Five years later, now a Catholic, she married a member of the Del Medico family, who controlled much of the Carrara marble trade, to the commercial benefit of her father, who was himself a major dealer in marble. Not all such affairs ended so conveniently. In 1763, all three daughters of the widow Gravier, an English silk merchant, declared their wish to convert to the Catholic faith and the eldest, Anna, successfully left home for this purpose. Anxious meetings of the British Factory were held, which resulted in assistance coming from the Emperor in Vienna. The authorities in Livorno were ordered to arrange for the return of the child to her mother and this was done, as we learn from a document written by the merchant Robert Rutherford, who, on 13 February 1765, acknowledged receipt of 'la persona della fanciulla Signorina Anna Gravier' on board a ship sailing for England.[60]

But Mary Earle still had to wait for a ship to take her and her daughters to England. Tom Earle was the problem. He was not ready to leave and Joseph Denham commended patience. Tom will want to leave sooner than Mary believes, he wrote, and this was confirmed by Bellamy, a bankrupt English merchant living in Leghorn and family friend: 'Bellamy says he is convinced that Tom Earle wants to come home.' And this proved to be true. Thomas and Mary tidied up the loose threads of their life in Italy and in 1766 returned by sea to Liverpool, complete with the children (still safely Protestant) and their maid Maddalena, whom they hoped would stay with them in Liverpool and serve to stop the children, especially five-year-old Maria, from forgetting the Italian which she spoke so fluently.[61]

---

60 TNA SP 96/98, 26 June 1762; SP 105/301, 24 June 1763; SP 93/70, 8 January, 13, 16 February 1765; many thanks to Cristina Bates for letting me see her unpublished paper on the marble trade and the Del Medico family.

61 D/EARLE/ 3/2/9, 16 October 1764; ibid., /3/2/17, 17 July 1765.

CHAPTER SEVEN

Thomas Earle of Hanover Street

'To the Messrs. Earle … everything arriving from
the coasts of the Mediterranean, from the Pillars
of Hercules to the Pillar of Pompey, used to be
consigned.'[1]

Thomas Earle was 47 years old when he and Mary returned from
their sojourn in Italy. At this age, many merchants began to think
about winding down, transferring funds into rentier investments and
beginning to anticipate the joys of retirement. But this was not to be
Tom Earle's way. He relaxed a bit, took pleasure in riding and gardening,
for instance, but overall he was pretty active in business right up to his
death, 25 years later, in April 1781. The family stayed with relations on
their return to Liverpool, but soon set up on their own in a large house
in Hanover Street, the street favoured by the mercantile élite.

The correspondence between Joseph Denham and Mary Earle
became much more irregular after her return to Liverpool, but Denham's
surviving letters do allow us some inkling of Mary's life in England.
In July 1768, for instance, Denham wrote that he believed her life was
now preferable to what she had enjoyed in Italy, 'on account of your
numerous friends and relations', suggesting that she had a lively social
life in England. Lack of English friends in Italy had been a major contribution to her homesickness. It is also clear that Mary had successfully
encouraged her two girls to keep up their Italian and to take advantage
of the best education available, although sadly no details are available. 'I
am glad to find your two daughters are well situated at school', Denham
wrote in 1774, when the girls were 13 and 10. 'Your plan of education
enraptures me. How different from this country!'[2]

1 Boardman, 1871, p. 13.
2 MMM D/EARLE/3/2/28 & 29.

Meanwhile, Thomas was busy as a shipowner and merchant. The shipping database shows him to be sole or part-owner of 11 ships which made 43 trading voyages between them from 1762 to 1780, two or three voyages a year, and he also had shares in seven slaving voyages in partnership with his younger brother William. Some of these non-slaving ships gave him very good service, the best coming from the snow *Polly* (the nickname of his daughter Maria), which made 11 voyages between 1762 and 1772, the *Vigilant* (nine voyages, 1763–73), *Leghorn Galley* (seven voyages, 1769–76) and *Lord Stanley* (five voyages, 1771–76). The average voyage length, as these dates suggest, was about a year from Liverpool to Liverpool. Although the main business of 'la flotta Earle' was to carry cargo, several of the vessels also had cabins for passengers, such as the *Experiment*, advertised in May 1774 as ready to sail for Marseilles and Leghorn 'with excellent accommodation for passengers … Apply Thomas Earle or Captain Peter Maddocks.'[3] Most of these ships were the sole property of Thomas, though his business partner Thomas Hodgson and one or both of his brothers joined him as part-owners of some of them.[4] In addition to his trading ships, Thomas had shares in several privateers, which shall be discussed in the next chapter.

Information on shipping movements comes mainly from newspapers, especially *Lloyds List* (the national shipping paper which began in 1741), the *Liverpool Advertiser* and the *Manchester Mercury*, which report arrivals and departures as well as any incidents or casualties such as capture or shipwreck. For some years there are, in addition, entries in the Liverpool and Manchester newspapers of 'goods imported', ship by ship, with the quantities imported and the names of the consignees. These entries provide the best information on goods coming into Liverpool between the end of the port books around 1720 and the Liverpool Customs Bills of Entry, which start a century later and will be discussed in Chapter 12. The lists of 'goods imported' are far from perfect; on many occasions the amount of goods listed hardly looks like the full cargo, and quite often this part of the paper is simply omitted to provide space for more important information such as advertisements or the results from the latest race meeting. Nevertheless, these entries are the best we have and, since they are fullest in the years 1768 to 1774, the discussion below shall concentrate on this short period.

3 *WLA*, 13 May 1774.
4 Ownership, voyage patterns etc. from LTS.

The pattern of utilisation was very much what one would expect from a man who had learned his trade as a merchant in Leghorn, as can be illustrated by the last five voyages of the *Vigilant*. This ship was jointly owned by Thomas Hodgson and Thomas Earle and at 130 tons, with a crew of 11 and four guns, was the largest ship employed by Thomas. She made voyages to Leghorn and back in 1763, 1765 and 1766–67, and in 1765–66 she sailed to Virginia via Dublin and then to Cadiz, Leghorn and back to Liverpool. Her next voyage was in 1768 and this is the first for which there is information on her cargo. She sailed in January via Dublin to Newfoundland for a cargo of salt cod, which she carried to Italy, returning to Liverpool in November of the same year. Goods imported into Liverpool and recorded in the *Manchester Mercury* comprised some oil, a bundle of prints and a case of statues consigned to Earle & Hodgson themselves, six blocks of marble to Charles Bromfield (a regular marble importer), lambskins and anchovies to a firm called Corles & Sorton, argol, oil, wine, anchovies and cases of marble to other unknown consignees and a large shipment of beads for William Davenport & Co., whose business shall be discussed below. The *Vigilant* also had aboard 'the finest Newfoundland dog that ever was seen' as a present from Joseph Denham to Thomas Earle. The quantities listed hardly seem like the full cargo of a vessel registered at 130 tons and one suspects that here, as elsewhere, the newspaper omitted many imports through ignorance or simply lack of space. Nevertheless, the types of goods listed are what one would expect a ship trading from Leghorn to Liverpool to carry.[5]

The next voyage of the *Vigilant*, in 1769, was very similar, via Dublin and Newfoundland to Gibraltar and Leghorn and then back home, arriving in Liverpool at the beginning of September 1769. Both the cargo imported into Liverpool and the consignees were also much the same. Earle & Hodgson imported hemp, wool, oil and wine, Charles Bromfield another 100 blocks of marble, 600 marble flags (paving stones) and 36 marble mortars (many of these are imported during this period), and William Davenport & Co. more beads and a case of coral. The *Vigilant* spent just a few days in Liverpool before setting off once again

---

5   Full cargoes are often listed in merchants' correspondence. See above pp. 125–27 for some examples. *MM*, 22 November 1768; D/EARLE/3/2/27, 27 July 1768; Denham seems to have made a habit of importing Newfoundland dogs as gifts; see TY 7/321, Thomas Jenkins to Charles Townley, 27 November 1773.

on a similar voyage, arriving back just over a year later, in November 1770. 'Waste silk', anchovies, oil and wine were consigned to Thomas Earle and the other consignees remained the same and imported the same sort of goods, Bromfield importing marble gravestones as well as 302 marble paving stones on this occasion.[6]

Once again, little time was wasted before the *Vigilant* set out again, this time trading in Sicily as well as Leghorn before returning home in August 1771 to serve quarantine at Hoylake before unloading in Liverpool a month later. This time there was one new customer, Cunliffe & Co., who imported brimstone (sulphur), which would explain the trip to Sicily, the main source of sulphur at this time. Finally, on 25 October 1771, the *Vigilant* set out on her ninth and last voyage for Earle & Hodgson, which seems to have been much like all the others, except that the ship was reported at the wine port of Malaga on her way home, where she arrived in April 1773.[7] Although the *Vigilant* was the most important of Thomas Earle's ships during these years, there were at least seven other vessels in which he had an interest sailing to the Mediterranean, most often to Leghorn itself, but also to Gibraltar, Cadiz, Alicante, Mahon (Minorca), Cagliari (Sardinia), Marseilles, Genoa, Civitavecchia, Venice, Trieste and the Levant, to which his ship *Lord Stanley* made two voyages, one in 1774 to Scanderoon, the port of Aleppo, and the other in 1776 to Smyrna in Anatolia. One voyage in which Thomas (and no doubt Mary) Earle must have had a special interest was that of the *Diana*, which arrived back in Liverpool from Leghorn in May 1768. She was carrying for Thomas Earle, in addition to such staples of the trade as oil, wine, olives and anchovies, a chair, a hamper of house furniture and six chests of apparel, all no doubt destined to give an Italian touch to the family home in Hanover Street.

A few of these Mediterranean voyages simply involved a passage from Liverpool to Leghorn and back, sometimes with passengers as well as freight, but most included at least one other leg to produce a variety of 'triangular' voyages, Liverpool to Ireland for a cargo of foodstuffs and then Leghorn and so back home, Liverpool to New York or Philadelphia (sometimes with emigrants) and then to Leghorn, Liverpool

6 *MM*, 5 September 1769, 6 November 1770; Benjamin Bromfield of 6 Marble Street is listed as a marble merchant in the Liverpool Directory of 1790.
7 *MM*, 1 October 1771, 11 April 1773.

to Newfoundland and then to a port in Italy with a cargo of salt cod (*baccalà*). In the Earle Collection, there is a passenger and crew list for the *Speedwell*, which sailed from Liverpool to Philadelphia in 1769 and then went on to Newfoundland, Italy and so back to Liverpool. She had a crew of 12, including four listed as servants, which probably means apprentices. On her passage to Philadelphia, she carried 13 passengers, seven men, four women and two children, the normal fare being £5 for an adult. No details are given, but passengers were probably required to find their own food.[8]

Thomas Earle (all the Earles, in fact) was always interested in new routes and new products. One new direction was indicated by the voyage of the *Betty* in 1766–67 to Jamaica and Honduras, this Central American territory being a major source of logwood (used in dyeing) and of mahogany, very fashionable in the later eighteenth century, both of which Thomas dealt in, as well as importing sugar, indigo and the other staples of Jamaica. This Jamaican interest became very important in the 1770s, when five of Thomas's ships ventured there, one of them, the *Leghorn Galley*, making six voyages, sometimes returning directly to Liverpool, and sometimes incorporating a visit to Leghorn. There was nothing particularly new about engaging in Jamaican trade, but such a change in direction seems to have rather alarmed Joseph Denham. In a letter written to Mary Earle in December 1779, he described her husband as a great 'enterpriser' who 'risks his money in insurance and the Jamaican trade.' We do not have much information on his insurance activities, but Jamaican trade was certainly important to Thomas in the twilight of his career.[9]

Most trade from Liverpool, including that engaged in by Thomas Earle, followed well-worn tracks so that there are few surprises in the listings of incoming cargoes in the Liverpool and Manchester newspapers. Ships from Leghorn carried the heterogeneous cargoes discussed in the last chapter and illustrated above; ships from the West Indies brought in the staple products of that region – sugar, cotton, indigo and so on. Occasionally, one does get a bit of a surprise. Almost every one of Thomas's ships which sailed to Liverpool from New York, for instance, carried in their cargo American pig and bar iron, usually about 100 tons on each ship. American iron benefited from the abolition

8 MMM D/EARLE/1/3.
9 MMM D/EARLE/3/2/30.

in 1757 of duties on imports into Britain and, by the early 1770s, over 5,000 tons a year were being exported. This iron competed with imports from Sweden and, increasingly, Russia in these early years of the Industrial Revolution when England was not yet able to produce enough of her own iron to satisfy the demands of manufacturers.[10]

An interesting trading innovation arose from an initiative of William Davenport, who was keen to develop a new source of supply for the beads used to trade in Africa. His accounts show that beads made up between a quarter and a half of the total value of cargoes shipped from Liverpool to the Cameroons, a major source of slaves, figures which suggest that Daniel Defoe's famous jibe against slave traders in his poem *Reformation of Manners* – 'They barter baubles for the souls of men' – had some basis in fact.[11] Most of the beads and similar baubles used in the Liverpool African trade came from India and were acquired in London or the Low Countries and, although satisfactory in quality, were expensive. Discussion with the Earle brothers suggested that a wide variety of good quality beads could be acquired in Venice, a city famous for its decorative glassware, and exported to Liverpool either direct or via Leghorn.[12]

In 1766, Davenport established a bead company in partnership with all three Earle brothers, together with Thomas Hodgson, partner in the Leghorn house, and Peter Holme and John Copeland, merchants who were regular investors in Earle and Davenport shipping and slaving ventures. The maximum capital of the company was to be £20,000 and a bead warehouse was acquired which, like William Earle's shop with its stock of knives and so on, could supply slaving vessels with what they required in beads, cowries and similar products. The partnership also acquired shares in the 90-ton snow *Polly* which had previously been owned by the Leghorn house of Earle & Hodgson. The newspapers show this vessel shipping beads from Venice and Trieste in the late 1760s and early 1770s, but the partnership used many other vessels as well, such as the *Lark*, on which 88 cases of beads were shipped by Earle & Hodgson in Leghorn in March 1767 for consignment to William Davenport & Co. in Liverpool. Nearly all the shipments were consigned to Davenport (there were a few to John Copeland) and consisted of beads and 'bugles',

---

10   Faulkner, 1960, pp. 88, 111.
11   Defoe, 1702, p. 17.
12   Richardson, 1989, pp. 66–67; Radburn, 2009, pp. 71–72.

a tube-shaped glass bead in great demand. Small quantities of coral were also shipped by the bead company.

There were vast numbers of different sorts of beads and it was easy to confuse one with another, so Earle & Hodgson also sent a sample book 'with numbers for us to refer to, having another of the like kind in our possession which will enable us more perfectly to comprehend any order.' And they promised that 'our friends in Venice' would produce another 'more thorough' sample book, as well as sending samples of goods not ordered 'by way of essay', i.e. trial. The bead warehouse also continued to stock beads and cowries and so on of Indian origin, as well as beads made in Amsterdam and Prague, even today a centre of bead manufacture, and Davenport can be found in the records shipping such goods through Amsterdam, Rotterdam and Bremen, like the 11 casks of beads, 99 casks of cowries and one box of hawks' bells shipped on the *Henry* at Rotterdam in 1772. A letter of March 1779 notes the very large stock of beads that had built up in the warehouse during the early years of the American War of Independence when there were few Liverpool merchants prepared to risk their ships in slaving voyages. It was proposed to fit out three or four ships to sail direct to Africa with the accumulation of beads 'in order to work off the stock and to reap benefit by the adventures, as negroes may now be bought for 50 per cent less than they were 12 months ago.' Beads may seem innocent enough, but they could and did contribute to the purchase of African men, women and children, and one wonders if the Venetians and Czechs are aware of their role in the eighteenth-century African slave trade.[13]

Both Thomas Earle and Thomas Hodgson, the founding fathers of the trading house in Leghorn, now lived in Liverpool, but the house continued to trade in Italy under the same name, Earle & Hodgson ['& Drake' was added in 1782]. Joseph Denham provides a description of it in a letter to his estranged wife Sukey written in December 1767. He claimed that it was 'one of the first houses in Leghorn', but it seems to have been seriously understaffed as all the business was done by Robert Hodgson, Thomas's brother, who was a partner, and Denham, who was as yet only a salaried clerk. They had 'a great rambling house and live comfortably enough. We keep only two servants, a cook and a footman, who make up the sum total of our family.' In 1768, Robert Hodgson

13 MMM D/DAV/5, fols 6–12, 13 and 20 March 1767, 23 March 1768; D/DAV/1 f.4b, Davenport to C. Ford, 23 March 1779 and reports of imports in *MM*.

was joined by 'a young gentleman' who came out as a junior partner, while Denham, after several years of scheming, went south to open a branch office in Civitavecchia, the port of Rome, a new partnership being established between the existing partners in Liverpool and Leghorn, and Denham was generously given three-quarters of the profits from the Civitavecchia house.[14]

The Leghorn house grew considerably in the next 30 years and was described in 1797 as 'a great establishment of clerks and dependents, a country house, warehouses, coach-house and box at the theatre,' an early example of a hospitality box.[15] But, both in 1768 and 1797, the business seems to have consisted of much the same sort of thing as when Thomas Earle was resident in Italy; there was just more of it. The Leghorn house was autonomous and made its own commercial decisions, subject to a flow of advice, orders and general information contained in letters from the Liverpool-based partners. The number of ships sailing from Liverpool to Leghorn would hardly have been sufficient to have kept the Leghorn house fully occupied and most of its business was in fact with London, which remained much the most important destination for English ships sailing to England from Leghorn. Correspondence to and from the Leghorn house has not survived, but it is clear that its business involved touting for commissions in both Italy and England, sending home information on markets, prices and availability of goods, carrying out commissions from Liverpool and elsewhere in England or from Italian merchants and Englishmen resident in or visiting Italy, arranging freight on their own or other ships, paying expenses in the course of shipment and, as the house's capital grew, discounting bills for customers and for well-heeled visitors who needed money to finance their Grand Tour.

Few documents exist to give details, except the shipping lists in the Liverpool and Manchester papers.[16] There is, however, a small collection of correspondence in the Hertfordshire Record Office which nicely illustrates the sort of business that houses like Earle & Hodgson carried out for wealthy clients. These papers relate to Earl Cowper, who first

14 MMM D/EARLE/3/3/7, 14 December 1767 and /3/3/13, 9 September 1768.
15 MMM D/EARLE/3/4, p. 56.
16 Much more information on the business of the Leghorn house in its final years is contained in a letter book titled *Livorno* covering the years 1801–08, MMM D/EARLE/2/3. This shall be discussed in Chapter Eleven, below.

came to Florence in 1759 and liked it so much that he stayed there until
1786 and became a leader of Florentine society.[17] Most of the letters from
Earle & Hodgson were written to Pierre Louis Jordan, Earl Cowper's
house steward, between 1774 and 1780. Much of this relates to the arrival
in Leghorn and consignment on barges up the Arno to Florence of a
range of delicacies not available in Italy. From England came hams, beer,
cheese, mustard, potatoes, red herrings and three dozen bottles of 'the
true Jamaica rum'; from Holland two cases of dried salmon; and from
Cadiz a cask of sherry wine. Jewels and silver plate were also imported
for Earl Cowper and Earle & Hodgson were kept busy paying freight,
customs duties and other charges on all these goods on behalf of their
aristocratic client. Cowper, like most upper-class Englishmen in Italy,
was also acquiring pictures and statuary for shipment to England and
Earle & Hodgson busied themselves with these precious objects with the
same care and attention they applied to the import of beer and potatoes.[18]

This business of exporting art and antiquities from Italy to England
has received much attention recently as a result of an exhibition held
in 2012 at the Ashmolean Museum in Oxford.[19] The exhibition was
called *The English Prize* and focussed on the capture by the French of
the *Westmorland*, an English ship sailing from Leghorn to London at
the beginning of January 1779. The prize was taken to Malaga, Spain
being an ally of France at this date, and the cargo was sold mainly in
Spain. This was a typical Leghorn cargo – silk, olive oil, drugs, marble,
anchovies and so on – but amongst these fairly mundane goods were
23 crates of marble statues and 22 of prints, portraits and books. Most
of these objects of cultural interest were acquired on behalf of Carlos
III, King of Spain, and deposited in the Real Academia de Bellas Artes
in Madrid, where they remain to this day. These statues, paintings and
books, together with supporting material, provided the attractive display
at the exhibition.

Unheralded among all these treasures was a bill of lading, dated
Leghorn 19 August 1778, for a case containing pictures shipped 'in
good order and well conditioned' by Earle & Hodgson on board the
good ship *Westmorland* which were to be delivered in London to the

17   Ingamells, 1997, pp. 245–47.
18   Herts RO, D/EPF 327, A/528–557, 1774–1780.
19   See Sánchez-Jáuregui and Wilcox, 2012, for the catalogue and associated
     essays.

Right Honourable, the Earl of Dartmouth.[20] It is more than likely that Earle & Hodgson were also responsible for many more of the crates and boxes loaded on the ill-fated vessel, for they were by this date the most important shippers of art from Leghorn to England. The best proof of this lies in the letters written by Thomas Jenkins, the leading English dealer in art and antiquities in Rome, to Charles Townley, the very important London collector whose collection of marble statuary was left at his death to the British Museum. Jenkins's letters are mainly to do with the art and not with the trivia of getting it to London but, when such matters are mentioned, we find that he used just two Leghorn houses as agents and shippers, Earle & Hodgson and Francis Jermy; after the early 1770s, he employed only Earle & Hodgson. This was a big business and must have played an important part in the activities of the House.[21]

We cannot leave Italy and rejoin Tom and Mary in Liverpool without a brief description of what happened to Joseph Denham, for this was truly amazing and goes to prove that charm and a facility in speaking one's own language and those of foreigners can take a man a long way. It was seen above that Joseph Denham left Leghorn to open a branch merchant house in Civitavecchia in 1768. This port was becoming increasingly important and Denham could expect to do well from the opportunity offered him, as he had plans to speculate in the grain trade to Rome and to become the British Consul in Civitavecchia. But he could hardly have foreseen just what a goldmine this Civitavecchia posting would turn out to be.

The key to Joseph Denham's success lay in his charm since, for some reason that is never spelled out, he became a great favourite of Pope Clement XIV (1769–74), 'molto favorito da papa', and from this favour everything else flowed. He was appointed manager of the Papal Navy, with a responsibility to maintain the ships and galleys, at a salary of 120,000 *scudi* (£24,000) a year. He was given a castle and an estate at Onano, on the borders of the Papal States and Tuscany, and was granted an income from the local customs duties to support his new aristocratic lifestyle. This papal largess enabled him to escape the heat of Rome by

20 Sánchez-Jáuregui and Wilcox, 2012, p. 37. My thanks to my brother Robert, whose sharp eyes noticed this little piece of paper.
21 Jenkins' letters to Townley in BM TY/295–550; see also Bignamini and Hornsby, 2010, *passim* and especially ii, p. 262, n. 2.

a seasonal migration to Onano, 'where the air in the summer is perfect and as cool as in England.' Pope Clement died in 1774, but Denham was just as successful in charming his successor, Pope Pius VI, as Thomas Jenkins reported in a letter to Charles Townley: 'The present Pope although he has annulled several farms [i.e. concessions] belonging to the Government, given by his predecessor, has confirmed Denham's which is a sort of complement of your humble servant.'[22]

Jenkins was referring here to the fact that Denham was his partner in the Roman art trade, both men cementing their positions by being favourites of the Pope, the source of all favours, export and excavation licences and so on. Denham also conducted a sizeable shipping business from Civitavecchia, Jenkins referring in 1773 to shipping goods on 'one of Denham's ships', so presumably he had several. One major aspect of this business was the route to Leghorn, where his small coasting vessels could link up with those employed by Earle & Hodgson for the long voyage to England. It seems that, between them, they had the business of transporting art from Rome to London all tied up. Denham and Jenkins were mocked for their artistic pretensions, but it was noted in 1774 that they 'survive all the rigour of satyre and effect a triumph, and well they may, for they are both as rich as ever.' Thomas Earle had done quite well in Italy, but he did not do half as well as his former employee Joseph Denham.[23]

Denham was no longer the carefree *cicisbey* of his Leghorn days, as he coyly admitted to his estranged wife Sukey in April 1771, after three years' silence. He informed her that, receiving no letters, he had assumed she was dead and so sought comfort elsewhere. His chosen partner, a young Italian lady 'of unblemished character', became pregnant and her family insisted that Denham marry her which, although married already, he was able to do with the help of a dispensation from his benefactor, Pope Clement. By the time he wrote to Mary Earle in April 1774, Denham's new wife Louisa had given birth to no less than five children, John, Charlotte, Caroline, Anthony and Wilhelmina. 'What a tribe!' wrote Denham. And what a rascal![24]

22 MMM D/EARLE/3/2/29, 16 April 1774; 3/2/32, 25 August 1781; BM TY 7/345, 4 March 1775.

23 For Denham see Ingamells, 1997, p. 291; Guglielmotti, 1884, pp. 219–21; Cryan, 2005; Bignamini and Hornsby, 2010, i, p. 262.

24 D/EARLE/3/3/15, 29 April 1771; /3/2/29, 16 April 1774; Cryan, 2005.

Denham continued to write to Tom and Mary Earle with no apparent shame at the way he had treated Sukey. He jokes about the bad table manners of the Duke of Cumberland when he was in Civitavecchia on his way to Rome. He extols the beauty of his eldest child John and warns Mary to be careful if he should send him to England, as 'one of your daughters would certainly fall in love with him.' He jokes that prosperity has made him so fat that even the Pope laughs whenever he sees him. He remains indeed very much the same amusing fellow that we met in the earlier letters. A letter written in April 1771 to Sukey which was clearly meant to be read by Thomas Earle as well was vaguely apologetic about his behaviour, but its main import was to record how glad he was to find 'that upon the whole you have both put a more favourable construction on my behaviour than I expected.' And, in the one letter in the collection written by Sukey herself, three years later (to an unknown friend), she says that she has heard 'of his health and additional good fortune with the greatest pleasure.' The Joseph Denhams of this world are usually forgiven, even by their victims.[25]

What exactly Thomas Earle did at his counting house in Hanover Street is difficult to say, since no correspondence or account books have survived so that we cannot discuss his business in the same detail as that of his younger brother William. He ran a substantial shipping business with several of the ships solely owned by himself as has been seen, which meant presumably that it was he who undertook the onerous job of ship's husband. For the last three years of his life (1778–81), he was heavily involved in privateering, a subject which shall be considered in the next chapter. He also continued to play an active part in the running of the Leghorn house, though Joseph Denham bemoaned Tom's failure to answer letters on more than one occasion. He must also have corresponded with contacts in Antwerp, Amsterdam, New York, Philadelphia, Jamaica, Honduras and elsewhere in order to arrange for the shipment of goods to Liverpool which are recorded in the newspapers. But the only aspect of his business on which we have direct evidence relates to the sale of the various imported goods in which he dealt. This, like the movements of his ships, can be traced in the local newspapers. Advertisements for the

25 D/EARLE/3/2/29 Denham to Mrs Earle, 16 April 1774; D/EARLE/3/3/15 Denham to Sukey, 29 April 1771; /3/3/16, 8 March 1774.

sale of mahogany imported from Jamaica and Honduras appear most frequently, as on 14 May 1773, when notice was given of an auction to be held at his brother Ralph's timber yard on Salthouse Dock. Here would be sold, on 7 June,

> a cargo of mahogany (in lots suitable to the purchaser) now landing from over board the ship *Venus*, from the Bay of Honduras; the logs are loose and the quality supposed to be the best of any cargo arrived here of a long time. Any one desiring to view the same may apply to Mr Thomas Earle, merchant.[26]

Other goods offered for sale at Thomas's own warehouse include Jamaica rum, American bar and pig iron, Carrara marble, 'fine Lucca oil in jars and chests', anchovies and Smyrna cotton, so reflecting both his Mediterranean and transatlantic trades. These were all to be sold at auction, but Thomas may well have had some more permanent arrangement, a shop for instance, for selling his imported wares. There were a few specialist grocers selling Mediterranean foodstuffs in 1770s Liverpool, such as Haliday & Bamber, who advertised raisins, currants, nuts and best Lucca salad oil. In the next decade there were shops whose advertisements make them sound like a modern delicatessen, such as T. Oakes of the Oil and Italian Warehouse, who advertised in the *Liverpool Advertiser* on 2 July 1787. He sold 'Florence and Lucca oils, French olives, Parmesan cheese, real Genoa macaroni vermicelli, Genoa and French capers, true Gorgona anchovies, India curry, tapioca etc.' Thomas Earle never had a shop quite like this, but it was as a result of his and Thomas Hodgson's efforts that such delicacies were known at all in Liverpool.

Thomas died on 18 April 1781, aged 62, the first of the three brothers to die. The *Liverpool Advertiser* of 26 April carried a brief but flattering obituary. 'DEAD. At Bath, where he went for the recovery of his health, Mr Thomas Earle, an eminent and worthy merchant, universally esteemed whilst living, and death most sincerely lamented.' A letter from Joseph Denham to Mary Earle, written from Rome on 25 August, referred to Thomas's death obliquely but reflected Joseph's great attachment to his mentor. 'I would avoid mentioning my dear departed friend and father [*sic*] if possible, but must always acknowledge my very great obligations both to him and you.' He offered her a refuge in his

26 *WLA*, 14 May 1773.

castle at Onano, 'an agreeable place to live in', but Mary never went and in fact died herself just two years later.[27]

Mary's death made orphans of her two daughters, Maria aged 22 and Jane aged 19, though they were orphans with plenty of uncles, aunts and cousins to look after them and give them advice. The future of Maria had probably been planned ever since she was a child, or at least since the return to Liverpool of the Leghorn Earles or 'Italians' as Tom's brother William called them. In a typical example of mercantile dynasticism, she was destined to marry her first cousin, Thomas, the eldest son of William Earle, and so provide the means for an amalgamation of the assets, estates and goodwill of the two most successful sons of the Liverpool family's founder, John Earle. This marriage duly took place on 20 April 1786, when Maria was 25 and Thomas 32, though Thomas Jr, who was clearly precocious in his understanding of business, had been managing the affairs of both his father and uncle since the beginning of 1781, when his uncle Thomas senior was still alive.

Maria was well educated and this shows in two letters to her future husband, her 'Dear Cousin', written while she was visiting relations on 2 and 23 October 1785. These are written in an elegant style and a beautiful hand, but do not really throw much light on her relationship with Thomas, which was presumably very much taken for granted. She refers to 'your partiality for me', but the closest she comes to declaring her own partiality, let alone love, is to sign herself 'yours affectionately'. This may be put down to convention rather than coldness, as the letters reveal her to be a thoroughly pleasant, responsible and warm-hearted young lady. Her main worries related to the behaviour of her sister Jane, whose 'lively manners will I fear gain her many admirers' and whose 'laughing way' will get her into trouble. Since Jane's parents were dead, it would of course be Thomas who, once married, would head the family and so be responsible for his laughing sister-in-law's behaviour. 'I foresee you will have a great deal of trouble with her', predicts Maria. However, 'she joins me in love and compliments which I must beg you to distribute as you think proper.'[28]

These letters may not disclose much, but they suggest that both young ladies were attractive in rather different ways, one laughing and

---

27 *WLA*, 26 April 1781; D/EARLE/3/2/32, Denham to Mary Earle, 25 August 1781.

28 D/EARLE/7/8, Maria Earle to Thomas Earle, 2, 23 October 1785.

the other more serious. Maria in fact reminds one of her contemporary Hannah Lightbody, whose delightful diary has recently been published.[29] Both were the daughters of Liverpool merchants and their families regularly entertained each other, both were well educated and well able to express themselves. Both liked dancing and they even shared the same doctor, the famous Dr James Currie. Hannah's family was more religious and more involved in politics, being abolitionists, but they both belonged to the same world as that depicted in the novels of Jane Austen. And Maria's husband, Thomas Jr, was every inch a Liverpool merchant whose activities in partnership with his younger brother William Jr shall be discussed in the last three chapters of the book.

29 Lightbody, 2008.

CHAPTER EIGHT

Privateering in the American War

'When these two privateers are out your Lordship
will enjoy the pleasures of a chace; it is really
such, and there is a pleasing anxiety in it – I
speak from experience.'[1]

Thomas Earle, like virtually everyone else in Liverpool with any money,
was interested in privateering, especially during the American War
of Independence. The first commissions against the rebel Americans
were not issued until April 1777, two years after the first shots were
fired at Lexington, as the British government was not sure of the legal
position of issuing commissions against rebels and, in any case, was
worried that such commissions might be interpreted as recognition of
American independence. Meanwhile, American privateers were receiving
commissions from Congress and many British (and Liverpool) ships were
captured, though quite a few of these were recaptured by ships of the
Royal Navy.

Even after April 1777, British shipowners were not all that enthusiastic
about making war against the rebels, whose ships tended to be well
defended, did not often carry very valuable cargoes and mainly cruised
in areas not much frequented by British privateers. All was to change,
however, in August 1778 with the authorisation of general reprisals
against France. Almost overnight, Britain and especially Liverpool was
engaged in a privateering craze greater than ever before. The newspapers
were suddenly bursting with news relating to the Liverpool privateers,
with advertisements appealing for men, fitting-out news, reports on
cruises and successes, information on prize cargoes and, quite soon,
flyers for the auction of these prize goods, the High Court of Admiralty

---

1 George Forbes to Lord Cowper, 15 March 1780, Herts R.O. DEP/F
310/46/2.

being speedy in its hearing of evidence and condemnation of captured ships as 'good prize'.[2]

On 25 September 1778, just seven weeks after the first commissions against France, the *Manchester Mercury* published a list of 18 ships with crews from 60 to 150 men which had fitted out or were in the process of fitting out in Liverpool, and it was noted that 'prizes have been brought in here worth upwards of £100,000.' Amongst these first comers was the *Viper*, Captain Philip Cowell, with commissions against both the French and the American rebels and owned by a syndicate of four Liverpool merchants, including Thomas Earle. On 1 May 1779, William Davenport wrote with great enthusiasm to his agents in Jamaica. 'Our privateers since my last have continued to be remarkably successful and, upon the whole, I suppose £800,000 have been taken into this port during the war, an immense sum indeed you'll say.' And Davenport was one of the Liverpool merchants benefiting from this craze, despite the hint of disapproval in a letter written in March 1781: 'We have 30 privateers ... and the seas are swarming with these licensed pirates, for you can call them nothing else.'[3]

The most prolific period of Liverpool's privateering war against France was the first nine months, though activity was to continue at a less hectic level right through till 1783. Commissions against the Americans and the French were amplified from June 1779 by the authorisation of general reprisals against Spain and, from 26 December 1780, against the Dutch, in revenge 'against that treacherous and self-interested nation' whose merchants and sea captains were thriving on the clandestine carriage of goods for the French. Overall, Liverpool set out 390 vessels between 1777 and 1783. So many ships could not all be successful and the High Court of Admiralty condemned only 154 vessels captured by Liverpool privateers, 15 in consortship with privateers from other ports. There were then a lot of unhappy or unlucky investors in Liverpool but, as will be seen, the Earle brothers and their sons did not belong to that number.[4]

During the American War, there were ten 'marks' (trading ships carrying letters of marque) whose owners included members of the

2 Many of these newspaper notices can be found in Williams, 2004, ch. 4.
3 MMM D/DAV/1/6a, Davenport to Messrs Vance, Caldwell & Vance; D/DAV/1, Davenport to Capt. William Begg, 16 March 1788.
4 Starkey, 1990, pp. 194–238.

Figure 8. Liverpool Privateer.
Detail from J.T. Serres, "Liverpool from the north–west", 1796

Earle family, William and Thomas until the latter's death in April 1781, and William's two sons, Thomas Jr and William Jr, in the later years. All but one of these ships were slavers and they carried powerful armaments and large crews, several having over 50 men aboard. Two of these slave ships were captured, both by American privateers from

Boston on the homeward voyage after delivering their complement of slaves in the West Indies. This naturally reduced the loss, as did the fact that one of these ships, the *Mars*, was later recaptured and had herself taken a prize on an earlier voyage, a Dutch snow laden with French brandy, wine and corkwood, which was taken on the outgoing passage to Africa. Two more Earle marks encountered setbacks; the *Ann*, Captain Smale, was wrecked in 1783 after disembarking her cargo of slaves in Havana and, more dramatically, the *Othello*, whose crew mutinied and took control of the ship on the African coast in the spring of 1783, but was then retaken by the second mate and the doctor, but not before the captain, James Johnson, had been murdered while attempting to quell the mutiny. More trouble was to follow, for the *Othello* was wrecked in July on the island of Tortola, though her cargo of 213 slaves was saved. This ship had, however, more than repaid her cost and outfit two years earlier when she captured and sent into an Irish port the *Santa Anna*, which was on her way home from Buenos Ayres to Cadiz with a cargo valued at £20,000. So, overall, it seems that Earle investment in letter of marque ships had paid off.[5]

In addition to their investment in marks, the Earles and their partners had shares in four true privateers or private men-of-war, all four of which were successful. First on the scene was the *Viper*, Captain Cowell, which had 16 guns and a crew of 40 men and was commissioned on 4 September 1778. She was owned by a syndicate of four Liverpool merchants, James Bridge, Thomas Birch, William Gregson and Thomas Earle, who were normally described collectively as Gregson, Bridge & Co. The *Viper* sailed for the favourite cruising ground of Liverpool privateers in the Bay of Biscay and did not have to wait long for success, taking *Le Judicieux*, a 400-ton West Indiaman on 3 October 1778 and *L'Aimable Annette*, a 160-ton snow, on 17 November, both on their way to Nantes with typical West Indian cargoes of cotton, coffee, sugar and indigo. It was generally accepted that these homeward-bound French West Indiamen were worth on average £15,000 each for their cargo

5   Williams, 2004, pp. 565–66. Information for this section is drawn from the slaveship database (TSTD), the declarations for letters of marque in HCA 24 and 25, and notices in newspapers. The ships with Earle investment were *Ann* (date of commission 1777), *Swift* (1777), *Mars* (1779), *Hawke* (1779), *Loyalty* (1780, not a slave ship), *Othello* (1781), *Bellona* (1781), *Neptune* (1781), *Rodney* (1782) and another *Ann* (1783).

and the ship itself, though some were worth a lot more. Neither of these two prizes gave any resistance, *L'Aimable Annette* being described as 'a defenceless vessel', which certainly seems to have been true, one of her officers deposing that she had only one cannon and not much gunpowder for that.[6]

No time was lost in getting these prizes back to England, where they were quickly condemned by the High Court of Admiralty and their cargoes and the ships themselves put up for auction. Advance notice of the auction of the cargo of *Le Judicieux* was placed in the *Liverpool Advertiser* on New Years' Day 1779, just under three months after her capture, and on 5 March there was a notice for the sale of *L'Aimable Annette* and her cargo at St George's Coffee House. In July, there was a general notice advising the former officers and seamen of the *Viper* that they could now be paid their shares of both these prizes at the offices of Gregson, Bridge & Co. Liverpool was awash with prize cargoes, mainly from the West Indies, and the town was enjoying a collective excitement similar to that engendered in modern times by a series of successes at football.

The most exciting news of all was the capture in October 1778 of the homeward-bound French East Indiaman, the *Carnatic*, by the Liverpool privateer *Mentor*, which was jointly owned by her captain John Dawson and his father-in-law John Baker. She was captured off the west coast of Africa and taken quite easily by the well-manned Liverpool ship, whose captain had cleverly detected that many of her guns were wooden dummies, a common practice to save money and to make the ship less top-heavy but in this instance a fatal one. She was generally believed to be the richest prize ever captured by a Liverpool privateer, mainly because of the discovery of 'a box of diamonds of an immense value' hidden away on the ship, though most contemporary estimates of her value were grossly exaggerated. Baker and Dawson built themselves a splendid mansion, nicknamed Carnatic Hall, and invested most of the rest of their gains in shipping, mainly privateers and slave ships, a fine advertisement for the privateering business. Amongst the many who gasped with excitement at the news was Jane Earle, Thomas's younger daughter, who reported the capture to her aunt, Mrs Hardman Earle, in a letter dated 14 November 1778. She listed the cargo and estimated

6 Prize papers for *Le Judicieux* in HCA 32/378/13 and for *L'Aimable Annette* in HCA 32/263/6.

the prize to be worth 'above £300,000' and the letter brings home to the reader what a personal and family triumph such a success could be. 'All this belongs entirely to the Captain and his wife's father', she wrote, somewhat of an exaggeration but one gets the general point. The proprietors of the Theatre Royal were quick to realise the drawing power of such privateering success and, on 4 June 1779, were advertising 'The Liverpool Prize. An entertainment much applauded at Covent Garden Theatre … which will be performed here next week.' Later issues gave more details:

> The Liverpool Prize or Who's Afraid, with the arrival of the *Mentor* and her prize the *Carnatic*. Mr Aldridge plays the captain of the *Mentor* and will introduce his much admired dance of the Merry Sailors. The First Lieutenant is played by Mr Moor with the favourite song of A Cruising We will Go … and the entertainment will be concluded with a medley dance of English and French sailors.[7]

Two more private men-of-war with Earle investment were in operation at the same time as the *Viper*, the *Sturdy Beggar*, Captain Cooper and later Peter Humphreys, and the *Enterprize*, Captain Thomas Pearce and later James Haslam, both of which received their commissions in the autumn of 1778. *Sturdy Beggar* was quite a common name for a privateer, an epithet normally used for vagabonds who were fit and strong and liable to be violent, not a bad description of a privateer. This vessel was described as being owned by Messrs Davenport & Co. and William Davenport's partners were John Parker, William Earle, John Copeland, Robert Jennings and James Penny, all merchants of Liverpool. She weighed 160 tons and had 16 carriage guns and 160 men, and was commissioned in October 1778 against both the Americans and the French, amplified in June 1779 with a commission against the Spaniards. She was reported at Milford on New Year's Day 1779 and then, on 15 March, a French prize of hers called the *St Michael*, a 450-ton ship from San Domingo, was brought into Limerick by a prize crew, these southern and western Irish ports playing a vital role in support of the Liverpool privateers, providing stores, provisions and the facility for repairs as well as extra men to bolster the usually small numbers in the prize crews. The vessel was then brought round to

7   MMM D/EARLE/7/4, letter to Mrs Hardman Earle, 14 November 1778; *WLA*, 4 June, 3 September 1779; Starkey, 1990, pp. 231–33, 281, 313–15.

Liverpool and, on 11 June, the prize herself and her cargo of sugar, indigo and cow hides was advertised for sale.[8]

The *Sturdy Beggar* now acquired a new captain, Peter Humphreys, and two more guns before setting out again. On 18 August, near the Azores, she captured *Le Moissonneur* [the reaper or harvester], a 180-ton vessel on her way from Cayenne in French Guiana to St Malo with a cargo of cotton, cocoa, redwood and orchil, a valuable lichen from which red or violet dyes were prepared. Like most of the other ships captured by Liverpool privateers, she made no resistance, which would have been foolhardy as she had only 'two guns mounted carrying ball of one pound weight ... but no ball on board, two or three muskets and two sabres.' Such a feeble armament seems astonishing in the middle of a war, especially as *Le Moissonneur*, like many ships out of St Malo, was a great traveller which had sailed to Pondicherry in India and then made several trading voyages in the Indian Ocean before making her way to Cayenne, a more adventurous set of voyages than anything done out of Liverpool at this date. Presumably, her owners calculated that, unless she had a very powerful armament, she would have no chance against a British privateer so she might as well be armed with virtually nothing, making a great saving in outfit costs. And of course ships without a weighty armament of cannon were more likely to be able to evade their pursuers.[9]

The French prize was sent home to the Mersey, where she arrived on 4 September, and was joined four days later by the *Sturdy Beggar* herself escorting another prize, *Nuestra Señora del Rosario*, a 200-ton *polacca* belonging to Barcelona on her way from Montevideo and Buenos Ayres to Cadiz with a cargo of 10,000 bull hides, sheep's wool, furs and about 10,000 dollars in specie, around £2,500. She had set sail from Montevideo on 6 June 1779, unaware that hostilities between Great Britain and Spain would be declared a few days later. On 26 August, some 600 miles from Cape St Vincent, she sighted the *Sturdy Beggar* and the Catalan captain sailed up close to check his position, still unaware that British ships were enemies. So she was very easily taken, though resistance would have been suicidal as she had only 16 mariners and her armament consisted of four cannons, two mounted and two unmounted,

8 *WLA*, 15 March, 21 and 28 May 1779.
9 Prize papers for *Le Moissoneur*, Jacques François Santos, master, in HCA 32/403/5.

about three dozen muskets and blunderbusses and one dozen pikes, 'for their defence and protection against the Moors and pirates.' Back in Liverpool, both ships and their cargoes were sold in George's Coffee House on 8 November 1779.[10]

The *Sturdy Beggar* had obviously had a very successful cruise, and in this case it is possible to calculate just how successful this was, as the accounts of one of the co-owners, William Davenport, have survived. These show that Davenport owned just 1/24th of the ship whose cost to him was £250, making the total cost of the ship and outfit £6,000, about average for a privateer at this date, most of them being between £4,000 and £8,000. The total value of the prizes to be distributed amongst the owners was £29,808 (i.e. 24 x £1,242) and so the profits were an enormous £23,808, nearly four times the cost of the ship and outfit, a profit far, far higher than could ever have been earned on a slaving voyage. What share William Earle had is not shown in Davenport's accounts, but it was probably more than that of Davenport, some consolation no doubt for the fact that the *Sturdy Beggar*'s next cruise was to have a less fortunate end. On 29 October 1779, at Fayal in the Azores, her anchor cables parted in a gale and she was driven ashore, 'and in ten minutes went entirely to pieces, four of her crew being drowned.'[11] The human cost might have distressed Davenport and Earle but, from a financial point of view, they had already earned very large profits and were in any case almost certainly insured.

Coinciding in time with the *Sturdy Beggar*, but surviving rather longer, was the private ship of war *Enterprize*, the best documented of the privateers in which the Earle family had an interest. She measured 315 tons, and had 16 six- and nine-pound cannon and a crew which varied in numbers from 50 to 106. She was owned by a syndicate of Liverpool merchants headed by Francis Ingram. Ingram owned 2/16ths of the ship, but the Earle share exceeded this, with Thomas owning 3/16ths and William 2/16ths. Some of the privateer's accounts and papers have survived and these have some interest. The crews of private men-of-war (unlike those of marks) are normally thought to have been unpaid, relying for their gains on the old privateering contract of 'no purchase, no pay.' But this was not true

10 Prize papers of *N.S. del Rosario*, Captain Buenaventura Pruna, in HCA 32/415/15; see also *WLA*, 10 September, 1 October 1779.
11 Radburn, 2009, pp. 100–01; Williams, 2004, p. 253.

for the *Enterprize* in 1779, all but three of whose petty officers and seamen did in fact receive wages. Indeed, not only were they paid wages but they received two months' pay in advance, as they would have done if they had been serving on a slave ship. This suggests that it was not quite so easy as sometimes believed to attract men into the service of privateers with the lure of plunder alone. The accounts also give details of what was paid to tradesmen and others for food, equipment and other fitting-out expenses. The list includes William Earle & Son and Earle & Molyneux, both of these partnerships being credited for supplying 'ironwork', and a considerable quantity of rum was supplied by Messrs Baker & Dawson, the captors of the *Carnatic.* Other drink included brandy, wine and bottled beer, while the food supplied for the crew sounds healthier than one normally associates with merchant ships of this date – beef, pork, fowls, fish, flour, pease, barley, potatoes, greens, butter, cheese and groceries, surely enough to make the Liverpool seaman's favourite, lobscouse or scouse. Much of this would have been fresh and more fresh food could be bought on the cruise as Liverpool privateers tended to stay fairly close to land and food could be bought in Ireland or the Azores or even on the west coast of France. 'The odds [of finding a prize] is considerably against rambling in the wide ocean', advised the privateer's instructions, 'whereas headlands and islands usually run down by vessels are the surest places to find prizes', the running down being along the lines of latitude which, in the current state of navigation, were far easier to determine than those of longitude.[12]

The instructions give details of the areas in which the *Enterprize* was to cruise off the west coast of France and the Azores, these being similar to those already considered for other privateer ships. Captains were ordered to escort back to Liverpool any prize worth more than £10,000, but otherwise to send prizes home on their own with a prize-master and crew, 'taking care not to put too many of the enemy in proportion to your own men on board.' They were strictly required to take possession of all papers which would help prove that the prize was legal and any letters or other information giving the whereabouts of French naval vessels or other potential prizes. Great care was to be taken 'to prevent the prisoners from being plunder'd of any article

---

12 For the *Enterprize* see LRO 387 MD 45 and Williams, 2004, pp. 18–30, 27, 661–64.

whatever, to prevent any insult to the meanest of them, ... treat them with humanity and all the tenderness that is consistent with the security of your ship.' Whether such orders were strictly observed is doubtful, though reciprocity in the treatment of prisoners was important, given the fact that there were plenty of British prisoners in enemy hands. In any case, Captain Haslam was also required to treat his own crew as well as his prisoners humanely and everyone should be made to 'do their duty with good temper; as harmony, a good look-out, and steady attention to the main point are all absolutely necessary to be attended to, the success of the cruise greatly depending upon it.'

The *Enterprize* made three cruises in the years 1778–80 and they were all successful. The first cruise started near the end of 1778 and success began with the capture on 20 February 1779 of *La Pauline*, a 300-ton ship on her way from Cap François in modern Haiti to Bordeaux and, four days later, the capture of the 160-ton brig *L'Hostilité*, going the other way from Bordeaux to Port au Prince. The *Pauline*, which was carrying sugar, coffee, indigo and cotton, had had to throw six of its 12 guns overboard to stabilise the ship in a terrible storm. After capture, she was taken to Crookhaven in County Cork and on her way shipped a great quantity of water during another storm, which forced her new owners to seek permission to unload in Liverpool before the ship had been condemned, so that the sugar aboard would not be spoiled. *L'Hostilité* posed problems to the Court of Admiralty since it was claimed by some London merchants that she should be considered as a recapture. According to them, she had previously been an English ship called the *Bordeaux Packet*, which had sailed from London on 9 March 1778 for Bordeaux. On her arrival, a fortnight later, she was seized by officers of the French Admiralty and detained under an embargo until hostilities with Great Britain began in July, when she was declared a legal French prize and sold to a syndicate of local merchants. The Londoners' claim was unsuccessful and so the cargo of beef, flour and wine which the ship was carrying on the French king's account became the property of the Liverpool merchants and their crew, as did the ship itself and the private 'adventures' being carried by some of the French sailors, such as the 'prunes, cheese, wax candles and fruit preserved in brandy' in which the First Lieutenant had invested.[13]

13 *WLA*, 5 March 1779; prize papers for *La Pauline*, Paul Labat master, in HCA 32/418/16 and *L'Hostilité*, Gerard Hirigoyan, master, in HCA 32/351/10.

A second six-month cruise began on 16 September 1779 and the *Enterprize* was back in Liverpool five weeks later, bringing with her a valuable prize, the 600-ton *L'Aventurier*, which had been captured between the Azores and Cape St Vincent on her way home from Martinique to Bordeaux. This was the most powerful ship encountered by the *Enterprize*, with 22 guns, a crew of 34 men and a letter of marque. Such a well-armed ship could not simply surrender without any resistance, as so many of the other prizes did, and the French ship did in fact fight for about two hours, 'but was obliged to submit, being boarded by the English, having had the mainmast and topmast carried away in a hard gale of wind.' Back in Liverpool, the prize's cargo was sold at auction on 30 November, but all does not seem to have been well, judging by a letter dated 17 November from Francis Ingram to Captain Haslam. The letter is a little ambiguous, but it reads as though the crew felt they had done enough and, happy with their prospect of prize money, were refusing to sail to complete the six-month cruise they had contracted to serve. 'We depend on the conduct of you and your officers', wrote Ingram, 'to carry a proper command on board the vessel and to prevent any disobedience or further attempts to mutiny.'[14] Nothing more was captured on this second cruise, but the third cruise which began on 18 June 1780 more than made up for this blip in the *Enterprize*'s productivity. The orders for this voyage required Captain Haslam to cruise and search close to the coasts of western France and northern Spain and this is what he did, sometimes on his own and sometimes in consortship with the *Stag* privateer of Jersey. The first ship taken was the brig *Le Courier* on her way from Bordeaux to San Sebastian. The cargo comprised a wide variety of goods, including sugar, claret, marble slabs, various kinds of furniture, eight new carriages and 41 new guns. Then, on 12 September, William Davenport reported gleefully to Anthony Kirwan, his insurance agent, that the '*Enterprize* privateer has taken three prizes, one a Spanish snow with sugar, one a brig with flour and wine ... and the other a sloop with wine and brandy.' These all belonged to a fleet of some 40 coasters which the *Enterprize* encountered 'in sight of the lighthouse at the entrance of the port of Bordeaux and within about two leagues distance from the French shore.' And finally, on 6 November 1780, the *Enterprize* seized the 80-ton brig *Le Moineau* [the sparrow] on her way

---

14 Williams, 2004, p. 25; prize papers of *L'Aventurier*, Joseph Curet, master, HCA 32/275/5.

from Nantes to San Domingo with a lading of 'wine, flour, linen, and many other different species of merchandize.' None of these five prizes gave any resistance to the *Enterprize*; in the case of the Spanish snow *San Pedro* because the men had taken to the boats 'so that when she was boarded she was totally abandoned by her crew.'[15]

On 2 November, the *Liverpool Advertiser* carried an advertisement for the sale of the first four prizes and their cargoes – *Le Courier* as above; *San Pedro*, the abandoned Spanish snow or *polacca* with flour and brandy; the *Saint Joseph* with amongst other things 484 casks of fine, yellow French rosin; the fourth prize, *Le Vaillant*, had been wrecked on the Burbo Bank off the mouth of the Mersey. The ship was lost, but salvage of the cargo was fairly successful and 141 casks of claret, 74 barrels of flour and some of the ship's fittings were added to the long list of other prize goods to be sold at St George's Coffee House. Two months later, the same coffee house hosted the auction sale of the brig *Le Moineau* and her cargo, a wonderfully miscellaneous collection of goods similar to the cargoes of Liverpool ships on their way to the sugar islands: 'flour, claret, nails, canvas, sailcloth, Castile soap, tallow and wax candles, butter, bread, cheese, pork, salad oil, linseed oil, linens, drugs, Epsom salts, thread handkerchiefs, stockings, shoes, hair powder, snuff etc., etc., etc.' By the time all this stuff had been sold, Liverpool must have been well stocked up with French and Spanish food, drink, clothing, haberdashery and bits and pieces.[16] And William and Thomas Earle must have been well pleased with their investment of 5/16ths in such a successful privateer, even if in percentage terms the *Enterprize* was not quite as successful as the *Sturdy Beggar*, according to Davenport's accounts. The total profits to be shared between the owners for this 1780 cruise were £16,440, just under three times the cost of setting forth the privateer, and of this the Earle share was £5,137.[17]

The last of the four private men-of-war in which members of the family had an interest was the *Harlequin*, which was commissioned for six months on 10 January 1781. Thomas Earle the elder had just three months to live by then but, as he lay dying, he could surely take some

15 Williams, 2004, pp. 249–50; prize papers of *San Pedro*, HCA 32/449/5; *Le Moineau*, Joachim Gillard master, HCA 32/403/4; MMM D/DAV/1, Davenport to Kirwan, 12 September 1780.

16 *WLA*, 2 November, 20 December 1780.

17 Radburn, 2009, p. 101.

pleasure from the knowledge that this was truly an Earle ship whose owners comprised his brother William, his two nephews Thomas Jr (aged 27) and William Jr (aged 20), and four other Liverpool merchants, the partnership being styled William Earle & Sons. The ship was sold at auction at the end of the cruise and the sale notice gives more detail than usual. She had been built in America two years previously 'on purpose for a privateer'. She was 150 tons and mounted 20 six-pounder guns and was 'copper sheathed, a most remarkable swift sailor, well calculated for a packet [i.e. ship to carry mail], or any trade where despatch is required.' Her captain was Joseph Fayrer, who had a fine fighting record, and she had a crew of 80 men. All of which was likely to make her a very effective privateer though, the privateering war being what it was, she never in fact had to fight for her prizes.[18]

The *Harlequin* sailed from Liverpool on 8 February 1781 and was reported safe at Belfast a week later. The next news comes in a letter written from the Azores on 7 June 1781. Captain Fayrer reported the capture of a Swedish brig and a ship from Ostend, both engaged in giving advice of enemies to the homecoming French East Indiamen and so enemies themselves. He also mentioned that he had been in company with the *Caesar* of Bristol when she took a ship from Curaçao and the *Liverpool Advertiser* noted that this prize had arrived at Bristol. In early August, the *Harlequin* was back at Liverpool, bringing with her two more prizes, the *Swallow* (presumably an American vessel) and a French snow. By this date the ship from Curaçao had been identified as the *Eendracht* [Unity], a 600-ton Dutch ship sailing from Curaçao to Amsterdam 'deeply laden with a cargo of sugar, coffee, indigo, money and hides.' The owners of the Bristol privateer *Caesar* successfully set in motion the process by which the ship would be condemned and on 8 October the cargo was sold in Bristol 'for near £36,000 and the ship sold for £2,400. She is the most valuable Dutch prize brought in here [i.e. Bristol].'[19]

William Earle & Sons had been strangely quiet during this process. It was a rule of the privateering game that all ships present at the time of a capture had a right to share in the proceeds, even if they had played no actual part in the capture, 'present' being defined as in sight. Both Captain Fayrer in the *Harlequin* and his consort, another Liverpool ship

---

18 HCA 26/40, 10 January 1781; *WLA*, 9 August 1781.
19 *WLA*, 20 September, 18 October 1781.

called the *Patsey*, had in fact been in company, rather distant company, with the *Caesar* when the Bristol men boarded the *Eendracht* and seized her as a prize. It was dark when this happened and it was the contention of the owners of the Bristol ship that the Liverpool ships were no longer in sight. This was accepted in the first place by the Admiralty Court, but it was obvious that neither Liverpool ship was going to leave it at that and it was ordered that the money arising from the sale of the ship and its cargo should be lodged in the treasury of the Court while the owners of the *Harlequin* and the *Patsey* prepared for an appeal. This took some time, and considerable expenses were run up by Captain Fayrer and Thomas Earle the younger as they travelled around the country collecting evidence. Thomas claimed for travelling charges, dinners and other outgoings for visits to Bristol, Liverpool, Warrington, Shrewsbury and Harrogate to interview witnesses, and more money was laid out while he was waiting for the case to be heard in London.[20]

Prizes were normally condemned quickly in the High Court of Admiralty but anything more complicated, like an appeal, was likely to be a lengthy process and this appeal in what was known to the lawyers as 'a cause of joint chacers and captors' did not come on till January 1783. As usual in these disputed cases, the truth is not easy to determine but the most likely scenario was as follows. All three English ships were lying in wait for potential prizes on the west coast of the islands of Corvo and Flores, the most westerly of the Azores and a haunt of Englishmen seeking prizes since Elizabethan times. These ships had been visible since seven or eight in the morning of 9 April 1781 from the homeward-bound Dutch ship, whose captain and crew did not realise that the British had been enemies since 26 December 1780. The Dutch steered towards the *Caesar*, whose captain, John Shaw, quickly saw how best to take advantage of the situation. All ships carried all flags in wartime and Shaw ordered the American Stars and Stripes to be flown as the distance between the two ships narrowed.

A little before sunset, the *Eendracht* was within hailing distance of what appeared to be an American privateer (and so an ally) and Shaw asked whether they knew of the war between England and Holland and offered his protection against the other two ships which he said, correctly, were English privateers. Neither Captain Jan Bouset of the *Eendracht* nor any of the 18 members of his crew, a mixed bunch of Dutchmen, Danes,

20 All information regarding the appeal in HCA 42/121.

Swedes and Prussians, realised the danger, 'the people on board her not apprehending that she could possibly be an enemy'. The Dutch ship followed the *Caesar* for an hour and a half or two hours as night began to fall, by which time the men of the *Eendracht* were getting suspicious. But now it was far too late and Shaw's men were able to board and take the Dutchman quickly and quietly and on a night so dark that their claim that no other ship was in sight would appear to be truthful.

Witnesses for the two Liverpool ships naturally claimed they were able to see the *Eendracht* when the Bristol men boarded her. They were also able to throw serious doubts on the truthfulness and honesty of the *Caesar's* main witness, a seaman called George Graham, 'a person of a very profligate character and an unprincipled abandoned man', and this was sufficient to persuade the Court that this was in fact a joint capture, even though the Liverpool ships had no hand at all in effecting it. The success of the joint claimants had been long awaited in Liverpool and led to much rejoicing. The *Liverpool Advertiser* estimated the value of the prize at 'upwards of £40,000 ... the most valuable West Indiaman taken during the course of the war', a fact which provided much excitement among the women of the Earle family. 'I rejoice with you on the *Harlequin's* prize being deemed a lawful one', wrote Mrs Stanley of Bath to her sister, William Earle the elder's wife. 'I saw it in the papers on Saturday, which we all rejoiced at.'[21]

The Bristol-based *Caesar* was much the biggest of the three English ships with 32 guns and a crew of 186 men, while the *Patsey* also had far more men than the *Harlequin* and so would normally have been awarded a larger share of the proceeds of the appeal. But the two Liverpool captains had agreed 'to share any prize ... in equal proportion, notwithstanding their inequality in size and force.' The Court therefore ordered that the *Caesar* be awarded £17,664 from the £39,317 'proceeds of the ship' and that the *Patsey* and the *Harlequin* should receive half each of the remaining £21,653. But even this was not the end of the matter for the Bristol men appealed again and the final hearing did not come until five years later, on 14 March 1788, when the Court confirmed its previous judgment and condemned the owners of the *Caesar* to pay all the costs of the case out of their share. Such delays must have been tedious, but the Earles could hardly have complained at being awarded

21 *WLA*, 6 February 1783; MMM, D/EARLE/7/7, Mrs Stanley to Mrs William Earle, 3 February 1783.

£10,826 for doing nothing except lie in wait off the island of Flores. Such a windfall was a fitting climax to the privateering successes of the Earle family during the American War of Independence. It was certainly a much more profitable activity than buying slaves and shipping them across the Atlantic.

Before leaving the subject of privateering, we should note that in addition to these Liverpool-based privateers, the Earle family was also involved in privateering in the Mediterranean through its Leghorn subsidiary, Earle & Hodgson. This took two forms, an investment in privateering vessels based at Port Mahon in Minorca and, more importantly, a major involvement in the Leghorn prize market. After Admiral Byng's loss of the island in 1756, Minorca reverted to British rule in 1763 and was the base for a privateering fleet of some 20 vessels in the early years of the War of American Independence. These had considerable success until the Franco-Spanish siege of the island and its eventual capitulation rendered Mahon no longer viable as a base and a market, the last prizes being sold locally early in July 1781, shortly before the arrival in Leghorn of the wife of General Murray, the officer in command in Minorca, 'and 37 other passengers, mainly women and children.'[22]

Earle & Hodgson shared ownership of two of the vessels in this fleet with a Minorca-based English company called George Forbes & Co., Forbes being Paymaster of the British troops in Minorca as well as a merchant and so presumably a man with influence in government circles. The first was the 100-ton *polacca Tartar* with 12 four-pounder guns and 40 men commanded by Captain Thomas White, which was granted letters of marque early in 1780.[23] Both companies also acted for Earl Cowper, the English nobleman who lived in Florence, and they managed to persuade him to buy 1/8th of the privateer, calming any doubts he may have had as to the wisdom of such an investment by arranging insurance at £6 per £100 per month and assuring him that the ship would hold its value when resold. This did not prove a good

22 For Minorcan privateering at this time see Puig, 1990, and for a table of prizes sold see ibid., p. 215; TNA, FO 79/2 p. 35, letter dated 31 August 1781. Minorca was ceded to the Spanish in the Treaty of Paris (1783), captured again by the British in 1798 and returned permanently to Spain in 1802.

23 HCA 36/38, bail bond dated 29 February 1780; see also letters in Herts RO, DEP/F342 & /F310.

investment, most letters to Cowper being similar to the one written from Leghorn on 10 July 1780. 'The *Tartar*, Captain White, is still in the Levant, as unfortunate as ever!' Indeed, White's greatest success had come a few months earlier when he took a small Corsican vessel loaded with oysters, which, 'after regaling his ship's company with some' of its cargo, he had to release.[24]

Forbes managed to persuade Lord Cowper to invest in a second, larger privateer, the 22-gun *Hibernia*, which was said to be 'one of the fastest sailers in the Straights [i.e. Mediterranean].' To flatter her new owner, Forbes changed the ship's name to *Earl Cowper* and sent him a painting of his 'namesake'. 'She is a perfect beauty'. But, beauty or not, she was to have even less success than the *Tartar*, being captured by a French frigate on her way from Minorca to Leghorn before she had even begun to search for prizes. The capture was later declared illegal by the officers of the French Admiralty in Toulon, as she had been captured in Savoyard waters, so she was able to sail free to Leghorn, but this good fortune did not make her any more profitable. She sailed on one more cruise but had no success and it is no surprise that Forbes should write to Cowper on 17 September 1781, informing him that 'I am sick, very sick, of privateering.'[25]

Such sentiments were probably not shared by Earle & Hodgson in Leghorn for they had hit on a more profitable way of exploiting the privateering war than owning shares in the vessels. This was to trade in prizes. At first, this business was shared between Leghorn and Mahon but, from July 1781, Leghorn alone stood to gain as the Spaniards closed in on Minorca. Several privateers formerly based at Mahon sailed over to join the Leghorn-based fleet, while three of the strongest and fastest were bought for the service of the Crown.[26] As in the previous war, arrangements were made to speed up the business of condemning prizes by delegating it to people appointed for the purpose in Leghorn. On 29 December 1780, John Udny, the British Consul in Leghorn, was made head of such a delegation and invited to name 'some respectable merchants' to assist him. He chose two of the most respected merchants, Francis Jermy and Thomas Panton, as

24   15 March 1780; for more on Cowper see above pp. 152–53.
25   Herts R.O. DEP/F 310.
26   TNA, FO 79/2, 56, 74, 98. The privateers with Minorcan captains and crews made their peace with Spain.

joint commissioners and other merchants were later included in the commission.[27]

The sales of prizes in Leghorn are reported in the surviving registers of the *Asta Pubblica* from 26 January 1779 to 20 August 1782, during which period some 25 or 30 prizes were condemned and sold.[28] This business demonstrated two differences from the pattern in the Seven Years' War; Consul Udny was not a very important player in the prize market, as Sir John Dick had been, and there were virtually no prizes taken by royal ships, just one in fact, the tartan *Santa Rosa*, which was seized by two of the former Minorcan privateers which had been bought into the royal service.[29] All the other prizes were captured by the 13 or 14 privateers based at the port, of which the most successful was the *Fame*, the same name as the ships employed by Fortunatus Wright in the 1740s and by Captain John Patrick in the 1750s, both of which were very successful, so clearly a name with a deserved reputation for good fortune. This *Fame* of the 1780s was commanded by Captain Thomas Moor, who took at least seven prizes and probably more, whose cargoes and the ships themselves fetched about 150,000 pieces of eight at auction, around £40,000.[30]

A captain's share of so much money might have tempted many privateers to seek a quiet life, but Captain Moor had different ambitions and, in January 1782, he wrote to Sir Horace Mann, the long-standing British Resident in Florence, offering his ship, himself, his officers and crew for the king's service when he had completed his cruise, 'on the condition of his being appointed a Lieutenant in the Navy'. Mann supported this application and described Moor as 'that brave young man who had performed the most valorous exploits during the course of the war.' Moor was an Irishman whose ship was described as 'a three-masted cutter built in Dublin of about 250 tons which carried 20 guns, 130 men and was owned jointly by 32 persons in Ireland.'[31]

All these privateers had agents in Livorno who arranged the sale

---

27 FO 79/1 172, 182, 189, 200; see also Lo Basso, 2008, pp. 162–63, who writes on the authority of the Genoese Consul that Robert Hodgson of Earle & Hodgson was one of the commissioners.

28 AP vols 54–55.

29 AP 55, p. 88, undated; for the Seven Years' War see above pp. 139–40.

30 It is difficult to be sure one is counting accurately in these registers. Lo Basso, 2008, p. 162, credits Moor with 178,075 pieces of eight.

31 FO 79/3, pp. 6 & 10, 5 & 12 1782.

of the ship and goods at auction, the latter often being sold out of the warehouses where they had been stored, eight such warehouses and 'cantinas' being named in the sales records. Only three firms out of the 12 or 15 active in the British Factory were involved in this agency business. Gentil & Orr were reported as organising the sale of seven prizes and Arrigo & Abel Fonnereau sold six, but the leaders of the pack were Earle & Hodgson, who are credited with the sale of 12 prizes brought in by five separate privateers which were sold at auction for at least 250,000 pieces of eight. Thomas Moor of the *Fame*, incidentally, split his custom, sending his first three prizes to Earle & Hodgson and his last four to Arrigo & Abel Fonnereau, though just how significant this was is difficult to say, as there are clear signs of collusion between the three Leghorn firms in the prize business.

The prizes sold reflected the cosmopolitan alliance which had been cobbled together to try and take advantage of Britain's potential vulnerability at sea during this war. French ships were still the majority, as in the last war, most of them sailing from France to the Levant with valuable cargoes of French cloth and clothing, wine and so on, though there were also smaller vessels engaged in the food trades. There were also several Dutch ships, including some big *baccalà* ships from Newfoundland with cargoes of salmon and cod which were captured by the *Fame* on their way to Leghorn whither they had been consigned by their owners in ignorance of the outbreak of war between Britain and Holland. The route home from the Levant also became vulnerable, with the capture of two Dutch ships on their way from Smyrna to Amsterdam and a Danish ship coming from Smyrna to Ostend, all carrying similar cargoes to those captured from French ships on the same route in the previous war – cotton, raw silk, wool, raisins and all the exotic products which made trade with the Levant so profitable. Some variety was provided by the capture of a Spanish ship carrying wine from the Canary Islands and a Neapolitan *polacca* with a cargo of hemp. The capture and sale of these ships and their cargoes must have been much welcomed in Livorno, for the dangers of capture by French, Spanish, Dutch and American privateers had reduced to virtually nothing the shipment of goods from Britain and the other countries of the North Sea to the Mediterranean. Even those who were hostile to the British and would have welcomed victory for their enemies could hardly fail to be pleased to acquire French and Levantine goods at bargain prices.

It is impossible to say just how much money Earle & Hodgson made out of this business, though it is worth noting that in each war they expanded their role as dealers in prize goods, just as their significance in the sale and carriage of art from Rome and elsewhere via Leghorn to England was expanding as time went by. They continued to act as general merchants and agents for English companies, but they also clearly chose to specialise in a few of the potentially more profitable niches available for enterprising merchants in the Italian *entrepôt*.

The prize agency business would have brought in commissions, normally 3 per cent of goods sold, so about £2,000 sterling for the 250,000 pieces of eight listed in the registers of the *Asta Pubblica*. But, clearly, they did not do all that work just for £2,000. There is abundant evidence that the auctions were rigged in both Leghorn and Mahon, and one might assume that this would benefit the organisers of such auctions, who are no doubt hidden behind the mainly Italian names of the successful bidders. It is also clear that, in both places, private sales took place after the official auctions, such *revendas* or 're-sales' generally bringing in more than half as much again as the first auction.[32] And in addition to whatever profits might be made out of such essentially shady dealings, there was a whole range of perfectly legitimate business to be transacted in fitting out, repairing and provisioning the privateers. The Earle family certainly did well out of privateering during the American War of Independence, but such gains did not come only from investment in privateers.

---

32 Puig, 1990, p. 208; Lo Basso, 2008, p. 159.

CHAPTER NINE

Ralph Earle and Russia

> 'He has great expectations ... I am instructed to
> communicate to him', said Mr Jaggers ... 'that he
> will come into a handsome property.'
>
> Charles Dickens, *Great Expectations*[1]

Ralph, the eldest of John Earle's three sons who survived into adulthood,
was born in 1715. His early life is little documented. He is recorded in
the Liverpool Fines Register as receiving his freedom in October 1736,
when he was 21, but there is then no further record of him in the sources
searched until 17 May 1753, when he was a witness to the marriage
settlement of his sister Sarah to the Hon. and Rev. John Stanley. This
is interesting in itself as Stanley was the younger brother of the 11th
Earl of Derby and such a marriage, even if it was a second marriage for
the groom, seems a remarkable social achievement for the daughter of a
bankrupt merchant. Sarah, incidentally, seems to have been a favourite of
Ralph's as he was to name his biggest ship, 450-ton burden and wholly
owned by him, *Beloved Sarah* (sometimes written *Beloved Sally*). Many
shipowners named their ships after the women of their families, but
no other ship in the Liverpool shipping database carries the adjective
'beloved'.[2]

The first question, then, is what was Ralph Earle doing during
most of his twenties and thirties, between 1736 and 1753? He does not
seem to have been in Liverpool and the most likely hypothesis is that
he was in Russia (or possibly London) learning the business of a Russia
merchant. Just how the brothers' careers were planned is not clear, but
one can imagine John Earle in his retirement at Prescot dividing the
world up between his three sons, Thomas to make his way to Italy,

---

1 Dickens, 2002, p. 135.
2 Marriage settlement in D/EARLE/9/5; ship information here and elsewhere
   from LTS.

William to Africa and, since Ralph was to be principally engaged as a merchant in trade with Russia, it seems reasonable to suggest that he went there to learn the business. There is, it should be noted, no direct evidence for this. However, there does exist a good example of another young man serving his time in Russia, who may provide a model of Ralph's experience.

This was Jonas Hanway, born in 1712 and so three years older than Ralph, who lived almost entirely abroad from the age of 16 till he was 39. He first spent 12 years in the English Factory in Lisbon and then went to Russia, finishing with several years in St Petersburg before returning in 1750 to London, where he conducted a modest business as a Russia merchant. Hanway later became famous as a philanthropist and writer on social matters, but his first book was about Russia, *An Historical Account of the British Trade over the Caspian Sea*, published in 1753. This is mainly about a journey he made through Russia to Persia, but the book contains much of general interest about Russia and the British who lived and worked there. And perhaps most interesting for us is the fact that in 1743 he 'accepted the offer of a partnership in Mr Dingley's House at St Petersburg'.[3]

The brothers Charles and Robert Dingley were Londoners who were important in Anglo-Russian trade in the mid-eighteenth century. Charles Dingley, the older brother, was an enterprising man who in 1761 built the first sawmill in England using circular saws, a wind-powered sawmill at Limehouse in east London, a model soon adopted in the Liverpool timber yards. This innovation greatly increased productivity but had the effect of throwing the old pit sawmen out of work. Their Luddite attempts to protect their jobs by destroying the new circular saws were unsuccessful, as 'during the hours of darkness packs of ferocious dogs, fierce as Siberian wolves, were let loose to roam the timber yards.' Charles Dingley and the wealthy Liverpool merchants Jonathan and Joseph Brooks were partners with Ralph Earle in at least three ships trading to Russia in the years 1757–60. This connection tempts one to suggest that Ralph had previously learned the trade in Charles Dingley's merchant house at St Petersburg, but there is nothing in Hanway's book to suggest that this was in fact the case.[4]

---

3 Hanway, 1753, p. 71.
4 Latham, 1967, p. 5; Hanway, 1753, pp. 121–65 for British trade and the Factory in St Petersburg; for more on Hanway see Taylor, 1985.

Whether he had previously spent many years in Russia or not, there is no doubt that Ralph Earle was in Liverpool from the mid-1750s onwards and it is possible to find several snippets of information about him. In 1756, for instance, he was named, together with his two brothers, as a leaseholder of property in Oldhall Street and, in 1760, property in Wales was conveyed to him. There are also several references to him as the seller or assignee of bankrupt goods and estates, and this seems to have been something of a speciality of his. On 20 August 1756, in the first year of *Williamson's Liverpool Advertiser*, there was an advertisement for the sale of 'a parcel of good Carolina tar, at 12 shillings per barrel … apply to Mr Ralph Earle, merchant in Paradise Street.' On 20 October 1758, the same paper carried a notice which throws further light on Ralph's business life: 'Stolen, about three weeks ago, from a raft of timber near the pitch house, an iron chain … also on Sunday last … from the saw-pit in Mr Earle's timber-yard, three other iron chains … a reward is offered from Mr Ralph Earle.' And, on 25 April 1760, Brooks and Earle were offering for sale 'a parcel of Dantzick oak plank of sundry dimensions, for building or repairing ships … to be sold in quantities not less than ten planks.' In the same year, 1760, Ralph was granted the lease of a long frontage to the Mersey near Salthouse Dock. So it is no surprise to find him listed in the first Liverpool Directory of 1766 as one of nine timber merchants in the town, with a timber yard on Salthouse Quay. In 1757, Ralph was one of the two deputy treasurers of the Liverpool Infirmary and he continued to follow a socially responsible and political career, being elected to the council in 1760 and just nine years later becoming Mayor of Liverpool, 60 years after his father, John, had held the same post. Some time in the late 1750s, Ralph got married, to Dorothy Aldersley, daughter of Richard Aldersley of Liverpool and, like most merchants' wives, an heiress. His eldest son, Richard, was born on 18 September 1760.[5]

A more comprehensive survey of Ralph's shipping and mercantile interests can be put together from the Liverpool shipping database. The first reference to Ralph was in 1757 and relates to a 40-ton schooner called *North Pole*, which he owned jointly with the Russia merchant Charles Dingley, mentioned above, and the Liverpool merchants Jonathan and Joseph Brooks, who were to be associated in business

---

5 *WLA*, 20 August 1756, 20 October 1758, 9 March, 3 August, 23 November 1759, 4 and 25 April 1760 etc.

with one or other of the Earle brothers on several occasions in the next 30 years. This small vessel was listed as arriving at Liverpool from Archangel, the Russian port on the White Sea, on 9 August 1757. This was probably an exploratory voyage, for the next three ships in which Ralph was involved were all built in Archangel and were much bigger, all three of them being owned by the same syndicate and rated at 500 tons each. These were the *Onega*, which traded to Archangel, Riga and Dantzig in the next three years; the *Mezeen*, which traded to Archangel, Onega, also on the White Sea, Dantzig and Riga; and the *Friendship*, which traded mainly to the Baltic and whose cargo of oak and fir planks from Dantzig was advertised for sale in March 1763 after the ship had stranded on the coast of Scotland on her return voyage. None of these three ships seems to have been very successful. The last recorded voyage of the *Onega* was in 1760 and the *Mezeen* was put up for auction on 2 May 1761:

> The sails may be seen at Mr William Williamson's sail room, rigging at Sir Ellis Cunliffe's warehouse in Hanover Street, the hull, cables, anchors, masts etc. at Mr Ralph Earle's timber yard by the South Graving-Dock, at which place the sale is to begin with the hull of the said vessel.

Several similar advertisements appeared in the *Liverpool Advertiser* in subsequent months, suggesting that she was not easy to sell, which may have had something to do with the fact that all these ships built in Archangel had a tendency to run aground.[6]

Nevertheless, the very fact that Ralph should have invested in such ships and such voyages marks him out as an innovator amongst his fellow Liverpool shipowners and merchants. Very few Liverpool ships sailed to Russia at all before 1760, Anglo-Russian trade being mainly an east coast and especially London business. And only one other Liverpool ship sailed to the White Sea in these years, the *Northern Lass*, which was in Archangel in 1758. This White Sea trade had been developed by Londoners in the later sixteenth century, but Peter the Great's building of St Petersburg and encouragement of trade to his 'window on the west' meant that trade to the White Sea had fallen to a low level by the middle of the eighteenth century and only a little of this was conducted

6 *WLA*, 2 May 1761.

by the English, the Dutch and Hamburgers being the most important shippers on the northern route.[7]

By the 1750s, the trade with St Petersburg was well established and the Russian government was now keen to develop and export the vast timber riches in the northern regions around Lake Onega and Archangel for export to the Dutch and British markets. Count Pyotr Shuvalov, a financial adventurer at the Russian court, showed an interest and in 1752 he was granted an exclusive timber monopoly in this region. He in turn brought in William Gomm, a timber merchant from Bristol, eventually selling him the whole of his monopoly. Gomm was based in St Petersburg, where he did business with the Dingleys among others, and he rarely went to the remote area of his timber monopoly and had in fact only a hazy knowledge of its geography. However, through his agents he was very active in creating trading facilities both at Archangel and at the port of Onega, to the south-west of Archangel and hitherto completely undeveloped. In his first year as monopolist he organised the building of a harbour and two sawmills and his activities were given a great boost by the rise in demand for shipbuilding timber during the Seven Years' War, which began in 1756. More sawmills were erected, shipbuilding yards were established and trade boomed in this forested wilderness. George Macartney, the British envoy at St Petersburg, described the situation in 1767:

> Onega is a town on the White Sea ... a few years ago, there was not a single house there, but it is now a flourishing port, frequented by near 30,000 tons of shipping, [which] is entirely owing to the genius and industry of an English merchant at St Petersburg.[8]

Onega was mainly developed to exploit the virgin forests which surrounded it, but there was also much iron brought up the rivers and exported from these two ports on the White Sea.

Ralph Earle played only a small part in this boom in the northern forests, but it is intriguing that a novice merchant should have engaged at all in such a new and untried business. His interest in the White Sea was to last a few more years but, once the Seven Years' War was over in 1763, trade to the far north became more problematic, and Ralph settled down in a more conventional business as a merchant trading on

7 Kellenbenz, 1973.
8 Clendenning, 1977.

a fairly modest scale to Russia and the Baltic, with some side interests in the businesses run by his brothers, such as investments in slave ships and ships trading to the Mediterranean. He appears as a part-owner in ten slaving voyages on five different ships in which his brother William had an interest, and was also involved in the *Polly*, the ship run by his brother Thomas and Thomas Hodgson. And he invested in other businesses developed by his brothers, such as sugar refining and the bead company.[9]

Most of Ralph's Russian trade was conducted in ships belonging to other merchants and references can be found in the 'goods imported' sections of the local papers, which are fullest for the years 1768 to 1774. Ralph's own *Beloved Sarah* had been built in Russia. She made 11 voyages for him between 1764 and 1772, sailing mainly on return trips to various northern ports, such as Onega, Riga, Dantzig, Narva and Elsinore, the port of Copenhagen. She also made three roundabout voyages between 1767 and 1770 to Cagliari, Leghorn and Marseilles in the Mediterranean and then north to the Baltic with an attractive and no doubt profitable southern cargo.

On several occasions Ralph is recorded in the newspapers as importing bar iron from St Petersburg, a trade growing fast in these years as British governments provided incentives for merchants to import iron from Russia rather than Sweden, which was felt to be a vulnerable source of so vital a raw material in wartime. The iron was produced far away in the east, by the metallurgical industry in the Urals, and a complex system of canals and portages employing vast numbers of men and horses was necessary to get the iron and other goods to St Petersburg, progress being so slow that it was normally necessary for the caravans of boats to winter in the ice on the way and so take two years to get the iron to St Petersburg and so at last to the increasing numbers of British vessels waiting to ship it to supply manufacturing industries desperate for cheap iron in these early years of the Industrial Revolution. Liverpool was not very important as a destination for this iron, but shipments were growing, and Ralph quite often appears as an importer, usually being consigned around 1,000 bars but sometimes much more, such as the 7,791 bars of iron consigned to him on the *Antelope*, which arrived in the Mersey in August 1773. Whom he sold

9   See above pp. 150–51 for the bead business and MMM D/EARLE/4/1 for the
     sugar refinery at the Haymarket Sugar House in Liverpool.

the iron to is not stated, but it is probable that some of this Russian iron was sold on to his ironmonger brother William.[10]

Ralph was, however, principally a timber merchant and the majority of the goods imported by him comprised various sorts of timber. The huge growth of Liverpool's housing stock in the second half of the eighteenth century, combined with its sizeable shipbuilding industry, meant that the port had a voracious appetite for wood of all sorts and this is reflected in the great number of advertisements in the local paper for the sale of timber standing anywhere near convenient water transport in North Wales, north-west England or western Scotland, such as the 2,257 oak trees in Whiteford, Flintshire, which were offered for sale on 2 March 1764: 'They lie remarkably convenient for being shipped off.' Roger Fisher, a Liverpool shipbuilder and timber merchant who wrote a book called *Heart of Oak* in 1763, stated that the town's chief sources of timber were in south Lancashire, Cheshire, Shropshire, Staffordshire and Flintshire, but 'the far greater part has been cut down in the space of 30 years, consumption being much greater than the growth.' All this was good news for timber merchants. John Earle may have been a bankrupt, but he knew enough to direct his sons towards trades likely to make them handsome profits.[11]

It seems probable that Ralph was involved in this coastwise trade in timber, though we have no direct evidence for this. But there is no doubt of the considerable scale of his import business of timber and other forest products, nearly all from Russia, Norway and the Baltic, though there are some references to imports of tar from Carolina. Judging by the shipping information in the Liverpool and Manchester newspapers, his most important business was with Riga, the German-speaking capital of Latvia, which had come under Russian rule in 1710. Next in importance were various Norwegian ports and then Memel (Klaipeda) in Lithuania, Narva, the capital of Estonia, Elsinore and Dantzig. Ralph imported some flax from Riga, but otherwise the products consigned, apart from the iron from St Petersburg, were nearly all timber, mainly oak planks, fir balks (beams) and deals, but also manufactured products such as spars, masts, oars, clapboards and wainscot or wainscoting (oak panels used for lining walls). Many of the big Liverpool timber merchants were also

10 Kaplan, 1995, ch. 4; Jones, 1984; *WLA*, 20 August 1773.
11 *WLA*, 2 March 1764; Fisher, 1763.

shipbuilders, but Ralph confined himself to importing the wood and using his sawmills to prepare it for sale in suitable lengths and thicknesses.

The goods exported to Russia in exchange for the timber, iron and other products imported into Liverpool are not recorded in the local paper, but the general picture is clear enough. The favoured cargo of London ships sailing to St Petersburg was a heterogeneous collection of all that was best and most desirable in the English metropolis, such as clothing and textiles, furniture, metalwork, coaches, clocks, looking glasses and so on. These were consigned to the British factors in St Petersburg who, according to Jonas Hanway, were 'generally well esteemed. They inhabit the best houses on the banks of the Neva and are hospitable, not to say magnificent in their way of life.' These houses had splendid ground-floor rooms where such goods were set out for inspection and purchase by Russian merchants and the local plutocracy, nearly always on very long credit. Every effort was made to recreate the appearance of rooms in fashionable London, an effect enhanced by the hanging of very English pictures on the walls, such as those imported in the *Cornwall* in 1760 – 'one sett of Marriage à la Mode prints, 25 landskipps and ruins, four mezzotints of the Royal Family.'[12]

However, it seems unlikely that Liverpool merchants would or could compete in this luxurious style of business and the exports from the Mersey to the Neva and the Baltic ports were rather more prosaic, the main cargoes being salt, coal and re-exported colonial goods, especially sugar and tobacco. Ralph Earle, as has been seen, also directed his ships to sail to Russia via the Mediterranean in three separate years and these southern cargoes sold well in the north, so that we can find several other Liverpool shipowners doing the same, sailing to Spain, Portugal or Italy and then north, sometimes via Amsterdam, Hamburg or Bremen, before discharging their cargoes in Riga or Dantzig.[13]

There are few signs of trade being conducted by Ralph Earle after 1775, when he reached the age of 60, and it may well be significant that he was described in the 1777 Liverpool Directory as 'Esquire', while his two younger brothers were listed as 'merchants'. The word 'retirement' was not used in this context at this date, but in effect he was retired, as

12 Hanway, 1753, p. 123; Newman, 1992; see also the papers of the Russia merchant William Heath in TNA C 104/141–5, Jackson v. Nemes; the picture quotation from an invoice dated 20 September 1760 in C 104/141.
13 These voyages are traced from TLS.

he transferred his former trading capital into bank accounts, bonds and loans. He was also, like other merchants, prepared to use his business knowledge and expertise to provide assistance to single or widowed women who were friends or relations. Our best evidence of this very important service comes from the letters written from Boston in New England by Ann Hulton, a cousin of Hannah Lightbody's mother, who refers to Ralph and a colleague helping her to recover debts due to her from the West Indies, advising her on the conduct of a lawsuit in the Court of Chancery and also helping her choose investments. The money she recovered from the sale of an estate, for instance, she 'put into the Bank Stock, agreeable to Mr Earle's advice', elsewhere described as Mr R. Earle to distinguish him from his brothers.[14]

One might think that that was just about the end of Mr R. Earle, former Russia merchant of Liverpool, but in fact the most extraordinary (but long anticipated) event of his life was yet to happen. On 28 August 1788, when he was 73, Ralph inherited the estates of the Willis family in and around Whiston, an bequest which brought with it not only much land and a fine house called Halsnead Hall but also some of the most profitable collieries in the south Lancashire coalfield, together with the Willis coal staithe, a landing stage on the Mersey with shoots for loading coal.[15] Ralph and his two sons were the ultimate beneficiaries of a series of childless deaths in the Willis family, his cousins through his mother, the former Mary Finch. The process by which this property ended up in the hands of Ralph began with the will of Daniel Willis in 1758 (he died in 1761) and finished with the death of Thomas Willis (formerly Swetenham) in 1788, whose will transferred the estate to his kinsman on condition that he change his surname to Willis. And just to make absolutely clear to one and all that everything was above board, Ralph procured a private Act of Parliament, 'An Act to enable Ralph Willis Esq. (lately called Ralph Earle) and the heirs male of his body, to take the surname and bear the arms of Willis only, pursuant to the will of Daniel Willis Esquire.' It pays to be the eldest son.[16]

Ralph Earle was therefore to be called Ralph Willis for the last two

14 Hulton, 1927, pp. 53, 65, 80.
15 For Willis collieries and the staithe see Langton, 1979, pp. 183, 221 and see above p. 17 for the significance of the coalfield.
16 29 George III, c. 2; there is a lot of material on the Willis-Earle connection in Blinkhorn, 2004, pp. 51–53.

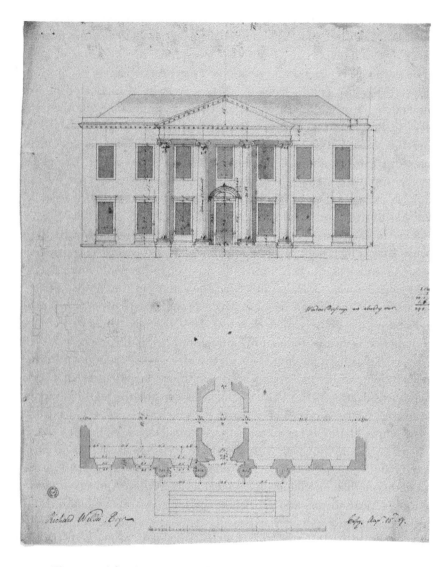

Figure 9. John Soane's 1789 drawings for refacing the south front
of Halsnead Hall. Commissioned by Richard Willis (formerly Earle)

years of his life and his eldest son Richard (1760–1837) became Richard
Willis. His second son had been known as Willis Earle from his birth
in the 1760s, some indication of how long the family had anticipated
these amazing changes to their lifestyle. Richard immediately set about
improving Halsnead Hall, the already handsome family residence set

in the centre of a circle of collieries – Whiston, Halsnead and Cronton – so there would be no doubt where the money came from. He commissioned John Soane (no less) to prepare drawings for refacing the south front of the hall and these drawings, showing a huge Ionic portico, have survived and seem to have been carried out as Soane intended, judging by the illustration in the sale catalogue of the hall, which was demolished in 1931.[17]

The younger son, Willis Earle, had been a partner in the Leghorn merchant house of Earle & Hodgson since the 1780s. There he married Annina Cecilia Lutyens, usually described as an Italian lady, but probably Dutch as members of this merchant family, including a sister Mary Cecilia Lutyens (1755–66), were buried in the Dutch-German cemetery of Livorno.[18] Willis Earle was described in the 1796 Liverpool Directory as a merchant living at 5 Great George's Street, but he is also listed as the owner of a counting house and coal and timber yards in South Dock. He had not only inherited his father's timber yard, but had also gone into business as a coal merchant in partnership with his brother.

Both of Ralph's sons appear from time to time in the Liverpool newspapers. In the 1790s, Willis Earle is still a major importer of timber from the Baltic. On 7 January 1799, for instance, he was the consignee of the entire cargo of fir balks and planks, oak planks, pipe staves and lathwood being brought in on the *Ann & Elizabeth* from Dantzig. He also dealt in American timber, as can be seen from the notice of a sale held in October 1797 of 'Riga, Dantzig, Memel, Stettin timber; also American pine, maple, birch etc.' Advertisements relating to the coal business of Willis and his brother are also quite frequent and in fact coal was probably more important than timber in Willis's business life by the early nineteenth century. On 24 February 1794, for example, Willis Earle announced to

the public in general, and more particularly the inhabitants of the south end of the town that he has opened a wholesale and retail coal yard at his timber yard, Cornhill, Salthouse Dock. Large quantities will be supplied at very short notice. The coals are from the pits of Richard Willis, Esq., Whiston, and of the best quality.

17 www.soane.org.uk/drawings and Blinkhorn, 2004, pp. 87–88.
18 Del Nista, 2004.

In the same month, Richard Willis announced that he was 'selling coal at a reduced price to help the poor of Liverpool.'[19]

Sales of coal and timber were certainly important, but Willis was also, like his cousins Thomas and William Earle, ready to start on the process of gentrification, very often the culmination of a mercantile career. Early in the new century he moved out of town into Wavertree, a country village south-east of Liverpool 'where the salubrity of the air is highly and very deservedly spoken of.' Here we find him engaging in activities which have little to do with either coal or timber. In 1805 he was, together with his two cousins, one of 17 great and good on the committee of the Liverpool Athenaeum. But this and similar committee work was standard fare for the socially ambitious in Georgian Liverpool. Willis's real interests in his new self-invented life lay outside in the fields. On 13 January 1808, a patent was granted to him 'for certain improvements in the tillage and dressing of land and the cultivation of plants.' And, on 10 May 1809, he was announced as Vice-President of the Agricultural Society of the Hundred of West Derby, responsible for giving prizes 'for the best crop of turnips, cabbages etc. or who shall drain the greatest quantity of land.'[20] And as was only fit and proper for the country gentleman he aimed to be, he had a house called Sandown Hall built for him in 1810. This was described in a sale notice of 1821 as comprising 'mansion, stables, outbuildings ... and 19 acres of grounds'. It may have been a bit smaller, but it was just as handsome as his brother's Halsnead Hall, as one can tell from an attractive drawing of the house made by James Brierley in 1830, one more sign that Ralph Earle's branch of the Liverpool Earle family knew how to make or at least preserve money.[21]

19 *BLA*, 10 and 24 February 1794, 16 October 1797, 2 July 1798, 7 January 1799.
20 *BLA*, 13 January 1808, 10 May 1809. For the gentrification of Thomas and William Earle see below, pp. 235–49..
21 Chitty, 1999; wavsoc.awardspace.info/sandown/page2.html.

CHAPTER TEN

Brothers in the Slave Trade

'The business of his uncle ... was amalgamated with his father's and [he] became exceedingly prosperous.'[1]

The 1780s was a watershed in the history of the Liverpool Earle family, as the men of one generation all died off and gave way to their sons and nephews and the husbands of their daughters. All three sons of John Earle left the scene, Thomas Sr in 1781, William Sr in 1788 and Ralph in 1790, leaving William's two sons, also confusingly called Thomas and William, to carry on the family's name in business and public affairs, Thomas continuing family tradition by being chosen as Mayor of Liverpool in 1787. Ralph's eldest son Richard (now bearing the surname of Willis) became a landowner and coal mine owner as a result of the quirks of inheritance which had left this branch of the family so wealthy, while his second son, Willis Earle, sold his brother's coal as a factor in Liverpool, and also continued to run his father's timber business.[2] This branch of the family will be mentioned from time to time, but the main focus from now on will be on Thomas Jr and William Jr, the two sons of William Sr, who will normally be described as just Thomas & William Earle & Coy or as T. & W. Earle.

Not much is known of the education and training of these two young men, which might have helped us understand how Thomas was able to take over both his uncle's and his father's businesses when still in his twenties. One just has to assume that he was a very precocious and talented young man. We do know that he was sent to Manchester Grammar School in January 1765, when he was 11, together with a younger brother, another Ralph, who died just two years later. This

1 Earle, 1890, pp. 48–49.
2 See above pp. 189–92.

was already a famous school, but it was famous for teaching classics not business.³ Where William went to school we do not know; not, apparently, to Manchester Grammar School, since his name does not appear in the admission register. Both sons were destined to become engaged in the slave trade, but there is no indication that either of them ever went to West Africa, let alone served as captain of a slave ship, as their father had done. Their names would be in the slave trade database if they had been captains and should have appeared in the muster rolls of ships belonging to their father if they had served on them or sailed as supercargoes.⁴ But there is no record of this, so one must assume that they picked up their undoubted knowledge of the trade through contact and conversation with their father and his associates and the group of former slave ship captains who were later to be investors in their ships. It must have been a subject that dominated family life during their childhood and adolescence.

The two young men also continued the family connection with the Mediterranean by overseeing the house of Earle & Hodgson in Livorno. Thomas was said in his obituary to have lived several years in Italy in early life, and maybe William spent some time there too. He certainly grew to love the country and was to die in Rome, where he spent every winter in his old age. A record of one of Thomas's visits has survived in two travel diaries. The first of these covers a journey from Livorno to Rome and Naples starting in April 1775. This mainly describes the sights he saw, in a rather perfunctory manner, and has nothing of much help to an understanding of his character or the business he would inherit five years later. The second diary covers the return journey from Leghorn to England starting in April 1776. This is more interesting, providing an account of the difficulties of long-distance travel overland, from Genoa to Turin and then on horseback over the Mont Cenis Pass, having sent the carriage on ahead. He came down from the pass into Savoy on a sledge towed very fast by a local on foot, and then travelled more sedately in the carriage through Chambéry, Geneva, Lyons and so to Paris. But we still do not learn very much about the young man.⁵

3 Smith, 1866, p. 133.
4 TNA, BT 98/33 is the first surviving Liverpool Muster Roll, covering ships sailing in 1772–73.
5 *BLA*, 18 July 1822; D/EARLE/8/1 & 2. Thanks to my brother Robert for information on these diaries.

Judging by the registration of their names as part-owners of ships, Thomas and William were in partnership from 1780, when Thomas was 26 and William just 20. This partnership lasted for over 40 years, until the death of Thomas in 1822 when he was 68. Thomas seems to have been the more enterprising of the two brothers. He was also the richer, as he inherited the business and half the fortune of his uncle Thomas when he married his daughter Maria in 1786 (the other half going to her sister, Jane), while the brothers shared equally in the assets of their father with their sister Mary, who was married to the banker Richard Heywood, a useful source of short-term loans. A real Earle clan was being built up, as can be seen in the listings for Hanover Street in Gore's *Liverpool Directory* for 1790. Hanover Street, running east from the Old Dock, was just about the smartest place for businessmen to live at that date and that is where the Earles and their relatives lived: Thomas Earle, merchant, at No. 40; John Copeland, merchant and former slave ship captain, who was related by marriage to Thomas's father and was soon to be father-in-law of his brother William, at No. 42; the banker Heywoods at Nos 45 and 46; while the counting house and warehouses of the Earle brothers stood on the corner of Fleet Street and Hanover Street, and no doubt there were other relations and business associates in close proximity if one only knew enough. Liverpool was famous for hospitality as well as business and one can imagine many a fine dinner party up and down Hanover Street, at least until the late 1790s, when growing wealth, age and children suggested to both brothers that it was time to move into larger and smarter houses outside the town, William moving into a villa in substantial grounds in Everton and Thomas building a fine house in Toxteth Park.

Combining as they did the assets and goodwill of the businesses of both their father and their uncle, the brothers in effect ran two substantial businesses, one focussed on the slave trade and the other on the Mediterranean and especially Livorno. They seem to have kept these businesses separate, if we can generalise from the only commercial document which has survived for this period, a letter book marked 'Livorno', which covers the years 1801–06, but contains nothing about the slave trade.[6] This was probably their biggest business when they started up in the 1780s and we can begin by considering their role as slave merchants.

6 MMM D/EARLE/2/3.

These were the last years of the British slave trade, which was to be abolished by Parliament in 1807. The Abolition movement is usually said to have begun on 22 May 1787 with the establishment of the Society for Effecting the Abolition of the Slave Trade and, from then on, it seems that people in England could think of nothing else. Adam Hochschild makes the point nicely in his book *Bury the Chains*. The *Gentleman's Magazine*, he notes, had no love for the abolitionist cause and, in 1787, there was no reference to slavery or the slave trade in its index. But in 1788 there were 68 references, though in more enlightened circles slavery had been recognised as morally wrong some years before that.[7] Not a word has survived which would allow us to ascertain the Earle brothers' attitude to abolition, but there are some interesting clues, not all of them what one might at first expect.

The most obvious point is that the Earle brothers were slave traders and the sons and grandsons of slave traders and so of course hostile to abolition. But this may be too facile a summary of their reaction to the problem which faced them and those like them. There was in Liverpool a small but distinguished group of abolitionists who of necessity kept fairly quiet about their beliefs, since they had no wish to antagonise their neighbours. The most important of these men were William Rathbone IV (1757–1809), a radical Quaker timber merchant 'who was at the heart of virtually all major political disputes in late 18th-century Liverpool'; William Roscoe (1753–1831), lawyer, poet, historian and 'Father of Liverpool Culture'; and Dr James Currie (1756–1805), a Scottish physician and man of letters who wrote among many other things a biography of Robert Burns.[8] All these men were nonconformists and all were passionately opposed to slavery and did what they could to promote the cause of abolition. But all three were also friends of the Anglican, slave trading Earle family, frequently visiting and having tea and dinner in each other's houses. In January 1797, for instance, the Quaker chemist and natural philosopher John Dalton wrote to his brother reporting a pleasant afternoon and evening spent with the Rathbones: 'We had a party of gentlemen to dine, chiefly literary – namely, Roscoe, Rathbone, Earle, Clarke etc … They staid tea, as usual … The etiquette in Liverpool is to sit down to

---

7   Hochschild, 2006, p. 129; Anstey and Hair, 1976, p. 239.
8   Sanderson, 1976, *passim* and p. 200 for the quotation.

dinner a little after three.'⁹ The Earles were particularly friendly with Roscoe and, with their knowledge of Italy and the Italian language, may well have helped him prepare his *Life of Lorenzo de' Medici*, which was published in 1797. They certainly acknowledged its publication in rather a dramatic way, launching a ship called *Lorenzo de' Medici* in the same year, a ship which it is pleasant to report was not employed in the slave trade.

The Earles were Whigs, as was Roscoe, and would have shared at least some of his political ideas, and they were also wealthy, well educated and sociable, people whom it was possible to like if not to agree with on every issue. This attitude is nicely alluded to in a memoir about Dr James Currie written in 1831 by his son:

> He was in the midst of many friends, who were embarked in the slave-trade, with whom he was in habits of daily intercourse and intimacy, and from whom he experienced much kindness. He knew that to be in the African trade did not necessarily render a man either unfeeling or dishonest. He knew that many of them (his own friends) were generous, affectionate and humane in private life.¹⁰

Most Liverpool slave-trading firms responded to the threat of abolition by making hay while the sun still shone, increasing the scale of their business if they could afford to, and buying and selling as many slaves as possible, while at the same time keeping an eye open for alternative investment opportunities. The period from the end of the American War in 1783 to the beginning of the French Revolutionary War, ten years later, was one of hectic activity for the Liverpool slaving community, which was to be brought to a sudden and, for some, disastrous end by the outbreak of war and the commercial crisis of 1793. This had much to do with over-investment in what was eventually to be Liverpool's answer to abolition, the cotton trade. Thomas & William Earle kept well clear of this crisis, as can be seen in a letter written to Thomas from Chester by Robert Hodgson, a family friend and former business partner:

> It gives me most singular satisfaction to learn that in these distressful

---

9   Rathbone, 1913, pp. 114–15.
10 Currie, 1831, pp. 110–11; see also Sanderson, 1976, pp. 200, 203, 232–33; Chandler, 1953, p. 408; Rathbone, 1913, p. 114. For the friendship of the Earles with the abolitionist Lightbody family see above p. 40.

times your situation has been free and undisturbed, a natural consequence of keeping yourselves as independent as possible of the fate of other people. The cotton speculations and all transactions of the kind ... are abominable – gambling to get a fortune in a hurry, merely to save the trouble of acquiring by progressive means.[11]

Instead of gambling, Thomas did his best to try to return the Liverpool commercial world to its normal state of prosperity, being appointed one of six men on a committee whose object was to recommend measures to restore confidence.[12]

T. & W. Earle may have been rich enough not to need to gamble to make a fortune in a hurry, but they were nevertheless extremely active slave merchants who operated on a scale even greater than their father. Between 1753 and 1787, William Sr invested in 97 slaving voyages carried out by 41 different ships, an average of just under two and a half voyages a year.[13] His sons, by contrast, invested in 73 voyages between 1780 and 1804, an average of over three a year, and between 1780 and 1794, when they were most active, they were involved in 58 voyages, over four a year. And in some years, they did over twice as much as this; in both 1783 and 1792, for instance, they were part-owners of nine ships engaged in the slave trade, which might suggest that they, like many of their competitors, were indeed in a bit of a hurry.

The place of T. & W. Earle in the league table of Liverpool slave merchants can be conveniently stated from data produced for the parliamentary commissioners by Robert Norris, a former slave-ship captain and merchant. He therefore knew a lot about the slave trade, though he was inclined to play down the nastier aspects of the business. This bias hardly matters here since he was merely giving evidence of the ships and shipowners engaged in the Liverpool slave trade on 3 March 1790, a subject on which he was certainly well informed. His table lists 140 ships owned by 38 separate slave-trading firms of which T. & W. Earle with six ships at that date came in at sixth equal.[14]

Heading the list was the firm of John Dawson, the man who captured the French East Indiaman *Carnatic* in 1778, with 19 ships, followed by William Boats & Co. with eleven. 'Billie' Boats (or Boates) was one of the

11 D/EARLE/11/8/1, Hodgson to T. Earle, 23 March 1793.
12 Baines, 1852, p. 495; Hyde et al., 1951.
13 For William Sr see Chapter Four.
14 For Norris's table see Lambert, 1975, pp. lxxii, 211–19.

more colourful men on the Liverpool waterfront. His peculiar name was said to derive from the fact that he was a waif who was found as a child in a boat. He was then sent to the charity Blue Coat School, apprenticed to the sea and hence into the slave trade in which he prospered amazingly. His great fortune was said to have come from his capture of a Spanish ship with large quantities of gold and silver aboard. This may or may not have been true, but there seems no doubt that the two most successful owners of slave ships at the peak of Liverpool's involvement in the business both derived much of their fortunes from privateering. This was also true to some extent of the Earles, as we saw in Chapter 8, and no doubt further research would produce more slave merchants in Norris's table whose capital derived to a considerable extent from a lucky voyage or two by their privateers in the American War. Other sources of windfall capital included lotteries, such being the good fortune of Thomas Leyland, 11th in the slave merchant table and later a banker, who in 1776 together with a partner won £20,000 in the state lottery.[15]

Overall, ten Liverpool firms in Norris's table owned five or more ships, a total between them of 85 of the 140 ships in the list. And, at the other end of the scale, there were 15 owners who invested in only one ship. The typical size of a Liverpool slave ship was between 100 and 300 tons. Great size could be a disadvantage as such ships took longer to 'slave', though this could be countered to some extent by the use of smaller feeder ships to fill the bigger 'mother' vessels. Big ships also tended to be slower. Many of the medium-sized ships were similar to privateers, built for speed and not bulk-carrying capacity, thus reducing times on the Middle Passage and so, theoretically, mortality.

The analysis of ownership above is rather misleading as the table drawn up by Robert Norris names only the one or two managing partners in each company – such as Thomas & William Earle & Co., or William Boats & Co. – without any mention of the other men who invested in the ships. But it was unusual for a slave ship to have only one or two investors, though there were exceptions such as Robert Bostock, who owned and managed four small slave ships entirely by himself, though he sometimes bemoaned having no partner to share his troubles and losses.[16] Other sources, such as Ship Registration books, show that

---

15 On Boates see Williams, 2004, pp. 484–85; for Leyland see Chandler, 1953, p. xv.
16 Hodson, 1953, p. 50.

there were normally many more investors, and the usual pattern for slave ships owned by Thomas & William Earle was to have between six and nine co-owners including the two brothers.

We can tell from this material that the business of Thomas and William, like that of their father, depended heavily on the financial support and sound advice of a solid core of loyal co-owners. The most important source of such men was the community of retired slave-ship captains, men such as John Smale, Francis Holland, Joseph Caton, John Copeland, Ralph Fisher and Thomas Jolly, all of whom were investors in over 15 of the slaving voyages carried out by T. & W. Earle & Co., though there were also substantial investors who had never been to sea, men who could be described as professional slave-ship investors, such as Arthur and Benjamin Heywood or William Davenport, who invested in the brothers' ships just as he had done in their father's. Davenport died in 1797 and his obituary in *Billinge's Liverpool Advertiser* described him as 'deservedly successful in his commercial pursuits, which were always conducted with pleasant manners, strict probity and exemplary punctuality.' And if such men did not want to raise the total capital required, there were always people in Liverpool only too happy to take a share for one or two voyages. 'Almost every man in Liverpool is a merchant', wrote the author of a description of the town in 1795. 'The attractive African meteor has ... so dazzled their ideas, that almost every order of people is interested in a Guinea cargo.'[17]

The slave-trade business of the Earles led to the carriage of large numbers of slaves, just under 22,000, of whom some 19,000 were delivered alive. At over 13 per cent, this was an appallingly high rate of mortality and one which does not seem to have been affected by the passage of Dolben's Act in 1788. This latter was intended to reduce mortality on slave ships by stating a maximum of slaves that could be carried on ships of a given tonnage and dimensions. Why mortality on Earle-owned ships should have remained so high is difficult to say. There is no evidence that they evaded the restrictions of the Act, which was quite thoroughly administered. They were not singled out by the contemporary parliamentary enquiries as particularly brutal or indifferent owners, though one of their ships was noted as having exceptionally high mortality. This was the *Liverpool Hero*, which in 1787 sailed from Calabar with 560 slaves aboard, of whom only 230 reached

17 *BLA*, 28 August 1797; *A General ...*, 1795, p. 229.

their destination at the island of Dominica alive. 'Have you ever heard that the Liverpool Hero had a great mortality?' the former slave-ship captain James Penny was asked in the following year. 'I have', he replied, 'but don't know the particulars.'[18]

This was not the only Earle-owned ship which lost over 100 slaves on the Middle Passage, though in fairness it should perhaps be noted that some of their ships lost very few slaves and one, the *Britannia*, which sailed from the Congo River in 1794, lost none at all. No one really knew why some ships had very high mortality (of sailors as well as slaves) and some very low. Enquiries focussed on overcrowding as that was fairly easy to measure, while the famous diagram of the slaves packed into the Liverpool slaver *Brookes* did more for the abolitionist cause than thousands of pages of 'evidence' and remains iconic to this day. Parliamentary enquiries also paid a lot of attention to the diet, exercise and cleanliness of the slaves and the degree and quality of medical attention available. But witnesses on both sides need to be treated with caution since they nearly all had entrenched viewpoints which coloured their evidence. Reading some of this material, one might think that cruise liners could learn a thing or two from slavers on how to organise a pleasant voyage through tropical waters. James Penny, who was quoted above, is a case in point. 'They are supplied with pipes and tobacco ...', he said of the slaves; when they were brought on deck for fresh air and exercise, 'they are amused with instruments of music peculiar to their country ... and when tired of music and dancing, they then go to games of chance.'[19] Though this seems obvious nonsense, logbooks do make it clear that slave-ship captains and their surgeons made great efforts to keep their cargo alive. They had every financial incentive so to do and sound as distressed as anyone might well be when both slaves and sailors started dropping down dead in one of the epidemics which periodically scourged the ships.

One factor which might help to explain the high mortality of slaves aboard ships owned by the Earle brothers was their predilection for Old Calabar as a source of slaves. This port on the Cross River in south-eastern Nigeria, a favourite destination for Liverpool slavers generally, was described in a captain's instructions as 'remarkable for great mortality in slaves' and this certainly seems to have been true.

18 Lambert, 1975, pp. lxviii, 41.
19 Quoted by Hochschild, 2006, p. 154.

The mortality rates on Earle ships sailing from Calabar was almost exactly twice that prevailing in ships sailing from the Cameroons and Bonny, the next two most important sources of slaves.[20] Nevertheless, this port had many advantages for Liverpool traders, not least being the close relations they had developed with the local African traders who supplied the slaves. These ties help to explain the growing emphasis on Old Calabar as a loading port for the ships sent out by T. & W. Earle. In their first 20 voyages as slave traders, between 1780 and 1783 inclusive, their ships acquired slaves at a number of ports, such as Bonny, Whydah and the Cameroons as well as Calabar. But then, from 1784 to 1792, the Earle ships focussed very heavily on Old Calabar, this port being the destination of at least half of their slave ships during this period.

Two unique documents have survived from the 1780s which help us get a better idea of what life was actually like at Old Calabar. The less important, but still interesting, document is the autobiography published in 1822 by William Butterworth, a runaway youngster from Leeds who, in 1786, was tricked into signing articles to serve as a boy aboard the *Hudibras*, a slave ship owned by the Earle syndicate, which sailed from Liverpool to Old Calabar under the command of Captain Evan Jenkin (described by Butterworth as Jenkins Evans). Since the book was published so long after the events it describes, it is no doubt affected by faulty memory and a desire to make the narrative and the author more interesting. But of course this is true of most memoirs.[21]

Like most sailor memoirs, Butterworth's book contains some entertaining accounts of shipboard life, the hard work, the rough games, the storms and 'the telling [of] long stories, as the custom is on board a ship', some variety being provided by his description of the 'ridiculous custom' of crossing the Tropic of Cancer, complete with Neptune and his trident and large quantities of brandy drunk and paid to the senior members of the crew as forfeits.[22] And so, after eight weeks, the *Hudibras* arrived at the bar where the Cross River meets the sea. Here they anchored and fired several guns as a signal to the English vessels moored upriver. They were at once surrounded by fishing canoes whose crews bartered yams and fish for salt beef and ship's biscuit, while the *Hudibras* waited for the arrival of a boat from the *Preston*, another ship

---

20 Williams, 2004, pp. 486–87; mortality rates calculated from TSTD.
21 Butterworth, 1822. A pseudonym for Henry Schroeder.
22 Earle, 1998, p. 96–97.

owned by the Earle syndicate commanded by Captain William Brighouse who piloted them upriver, 'as is customary for the oldest captain to do', the oldest or senior captain being recognised by both Englishmen and Africans as the leader of this temporary English community in the tropics.

Butterworth now becomes almost poetical in his description of the river, which was 'adorned and most agreeably shaded by large trees … wide and deep … the most beautiful sheet of water I ever beheld.' Captain Brighouse piloted them into the anchorage at Old Town, the part of Old Calabar favoured by the Liverpool men, where they found a large French ship, one from Bristol and four other slave ships from Liverpool. Two of these, the *Preston* and the *Rodney*, were owned by the Earle brothers and their associates, making Old Town in Calabar almost as much the focus of the Earle trading empire as Hanover Street on the Mersey. And now, as one might imagine, it was party time, with visits and exchange of news and letters between the ships and a continuous flow of visitors in canoes from the riverbank, as African traders and chiefs with their wives in colourful native garments came on board and were greeted with a plentiful flow of alcohol.[23]

All this must have seemed incredibly exciting and exotic to a teenage boy from Leeds. But now it was down to business as preparations were made for the reception of 'the unfortunate sons and daughters of Africa'. The *Hudibras* was completely transformed. The ship was unrigged and all the masts except the lower ones taken down and tarpaulins stretched across to make a waterproof shade, this later being replaced with thatch like that used in the houses ashore. A barricade, ten feet high with a fortified door in the middle, was built across the ship near the mainmast and the interior of the vessel was divided into three parts by means of strong partitions, with the men destined to be cooped up in the forepart of the ship as they were brought aboard, boys in the middle and women and girls aft. The 100-ton *Preston* and 150-ton *Hudibras* were designed to act as tenders to each other, the *Hudibras* having all her remaining cargo and other stores transferred to the *Preston* or warehoused ashore, leaving plenty of room to accommodate slaves as they were acquired, though in fact this plan to speed up the loading process did not work very well and it took nearly six months for the *Hudibras* to receive her allotted number of 360 slaves and set sail for Grenada.

23 Butterworth, 1822, pp. 25–27.

Billy Butterworth was a mere boy and he has little to say about the business of acquiring the cargo of slaves, though there are some passages of interest. On one occasion, he describes meeting a small war canoe, mounting a six-pounder gun in her bows and manned by 12 or 14 paddlers armed with fire arms and cutlasses. They informed Captain Jenkin that they 'were going to catch slaves' and made a bargain with him to take their catch when they got back to Calabar. Catching slaves was clearly seen as good sport by this jolly crew, who sang lustily as they paddled away upriver, 'apparently full of mirth and good humour.' Elsewhere, Butterworth described the custom of leaving pawns aboard as a pledge to guarantee the delivery of the slaves who had been bargained for. 'Pawns are the sons or daughters of inferior traders who ... pledge them for what they may want in trade', he wrote, the pawns becoming slaves themselves if the traders did not redeem them.[24]

Most of this information can be acquired elsewhere, as can his comments on other matters, such as the local propensity to lop off heads as a punishment for adultery or other crimes, or in large numbers to honour a recently deceased person of importance. Where Butterworth is most interesting is in the incidental insights his book provides, which are unusual in being written by someone from the lower deck who had a genuine affection for some of the Africans he met. He often went ashore to collect stores, wood, provisions, water and so on, to go on 'my favourite walk' on the sands near the edge of a wood or simply to amuse himself in the company of the locals. He made good use of these visits ashore, learning a smattering of one or more of the local languages as well as pidgin, the trade language of a few hundred words which provided a general means of communication between Africans and Englishmen. He had little of the ingrained racism so common among Englishmen in Africa and was able to wander about and make friends with the local inhabitants and also with slaves eager to discover from this friendly white boy some information about their eventual fate. Young Billy enjoyed the music played by the locals, who were 'very partial to singing in chorus'. He was sensitive enough to note that the women slaves, who danced so attractively, sang mainly 'slow airs of a pathetic nature', a sad observation echoed by Alexander Falconbridge, a former surgeon on slave ships who wrote an excellent account of the trade:

24 Butterworth, 1822, pp. 25–26, 97.

'Their songs are generally, as may naturally be expected, melancholy lamentations of their exile from their native country.'[25]

Butterworth punctuated his book with complaints about both the quality and quantity of the food served to sailors aboard the *Hudibras*. He made up for this by making friends with a hospitable family ashore, who often invited him to eat at their table and no doubt he fed well, as he considered even the slaves to be 'infinitely better fed' than the English sailors. This may seem unlikely, though it is one of the many ironies of the slave trade that the food supply of West Africa was much improved by the introduction of crops native to America but not to Africa, such as maize, cassava, sweet potatoes and groundnuts. At Calabar, however, the native yams remained the main staple, usually eaten in the form of *fufu*, i.e. boiled, pounded and made into balls which were moistened with a sauce of palm oil liberally spiced with pepper or served as an accompaniment to various sorts of stew. Another dish described was 'chop', sliced yams layered with fragrant leaves and smoke-dried fish, alligator, shrimps, pepper, salt and palm oil, the mixture being simmered in water for two hours.[26] Yams and oil were brought down to Calabar by river, and palm oil, used in England for the manufacture of soap and candles, as well as in the kitchen, was rapidly growing in significance as an export. Huge quantities of yams were also exported as food for the slaves on the Middle Passage, who each consumed between half a yam and two yams every day according to one account, one captain estimating that between 50,000 and 100,000 yams were required to feed a cargo of 500 slaves on their passage to the West Indies.[27]

Butterworth's book includes a dramatic description of the voyage of the *Hudibras* from Calabar to Grenada,[28] but one fears that this may be largely a product of his imagination. The main events were two 'revolts' and an epidemic which together killed off between 60 and 70 of the 360 slaves on board. Other sources do not mention these uprisings, while the slave ship database shows the *Hudibras* to have been remarkably healthy, with just ten slaves lost. It is a shame that we cannot trust Butterworth, as his descriptions of the slave insurrections is full of incident and quite moving as he was torn between his natural fear of the rebellious and

25 Falconbridge, 1788, p. 30.
26 Butterworth, 1822, pp. 32–33.
27 Masefield, 1967, pp. 284–86; Northrup, 1978, pp. 80–84; Sparks, 2004, p. 57.
28 Butterworth, 1822, pp. 98–132.

very violent slaves and his sympathy and indeed affection for many of the individual participants. So, perhaps, we can leave young Billy Butterworth at the island of Grenada, where he left the service of the *Hudibras* and engaged in a series of less interesting adventures before finally getting back home to Leeds, where he renounced the sea and 'followed copper-plate printing for a livelihood.'

The other document relating to Old Calabar in the 1780s is very different. It is the diary of one of the local slave traders, whom the English called Antera Duke, and so provides a record of the slave trade from the point of view of an African. It was written in 'pidgin' English, which is difficult to understand, though there is a modern edition in standard English.[29] Antera Duke was an *Efik*, a member of the powerful trading people who controlled the capture and sale of slaves at Old Calabar. The *Efiks* were animists who attributed spiritual powers to rocks, trees and particular parts of the river, as well as animals and birds and such deities as *Ndem Efik*, a serpent-like water god who dwelt in the river and had to be regularly appeased by the sacrifice by drowning of albino or light-skinned girls. Nearly everything, including most deaths, could usually be explained by witchcraft or magic, and much time was spent in offering libations or sacrifices to the many local gods, most commonly in the form of goats, but quite often of people (usually but not always slaves), whose heads might be lopped off in a fairly arbitrary fashion. The diary often records efforts to propitiate these gods by 'making doctor' in the 'god basin', making doctor meaning any sort of sacrifice or oath swearing as well as various forms of medicine.

Governing all was a secret society of males, called the *Ekpe* or Leopard Society, which had a vital part to play in the slave trade, since one of its many activities was to enforce the payment of debts and oversee the treatment of pawns. Several types of sanction were employed to overawe offenders, including fines and death, but the commonest was to 'blow *ekpe*' against them, a ritual which boycotted the offender until an accommodation had been agreed. Boycotts, such as a refusal to sell slaves to offenders, could also be employed against the European slave-ship captains and their crews if they were deemed to have offended. Maintaining trust and good relations between African slave-merchants and the slave-ship captains was obviously essential if the main business

---

29 Forde, 1956; Antera Duke, 2010. Quotations will be from this modern edition, giving the date of the diary entry.

of Old Calabar was to be carried on effectively. Both the *Efiks* ashore and the crews of slave ships tended to be violent and hot-headed, so the local leaders had pledged that no white man should be hurt ashore and, when they were, the perpetrator was likely to be punished, as was one man who had 'an ear cut off because of the fight' in which he had wounded the mate of the Liverpool slave ship *Ellis*.[30]

Human sacrifice was an essential element in *Efik* social customs and is frequently referred to in the diary, often very casually. 'We heard that … they were making a play for their father. They cut seven men's heads off.' 'One woman slave to be beheaded in honour of my father.' 'We heard about a new ship, three more heads were cut off.'[31] Antera Duke was not specific about the form such executions took, but Butterworth and other observers provide a detailed description:

> At these executions the sufferers are pinioned and tied in a sitting position to a stake driven in the ground, and round their heads, so as to cross their eyes, is fixed a rope, the end of which is held by some bystanders who participate in the sacrifice. The executioner comes up with a leaden-handled sword, and generally at one blow severs the head from the body, when it is instantaneously pulled away by the rope, and, while yet warm, is tossed up in the air, and played with like a ball.[32]

A nasty and bloodthirsty business, but maybe less so to the crew of an eighteenth-century slave ship than it would be to us today.

The most bloodthirsty sequence of events in the diary follows the sickness and death in July 1786 of a local dignitary called Duke Ephraim. In the weeks immediately following his death, the main emphasis was on trying to determine who if anyone was responsible for killing him by witchcraft, a process similar to that conducted in England for the same purpose in the previous century. Meanwhile, tension built up as the time approached when sacrifices would be made in honour of so great a man. 'All the men and women were crying in the town', Antera Duke recorded on 4 November 1786, while wisely sending his own people to safety in the woods until calm returned. Two days later, the slaughter

30 Antera Duke, 2010, 11 August 1787.
31 Antera Duke, 2010, 18 May and 8 November 1786.
32 Antera Duke, 2010, 13 April 1787, n. 207; see also Butterworth, 1822, pp. 58–60.

began. 'About 4 a.m. I got up, a great rain ... We got ready to cut heads off and at 5 o'clock in the morning we began to cut slaves' heads off, 50 heads in that one day. I carried 29 cases of bottled brandy and 15 calabashes of chop for everybody.'[33] More heads were removed on succeeding days until honour was satisfied.

It must have been a terrifying society to live in, but that is not immediately apparent from the diary, which records an impressive amount of party going and party giving, on board the ships as well as ashore. These involved substantial quantities of food: goat, cow and fish, as well as yams and 'chop' – and drink – *mimbo* (palm wine), brewed from local sources, and brandy, bottled beer and other European liquors supplied from the slave ships. Expressions such as 'we drank all day until night' were frequent in the diary, as was 'we played', 'play' being a catch-all word in pidgin for singing, dancing, drinking and generally having a good time. The English ships' captains were often invited to these parties and did their best to reciprocate with invitations for the local dignitaries to come and drink and play aboard their ships.

Interspersed with executions and parties are references to the slave ships and their officers and the trade they conducted in Old Calabar. Antera Duke usually identified ships by the surname of their captain and the diary refers to some 40 English vessels, most of them from Liverpool. Five of these were owned by syndicates in which the Earle brothers had an important share, *Rodney, Perseverance, Preston, Hudibras* and *Liverpool Hero*, this last ship sailing to Old Calabar twice in the period covered by the diary. Judging by the numbers of slaves he mentions as having been supplied by himself, Antera Duke was not a very important slave merchant, but he was nevertheless constantly active and there are references to just about every aspect of the business in his diary.

His first task was to greet new arrivals after their long voyage from Liverpool or Bristol, or indeed Nantes, though Antera Duke had few dealings with the French. On the afternoon of 5 February 1785, for instance, he was doing business with another, more important, slave merchant at his splendid two-storey house, named Liverpool Hall in honour of his best customers, when he 'heard news that a ship was coming up the river, so we ran to the landing to get five great guns ready to fire.' A few weeks later, he was introduced to Captain Peter Comberbach, a newcomer to Calabar, who had come upriver in his ship's

33 Antera Duke, 2010, 6 November 1786.

boat and said that his ship, the *Gascoyne,* was 20 miles downstream at
Parrot Island and needed a pilot to bring her up to Old Calabar. Keen to
oblige, Antera Duke and two colleagues 'dressed as white men and went
down in his boat with a big canoe to bring up his ship.'[34] Such occasions
were usually accompanied, as has been seen, with much merriment, but
on a more serious note this was also the time to extract 'comey' from the
visitors, a sort of anchorage tax, this often requiring much bargaining
in a 'comey palaver'.

The beginning of business is noted by the expression 'breaking
book', which meant the opening of a new account in a ledger. This would
acknowledge the details of a trading agreement, involving a promise to
deliver so many slaves for such a combination of trade goods. The next
task for the African slave traders was to acquire their quota of slaves.
Antera Duke only went upriver once in the diary period 'to catch men'.
Normally, he got other people to get him slaves, 'my fisherman came
home with a slave', 'sent my brother to Boostam [upriver] to trade for
slaves', thus gradually acquiring what was required by the English ships,
though these sometimes rejected the slaves delivered to them. 'Went on
board Captain Smale's ship [*Perseverance*] with three slaves. He took two
slaves and we came back.'[35] And then at last, after months of trading
activity, the English ships were fully slaved and nearly ready to sail,
so that all that was now needed were some last-minute exchanges. 'We
got alongside Captain Savage's ship', the diary reported on 22 April
1785. 'We got together to settle everything we owed him. He [another
African merchant] dashed one big great gun and he dashed us', 'dash'
(a gratuity, present or just a payment) being as common a West African
word then as it still is today. The numbers of slaves supplied by Antera
Duke were usually very small, one or two at a time, so it comes as a
bit of a surprise when he reports the departure of the English ships,
most of them with several hundred slaves aboard, a reminder that the
diary writer was just one of many local slave merchants with whom the
English captains and their officers did business.

The long-drawn-out process of trading for slaves was accompanied by
efforts to maintain and lubricate good relations between the English and
the Africans. Presents of all sorts were exchanged, including attractive
slave girls if so desired for the officers of the slave ships. Dinner parties

34   Antera Duke, 2010, 5 February and 26 May 1785.
35   Antera Duke, 2010, 28 and 30 January, 7 August 1785.

were given both ashore and aboard ship. 'About 7 o'clock at night I had all the captains to supper at my house'. 'We drank all day' at a party for a departing captain.[36] On a more practical level, the English captains were able to provide skilled services for their African customers from the human resources aboard their ships. 'Captain Cooper's carpenter to work for me ... I went on board Fairweather's ship to fetch his joiner to make windows for the big house.'[37] Captain Patrick Fairweather was a central figure in the development of close and mutually beneficial relations between Liverpool and this part of West Africa. He first came to Calabar in 1755 as an apprentice and retired from the sea in 1792, having trained large numbers of Liverpool men in African ways in the intervening 37 years.[38]

Fairly soon after the end of the diary period, Calabar ceased to be an important destination for ships owned by the Earle syndicates. In the five years between 1788 and 1792, eight Earle ships made their way up the Cross River but, in the next quinquennium, 1793–97, there was only one and there were no more after 1797. The sources give no reason for this change, but it was accompanied by a growing interest in shipping slaves from the area which is now Ghana and, from much further south, from Angola and the Congo River. This change in the sources of slaves was accompanied by a fairly rapid overall decline after the peak year of 1792. Only 13 Earle ships sailed to West Africa in the remaining years of the 1790s and only six more in the early years of the nineteenth century. The last slave ship owned by the Earle brothers was the 81-ton *Minerva*, which set sail from Liverpool for Cape Coast Castle on the Gold Coast on 10 April 1804 and was sold 15 months later to John Bridge and James Aspinall, a leading firm of Liverpool slavers, who set the *Minerva* out on two more slaving voyages, in 1805 and 1806, before the trade became illegal by Act of Parliament.[39]

So, we are left with the intriguing question, why did these successful slave-trading brothers, Thomas and William Earle, give up their trade three years before they were required by law to do so. It is possible, of course, that their friendship with such famous abolitionists as Roscoe and Rathbone persuaded them that slave trading was immoral and not

36   Antera Duke, 2010, 4 September, 26 October 1785.
37   Antera Duke, 2010, 23 August and 20 September 1785.
38   Antera Duke, 2010, p. 72; Behrendt, 1991.
39   Data from the TSTD.

the sort of thing with which a gentleman should be associated. But this seems unlikely. The answer probably lies in a fundamental change of focus in their transatlantic trading activities. The islands of the West Indies were the destination of every one of their slaving ventures from 1780 to 1800, when a change of pattern can be seen with the voyage of the *Harlequin* carrying a cargo of slaves to Demerara on the South American mainland. Similar voyages were conducted by the *Paragon* in 1800–01 and by the *Minerva*, all three of these ships acquiring their slaves at Cape Coast Castle or Accra on the Gold Coast, modern Ghana. As if to emphasise the change in pattern, the ships engaged in this new trade to Demerara were all owned by a completely different syndicate, consisting of the two brothers and usually just one co-owner, Thomas Leathom of Liverpool, a young merchant who was to be associated in trade and shipowning with the Earle brothers right up to the 1820s.

Demerara and Berbice, which was also important in the Earle trading schemes, were rivers which gave their names to two regions or colonies in Guiana and, together with Essequibo, they were to become the colony of British Guiana in 1831. This territory had been colonised by the Dutch, an ally of the French, and was seized in 1796 by the British, who held it till 1802, when it was returned to the Dutch at the Peace of Amiens, only to be seized once more when the war with Napoleon began again in the next year. These Dutch plantations produced sugar and coffee, but their main interest for the British at the turn of the nineteenth century was their cotton plantations. It was estimated in 1796 that there were 150 estates in the new colonies, the greater part of which were planted with cotton and worked by 50,000 to 60,000 slaves.[40] Cotton was a very attractive plantation crop as it was easy to increase the quantity grown, especially on virgin land, and it was very profitable in these early years of the Industrial Revolution as cotton-spinning factories mushroomed in and about Manchester and also spread towards Liverpool, which had eclipsed London as the leading port of entry for cotton by the middle of the 1790s.[41]

One tends to think of the southern United States as the main source of raw cotton and this indeed was to become true in the early nineteenth century. But there were many other sources. Liverpool merchants,

---

40 Dalton, 1855, i, p. 254. Guiana is spelled Guyana today but, to avoid confusion, the older usage will be employed throughout this book.
41 Dumbell, 1923; Edwards, 1967.

including the Earles, had been importing cotton from the West Indies since the early eighteenth century, but expansion was more and more difficult as the soil became worn out. The eastern Mediterranean was also an important source and one in which the Earles with their Livorno base had played a leading part. But here again there were problems, since the long voyage home to England was so vulnerable to French privateers in the 1790s that Mediterranean trade with England almost came to a stop. This all meant that the most important competitor to United States cotton was South America, especially Brazil, though Demerara and Berbice were also to have a significant part to play.

The Portuguese did not permit ships from Brazil to sail direct to Britain so Brazilian cotton had to be imported via Lisbon, though this was to change in 1808, when the Portuguese royal family fled to Brazil and Brazilian ports were opened to British trade. Reports of small quantities arriving in Liverpool via Lisbon can be found from the early 1790s and a few years later large consignments were being reported in the Liverpool papers. On 24 April 1797, for instance, *Billinge's Liverpool Advertiser* recorded the arrival of a fleet of nine ships from Lisbon, seven of which carried Brazilian cotton for the Earle brothers, a total of 803 bags. Growth continued into the following year, as can be seen in the *Liverpool Trade List*, a short-lived publication which ran from July 1798 to the end of 1799 and summarised material gathered from the Custom House books. This recorded the import of 4,400 bags of Brazilian cotton from Lisbon by T. & W. Earle. Demerara came a poor second with just 303 bags for the Earles, but this route was probably more profitable as shipping costs were lower than on the roundabout Brazil–Lisbon–Liverpool route. Guiana's 'golden age' was in the early years after British ownership was re-established in 1803. The new colonies were said to be so profitable that capital invested in the cultivation of coffee, sugar and especially cotton would double in value in ten years and often in just five.[42]

Given this potential and the continuing growth in demand, it is not surprising that the Earles, who had long been familiar with buying and selling in their Mediterranean and West Indian trades, should have decided that this was a cargo which could help to sustain their house for the foreseeable future. This encouraged them to become not just purchasers and shippers of cotton to Liverpool, but also slave merchants

---

42 *Liverpool Trade List*; Dalton, 1855, i, p. 317.

engaged in shipping slaves from Africa to Britain's new colonies. But, as far as can be seen, the Earles engaged in only four slaving voyages to Africa and Demerara, and no slaving voyages at all after the departure of the *Minerva* on 18 April 1804. Various reasons may be suggested for this change in policy, such as the risks inherent in the slave trade, especially in wartime, and the correct belief that the trade was on its last legs anyway, but probably the most compelling reason was the fate of the *Annabella*, a ship sent out under the command of John McClure for the Gold Coast and Demerara on 18 February 1804. Five months later, it was reported in *Lloyds List* that she had been seized at Cape Coast by the Royal Navy frigate *Inconstant* 'for illicit trade'.[43]

Just what this meant can be pieced together from the logbook of the *Inconstant*.[44] Her captain, Edward Dickson, appears to have been an energetic but rather irritating officer. His orders were to patrol the West African coast, seeking out any illegal behaviour and keeping an eye open for potential enemy prizes. On 23 April 1804, he was anchored at Cape Coast Castle when a canoe arrived from the west with the news that the *Annabella* of Liverpool was anchored at Elmina, a Dutch possession. Captain Dickson quickly weighed anchor and, later that same day, boarded the English slaver, which he discovered was carrying 140 male and 63 female slaves who had been bought from the Dutch Governor of Elmina in exchange for a trading cargo. Dickson arranged for the *Annabella* to be revictualled and then sent under the command of his lieutenant to Jamaica, where she was condemned for trading with the enemy and both cargo and ship were seized for the Crown.[45]

One has to assume that Captain McClure had specific instructions to behave in this illegal fashion. As long as he was not caught, it certainly made sense. Buying the whole cargo of slaves at once greatly reduced turnaround time, compared for instance with the slow procedure at Old Calabar. And there were probably some advantages in buying slaves from the Dutch if they were going to be sent to a former Dutch colony. As it was, Captain McClure did his best to defend himself, but his predicament was hopeless. He wrote to the Governor of Cape Coast Castle, who was sympathetic to his plight and forwarded his letter to London. Both the governor and McClure pleaded that trading with the

43 *LL*, 24 July 1804.
44 ADM 51/1571/4.
45 CO 138/36, 1 July 1804.

Dutch was common practice and was not condemned in West Africa, whatever might be the case elsewhere. McClure also protested that no attempt had been made to warn him of the danger of trading at Elmina and that he had only done so, 'with a view to further the interests of the owners as the rains approached and I perceived no other way open to expedite my purchase.'[46] But the fact remained that he had been caught fair and square and so his ship and cargo were forfeit.

This was a serious loss to his employers and, since it was the result of an illegal act, did not come within the scope of the *Annabella's* insurance. So, it is perhaps not surprising that Thomas and William Earle should consider it a suitable time to give up their family's connection with the slave trade, just over a century after John Earle, their grandfather, invested in 1699 and 1700 in the voyages of the *Liverpool Merchant* and the *Africa*, the very first ships from Liverpool to engage in this notorious but normally profitable trade.[47] The end of slaving voyages to Guiana did not, however, mean that the Earles lost interest in the new colonies. They sent out three ships direct to Berbice and/or Demerara in 1805–06 and were to continue to trade to this area in their own and other people's ships right up to the 1820s. From 1806, they also occasionally engaged in trade to Surinam, Brazil and Buenos Aires, but Guiana remained their main destination in South America.

There is a coda to the involvement of the Earles in the slave trade. On 25 October 1806, Parliament was dissolved and a general election called. Three candidates stood for the two Liverpool seats: the two incumbents, Lieutenant-General Banastre Tarleton and Major-General Bamber Gascoyne, both anti-abolitionists, and William Roscoe, a passionate supporter of abolition who had been persuaded to stand in the Whig interest. Since the subject of abolition was likely to be the main business of the new Parliament, it might seem a little surprising that Roscoe's two proposers were his business partner, Thomas Leyland, who had three ships, *Ellen*, *Enterprize* and *Fortune*, actually engaged in slaving voyages at the time of the election, and Thomas Earle, described by one historian as one 'of the leading African merchants of the town', though as has been seen this was no longer strictly true. Even more surprising, William Roscoe came top of the poll, some say helped along

---

46 T 70/1581, letter and enclosure dated 26 April 1804; T 70/34, letter of 31 March 1804.

47 See above, ch. 1, pp. 8–9.

by lavish bribery, and his supporters, including the Earles, paraded the streets of Liverpool as their band played 'Oh, dear, what can the matter be' before sitting down, 268 strong, to a celebratory dinner at the Golden Lion in Dale Street.[48] Once at Westminster, Roscoe behaved according to his conscience, making a maiden speech in support of abolition and casting his vote in favour of the measure.

This Parliament was short-lived and was dissolved on 27 April 1807, just a month after the slave trade was abolished. The passage of the Act caused consternation in Liverpool and William Roscoe was no longer the popular man who had been elected just six months earlier. A mob of sailors, now likely to be unemployed, threatened his and his supporters' safety, but nevertheless William Roscoe made a public entry into Liverpool on 2 May 1807, accompanied by a numerous body of friends, mounted and on foot. Bringing up the rear, 'after those on foot, came Mr. Roscoe, with Mr Earle on the barouche box uncovered.' Thomas Earle was a colonel in the Liverpool militia and was described in one of the election songs as 'brave Colonel Earle.' He was certainly brave on that day.[49]

48 Anstey and Hair, 1976, p. 223; Jones and Wright, 1806.
49 Picton, 1907, i, p. 279; Rathbone, 1913, p. 290; *Impartial*, 1806. Roscoe was not re-elected in the 1807 election.

CHAPTER ELEVEN

The Last Years of Livorno

'I cannot entertain a doubt of his friendship for he always said that whilst the name of Earle existed at Leghorn, he should never go elsewhere.'[1]

Thomas and William Earle may have been the sixth most important slave merchants in Liverpool in 1790, but this was by no means their sole mercantile activity. Like their father before them, they also invested in a variety of other potential sources of profit.[2] They were, as has been seen, part-owners in 34 slave ships which made 73 voyages between 1780 and 1804. They were also owners or part-owners of 19 other ships which between them made 59 voyages between 1783 and 1803, all non-slaving voyages with the exception of one to Africa and Jamaica carried out by the *Apollo* in 1792–93, her other two voyages for the Earles being slave-free. With this one exception, the ownership and management of slaving and non-slaving ships were thus separate activities.

From 1793 onwards, Britain was at war with France and shipowning once again became a hazardous occupation. Most of the non-slaving ships were very lightly armed, ships sailing to the Mediterranean usually having just two or four guns even in wartime, so it is no surprise to find that six voyages ended in capture, three or possibly four of them in the same year, 1797. But, since no vessels were wrecked, this means that the other 53 voyages were completed as planned. Since it was the brothers' policy to insure their ships, as their father had done, it seems probable that shipowning continued to be a profitable activity for them.[3]

---

1 MMM, D/EARLE/2/3, 3 May 1803.
2 This section is based on LTS until 1784 and then Liverpool ship registers in MMM, Mediterranean passes in ADM 7 and newspapers.
3 Captured ships identified from the ship registers in MMM: *Nevis* (1795), *Susannah* (1797), *Zebulon* (1797), *Diligence* (1797), *Lorenzo de' Medici* (1797 or 1798) and *Sea Nymph* (1799).

Most of these profits accrued to Thomas and William themselves since, unlike the slave ships, which had a minimum of six owners, they owned all or most of these vessels, the only one with more than three co-owners being the *Dispatch*, a 120-ton brigantine which in the 1780s acted as house ship to the trading company of Earle, Hodgson & Drake at Leghorn and was jointly owned by all five partners: Thomas and William in Liverpool; their first cousin Willis Earle, who owned 3/16ths of the business and was resident in Leghorn; John Drake, also resident in Leghorn; and Robert Hodgson, resident in Chester. All the other non-slaving ships were owned either by the brothers alone or, more commonly, by the brothers and just one other man, who normally owned 1/8th of the ship. These third owners were the masters in the early days but, from 1792, ten ships in sequence were owned by the brothers and Thomas Bradley, a former captain, who was replaced in 1800 by another former captain, Thomas Leathom, who was to remain in partnership with the Earles for over 20 years.

The brothers also tended to rely on the same fairly small pool of captains for their ships. On 40 of the 59 voyages, almost exactly two-thirds, the ships were captained by just seven men who each commanded on four voyages or more, the longest-serving being Simon Forbes, who was captain for nine voyages, six of them on the *Dispatch* and the other three on her replacement, the *Fame*. Such continuity was obviously an important factor in the success of a shipping business, since a man like Forbes, or John Tobin who commanded for eight voyages, would not only be thoroughly acquainted with the navigation and the ships, but would also get to know the brothers and their foibles well. And, once in their ports of destination, they would know the customers and the local petty bureaucrats, who to bribe and who to bow to, and the hundreds of other small details that made for a successful voyage.

The non-slaving ships owned by the Earles conformed to a general pattern, the great majority being medium-sized vessels – five ships and 12 brigs and snows – between 120 and 180 tons. The word 'ship' normally refers to a three-masted vessel, while the commoner 'brigs' and 'snows' were two-masted, a convenient rig which required a smaller crew. Crew size depended on destination as much as rig, with nine to 12 men being normal for the Mediterranean and sometimes over 20 for the West Indies. Only three of the 19 ships were newly built, all of them in Liverpool. Four of the rest were prizes, one Spanish, one Dutch, one French and one American. The remaining 12 ships were all second-hand

Figure 10. View of Livorno with canal and warehouses, *La Venezia Livornese*, from Mario Baruchello, *Livorno e il suo porto* (1932) pp. 343-347

English or Scottish ships, up to eight or nine years old at purchase, and built in Chester, Bristol, Whitehaven, Leith and Saltcoats in Ayrshire as well as Liverpool, the building of small ships requiring no more than a beach, a timber supply and a skilled workforce. Old ships were cheap ships, but that did not mean they were unfit for purpose. And if they did turn out to be unsuitable, they were easily sold and replaced, as the *Delaval* was in 1795 or the *Crescent* in 1799, in each case after just one voyage.[4]

The pattern of voyages was similar to that engaged in by their uncle Thomas Earle Sr in the 1760s and 1770s. Much the most important destination was Leghorn itself, with other Italian voyages calling at Ancona on the east coast and Genoa, Naples, Sicily and Salerno, famous for its autumn fairs, on the west. Some of these vessels sailed to the Mediterranean via Ireland, Newfoundland or Nova Scotia, and a couple of them fitted in a short voyage to Lisbon after their return, seeking cargoes of fruit and wine suitable for the Christmas market. The voyages undertaken by six of the ships were more enterprising, involving a West Indian or South American voyage. The *Apollo* made two voyages to Leghorn and back, but also one slaving and one non-slaving voyage to the West Indies. The *Globe*, a 12-gun snow, granted a letter of marque in 1793, made four voyages to Italy or other places in the Mediterranean, but also one to Antigua and, in 1797–98, one to Demerara, the first sign of Earle interest in this part of the world. Other ships sailed to Jamaica, Grenada and Honduras, but the most well-travelled of the non-slaving Earle ships was the 170-ton *Britannia*, which made six voyages between 1802 and 1810, the first to Naples, but then increasingly adventurous, to Barbados, Demerara, Buenos Ayres, Surinam and 'the Brazills', the main interest in these last four voyages being the cotton import trade.

The records of the quarantine authorities (*Sanità*) at Leghorn give voyage times for incoming ships and these show how slow travel was before the advent of steam. One very common voyage was that from Newfoundland or Nova Scotia with a cargo of fish to Leghorn, a passage normally broken at Gibraltar. Journey times to the Straits of Gibraltar ranged from 30 to 70 days depending on the wind or such maritime hazards as a visit by ships of the Barbary corsairs, who were very

---

4 Most of the information on the ships is drawn from the ship registers in MMM. There is also useful material on crew size, passengers and voyage times in the quarantine records at Leghorn (ASL, *Sanità*).

active during the long period of European warfare. These well-armed ships usually respected the 'Mediterranean passes' carried by English, Irish and Scottish ships, though occasionally they took a rather insolent advantage of their comparative strength. Ships might be relieved of some of their provisions or other items which attracted their visitors' attention. In May 1789, for instance, the Bristol brig *Pilgrim* with her crew of seven men was 'visited' by an Algerian corsair *polacca* with 20 guns and a crew of 300 men. The boarding party checked her 'passaporto' (i.e. Mediterranean pass) and bills of lading and then, 'having taken a quadrant and some other small things', left the brig free to continue her journey to Leghorn.[5]

There were many ways in which merchants could make money out of the ships they owned. The most obvious was simply to fill up the ship with cargo belonging to the owner or owners, and then carry it to its destination freight-free and sell it for a profit. This was always the situation on slave ships; the same men who owned the ship bought and owned the slaves until they were sold in the West Indies. This same pattern could be seen in several other trades, such as the coal, timber and whaling trades, but it was unusual in most of the non-slaving trades conducted by the Earle brothers.

Shipowners normally sent their ships to ports where they had agents who could facilitate the sale of the outward cargo, Newfoundland or Scottish fish perhaps in ships bound eventually to Leghorn or such typically English cargoes as salt, coal, lead and tin. These agents, in the Earles' case the firm of Earle, Hodgson & Drake, would then load cargo bought on behalf of their principals or else let out cargo space on freight to other shippers. The balance between shipping one's own goods and those belonging to other merchants required careful calculation since the merchant/shipowner had a split commercial personality. As a shipowner he sought the highest freights possible and if shortage of shipping pushed freights up he would be tempted to let the whole of his ship out to third parties. As a merchant, however, he hoped to buy and transport goods at the lowest possible price and so, as a very general rule, he or his agent was more likely to seek freights when other shipping was scarce and to fill his ship with his own cargo when it was plentiful. In the course

---

5 ASL, *Sanità* 698, p. 52, 20 May 1789. The range of journey times from British and Irish ports to the Straights was the same as from Newfoundland, from 34 to 70 days.

of the nineteenth century this dichotomy between the interests of the merchant and the shipowner began to vanish as shipowning became a specialist occupation in which the owners concentrated on maximising their revenue from freights and minimising their costs. But, in the 1790s, most ships were owned by merchants who had to address the problems mentioned above.

There were plenty of other problems. A shipowner might decide that the whole of his ship be chartered to other merchants on terms spelled out in a charter party which defined the route to be taken, the time to be spent in each port and the freight rate, this sometimes being calculated on a time basis, but usually at so much per ton or hogshead or some other measure of quantity. Sometimes rates were advertised in sailing notices published in the local papers, but usually cargo space was simply offered for freight and the rates were negotiated between the shipper and the captain or other agent acting for the owners of the ship. The skill of owners and their agents rested in finding potential shippers, negotiating beneficial freight rates, collecting these freights (not always easy) and deciding when enough was enough. Captains and owners obviously preferred their ships to be full when they sailed and space might well be filled up with the owners' own goods, but it was often more sensible to sail with space still available, even half-empty, rather than to hang about at great expense looking for shippers to take up the remaining tons of storage space.

All this made lots of calculations necessary, everything made more difficult by the need to get a balanced cargo, to load goods which had to be unloaded first near the top of the hold, to load heavy stuff like marble or sulphur near the bottom to act as ballast, and by the wartime necessity of waiting for a convoy from Italy to England. Three of the very few surviving letters written by Earle, Hodgson & Drake in the 1790s relate to a shipment to Charles Townley in London of a case of artistic objects forwarded to Leghorn by Thomas Jenkins in Rome.[6] This case had been loaded on the *Earl of Marchmont*, Captain James Hulme, which was just about to sail for London in February 1793 when letters arrived from Genoa reporting that the French had declared war on England. Earle, Hodgson & Drake would not ship the goods without convoy, even though the impatient Captain Hulme was threatening to 'be imprudent enough to go single [i.e. without convoy]'. If he did, they

6 See above pp. 152–53, 173–74 for descriptions of this important trade.

wrote to Townley, they would 'have your case unloaded and warehoused at your disposal.'[7]

Although the carriage of goods, either for themselves or for others, was the main business of shipowners, there were other activities which could earn them money. Ships often carried paying passengers as well as cargo and this passenger business was quite important, though not much is known about it. People wishing to travel to Italy, as many did (for their health, for culture or for business), had a choice. They could go overland by coach and then, if they did not fancy travelling across the Alps, take passage on a *felucca* from Marseilles, Genoa or elsewhere, normally to Leghorn. Or they could travel the whole way by sea, a much longer and sometimes very unpleasant journey if there was rough weather, but a lot cheaper and potentially quite entertaining if the ship was as well equipped as the *George*, which sailed to Lisbon in May 1797. She was advertised as having 'most excellent accommodation for passengers … and has on sale a constant supply of Port, Lisbon and Sherry wines, as also London porter in butts, barrels and bottles.'[8]

The Liverpool papers carried many sailing notices advertising the imminent departure of ships for Italy and these often mention the availability of accommodation for passengers, though unfortunately they never give fares, which were probably negotiated individually with the captain. Such advertisements were much commoner on routes on which travellers had no choice since they had to cross the sea. The busiest was the short passage to Dublin, the packet boats being advertised in 1787 as having 'elegant cabins and state rooms', rather less elegance being implied in the description of the brig *Fortune*, which had '18 bed places, with complete bedding.'[9] By the 1790s there was a considerable increase in transatlantic passenger business, with nearly every ship sailing for American ports offering accommodation, this nearly always being qualified by encouraging adjectives, such as good, excellent, superior, elegant or commodious. In wartime, most of these ships were owned by Americans, who exploited their neutrality to get a grip on transatlantic shipping which they were able to maintain in peacetime as a result of low costs and efficiency, and this dominance was not lost until the advent of steam.

7 BM TY 7/114–13, 8 February, 12 April, 2 August 1793.
8 *BLA*, 8 May 1797.
9 *WLA*, 26 November 1787; *BLA*, 28 December 1801.

American neutrality during the wars also allowed their shipping to play an increasingly important role in the Mediterranean carrying trade.[10] But there was one trade in which British merchants had a decided advantage, especially those based at Livorno. Much of the activity of the British Mediterranean fleet in the early years of the French Revolutionary War was spent in the siege of the French naval base at Toulon and the conquest of Corsica. Both activities benefited Livorno which, during the years 1793 to 1796, became an advanced base for the Royal Navy, 'and not less than 60 ships of the line and 20,000 sailors depended on the British Factory for supplies of all kinds.' 'This free port of Leghorn', wrote John Udny, the British Consul, to Lord Grenville, the Foreign Secretary, 'is the deposit, and general magazine and market for grain from Italy, Barbary (North Africa), the Levant and even the Black Sea … H.M. fleet may be supplied from here.'[11] This business was on a much bigger scale than in previous wars, though what share of it fell to Earle, Hodgson & Drake we do not know. It seems unlikely, however, that such a well-established firm did not benefit from this bonanza. They were certainly engaged in the grain trade from North Africa, as can be seen in the records of the *Sanità*. On 13 February 1792, for instance, the brig *La Maria* arrived at Livorno from Porto Farina [modern Ghar al Milh] in Tunisia after a voyage of 13 days. She was carrying grain for Earle, Hodgson & Drake.[12]

Wartime was also privateering time, though the scale was much smaller in the war of the 1790s than in the previous two. One good reason for this was that the French had far fewer merchant ships available for capture, as the British took over most of their West Indian colonies while the great sugar colony of Santo Domingo was seized by the slaves and free blacks after a truly dramatic slave rebellion. Nevertheless, Thomas and William Earle are recorded as taking out 14 letters of marque, 12 of them in the first year of the war.[13] Nearly all of these were simply armed merchant vessels, mainly slavers, and they seem to have fitted out just two true privateers. One of these, the

10 Keene, 1978; Galani, 2010, pp. 181–82.

11 Hayward, 1980, p. 265, n. 12, based on the records of the *Sanità* in ASL; FO 79/12, p. 161, 25 May 1795.

12 ASL, *Sanità* 699, p. 196. These records give tonnage, loading port, voyage time, crew size, cargo and consignees. See Galani, 2010.

13 HCA 26/81–86.

single-masted cutter *Hope*, Captain Thomas Hall, was armed with ten howitzers and 40 men. She was active in 1793, when she was involved in several recaptures either alone or in consort with other privateers and she also captured an American ship bound to France with a cargo of sugar, coffee, indigo and cotton and several French passengers. But, on 5 September, her career came to an end with her capture by two French luggers after a long fight in which several men were killed or wounded.[14]

Another *Harlequin*, 165 tons, had a slightly more illustrious career, though neither ship could rival the successes of Earle-owned privateers in the War of American Independence. She was captained by Jesse Topping, an American loyalist born in Virginia. In August 1796, she was employed as a slaver with a letter of marque and was captured on her way to Africa by a French privateer, *L'Aventure* of Bordeaux, after a long and very spirited fight which ended only after she had run out of ammunition and had to surrender – 'every shot was gone, every ounce of nails and copper dross finished, when the *Harlequin* struck to her opponent.' She did not spend long in French possession, however, being recaptured by the *Sugar-Cane* of London. She completed her slaving voyage and then, in the following year, was cruising as a privateer off the coast of Galicia, where she had two successes, both of them Spanish ships.

The first of these was the *Nuestra Señora de la Misericordia*, a 70-ton brig sailing from Vigo to Corunna and Bilbao with a cargo of ham, pilchards, herrings and 9,906 gallons of red and white wine. Her crew of seven men did not hang about when they saw the *Harlequin* approaching on 19 May 1797. They were near to Corunna and ran the brig close to shore, 'without leaving any person on board.' When Thomas Williams of Liverpool boarded the prize, he found 'her helm lashed, her sails set aback and the vessel put in the best possible position for her going on shore.' A prize crew took her to Waterford and then on to Liverpool. The *Harlequin*'s other Spanish prize was the *Nuestra Señora del Carmen*, also of Vigo, which was captured six days later off Cape Finisterre and was carrying even less; indeed, she was said to have no cargo at all. She was an 80-ton brig with ten guns and a crew of 70 men, most of them Spaniards but also including eight Frenchmen, a Sicilian and a Maltese, who surrendered after a running fight of an hour and a half. She was carrying a privateering commission and, in addition to her Spanish colours, 'had English, Portuguese and American colours on board for

14 Williams, 2004, pp. 317–18; letter of marque, 2 March 1793, in HCA 26/81.

deception.' François Maingett of Nantes, her second captain, deposed through an interpreter that 'at the time of the capture, they were on their cruizing ground in hopes of, and for the purpose of, seizing and taking any British ships or vessels they might fall in with.' But the *Harlequin*, like the *Hope*, was not to finish the war in English hands. In December 1798, on another slaving voyage, she was taken by a privateer of Bordeaux, *La Mouche*, on her passage to Africa.[15]

Livorno was very busy during the early years of the French Revolutionary War. One historian has estimated that the number of vessels calling at the Tuscan port more or less doubled between 1791/2 and 1794/5. This bonanza was not to last very long. The French revolutionary armies were on the rampage and the Army of Italy was commanded by a military genius called Napoleon Bonaparte, a young general of whom John Trevor, the British Resident at Turin, declared that 'if he was not a Jacobin, I should call him a fine fellow for his enterprize and abilities.'[16] Nearly all northern Italy fell quickly before the French and nobody believed they would respect Tuscan neutrality for very long. Within Tuscany, the main French interest was Livorno, currently being used as a British naval base, full of warehouses bursting at the seams with British goods, and virtually undefended by land. 'A desire for plunder' drew Napoleon's army southwards and the British in Livorno prepared for its arrival.

There was just one British warship in the Tuscan port as the French approached, the *Inconstant*, commanded by one of Nelson's 'band of brothers', Captain Thomas Fremantle. He was to do a very good job. In conjunction with the British Consul, John Udny, he organised the evacuation of the whole British Factory, all the contents of all their warehouses bar one and anything else British which could be seized. First of all, everything and everyone was loaded on the merchant ships in the harbour, ready to sail at once if it seemed the French were definitely coming to occupy the town. By 25 June 1796, it was quite clear that this was going to happen and Udny and Fremantle spent two days and nights of 'extraordinary exertions' supervising the loading of every ship in the harbour. The excitement of these exertions was described in her diary by Betsy Wynne, the 18-year-old daughter of an English family who had been drifting round Germany, Switzerland and Italy for several

---

15 HCA 32/769/94 (*Misericordia*) and 32/769/93 (*Carmen*).
16 Galani, 2010, p. 185; BL Add. 34904, 23 May 1796, Trevor to Nelson.

years. Betsy was having a very good time in Florence in June 1796 and
had no wish to leave, but her father was desperate to escape the French.
'We arrived to Leghorn [from Florence] at eleven in the morning', she
wrote, 'we went to Mr Udney's and found there a most terrible bustle
and noise – All packing up and getting on board the ships. We hardly
had time to get a little breakfast, they hurried us so terribly to quit
the place.'[17] By daybreak on 27 June, everything was ready and Captain
Fremantle was able to supervise the departure of '20 sail of square rigged
vessels and 14 tartans', remaining behind himself in the *Inconstant* to
provide a rearguard if necessary. A few hours later, a little after noon,
the French marched into the town. They were just a little too late.
'All the shipping, nearly the whole of the English property, and all his
Majesty's naval stores and provisions have been saved', Fremantle wrote
in his report to Admiral Sir John Jervis, 'and every English person and
emigré desirous of leaving Tuscany have [*sic*] been received on board
some of the ships.'[18]

Captain Fremantle was much praised for his conduct, but this paled
before the impression made on him by young Betsy Wynne and *vice
versa*, Captain Fremantle featuring in her diary as 'that kind best of
men'. He must have been incredibly busy, but the demands of war did
not stop him organising dinners, music on Mr Udny's harpsichord and
other amusements for Betsy, culminating in 'a famous Ball' aboard the
Inconstant. 'The deck was most elegantly drest up and looked really like
a charming large Ball room … We had a lively, gay dance' which lasted
until two in the morning. It seems to have been love at first sight and
the couple were married just six months later at Lady Emma Hamilton's
house in Naples. The Royal Navy fought their wars with style and
gaiety, especially in the Mediterranean, as was seen above in regard to
Captain Augustus Hervey, that 'naval Casanova' who provided Leghorn
with so much entertainment in the middle years of the century. Not
surprisingly, Betsy Wynne had nothing but praise for naval officers. 'All
these gentlemen are equally complaisant and good natured', she wrote,
'they live like brothers together and give all they have.'[19]

17 Fremantle, 1937, p. 97.
18 FO 79/14 pp. 220–21, Fremantle to Jervis, 30 June 1796.
19 Fremantle, 1937, pp. 99–102. For biographical information on Fremantle and a
    good description of the evacuation of Leghorn see Kennedy, 1951; on Hervey
    see above p. 117.

The fleeing British Factory went first to Elba and Corsica and then scattered further afield, to Naples, Sicily and Malta, while some made their way back home. Earle, Hodgson & Drake had three loyal Italian clerks who could be trusted to pay bills, collect debts and do whatever other business was necessary while their principals probably went back to Liverpool. Meanwhile, Admiral Jervis ordered Captain Nelson to blockade the port of Leghorn, so that the French would have no benefit from their occupation of the city. On 15 July 1796, Nelson reported that 'the blockade of Leghorn is as complete as is possible' and, judging by the complaints of neutrals unable to sail into the harbour, this was pretty complete. Napoleon stayed with the occupying troops for some time, so it is perhaps worth noting that this must have been the closest that those two great men of war, Horatio Nelson and Napoleon Bonaparte, ever came to meeting, one looking out from and the other looking into the Tuscan port of Livorno.[20]

This first French occupation of Leghorn lasted from June 1796 to May 1797. Some merchants of the Factory then returned to take up their business again, but not Earle, Hodgson & Drake, very sensibly since the British were driven out of the port twice more before October 1801, when the Peace of Amiens brought about a somewhat nervous end to the war. The promise of peace encouraged the Liverpool firm to re-establish its Italian house and a new co-partnership agreement was drawn up for seven years from 6 November 1801. The firm was to have a capital of 50,000 Leghorn dollars (i.e. *pesos*; worth about £12,500) and was to engage 'in the commission business and in the purchasing of goods and bills at Leghorn under the firm of Earle & Co.' There were 96 shares, of which Thomas and William Earle had 29 each, their shipowning partner Thomas Leathom had eight, and a new man, John Lewis Cailler, a merchant from Manchester, had 30. Cailler was to sail to Leghorn and personally manage the business. The brothers do not seem to have got on very well with their cousin Willis, so he was passed over for the new firm and left to concentrate on his coal and timber business.[21]

This new Leghorn partnership is much better documented than the one before the French occupation, as there is a surviving letter

20 On the clerks see D/EARLE/3/4. For Nelson see BL Add. 34904, Nelson Papers, vol. iii, p. 188 (3 July 1796) and p. 238 (15 July 1796).
21 For the various French occupations see Hayward, 1980, p. 265; Galani, 2010, p. 188; d'Angelo, 2001; for the partnership see MMM D/EARLE/4.

book which covers the remaining years of Earle involvement in Italy. This document comprises 227 double pages, with copies of 500 or more letters, nearly all written by or for one or other, or both, of the brothers in Liverpool to Messrs Earle & Co, Leghorn, though some of the earlier letters are written by Cailler before his departure by sea, in company with his sister and her maid, to take up his duties at Leghorn. Their voyage in the *Astraea* seems to have been a terrible one, as we learn obliquely from a letter congratulating Cailler on his safe arrival at Genoa: 'We are much concerned for the sufferings undergone, especially by the females, upon the passage. The gale must have been dreadful ... and it must indeed have been a most shocking business to your sister and her faithful attendant.' Such discomfort and danger endured by a partner and his sister aroused the compassion of the wives of both brothers: 'Mrs W. Earle will be very happy to receive the interesting narrative from Miss Cailler's own hand. She and Mrs. T. Earle unite with us in congratulations on your safety.'[22]

The new partnership had no English staff at its inception and had to rely on the loyal Italian clerks. This situation was soon rectified. Long before Cailler and his sister arrived, the former partner Robert Hodgson made his way south to get the business going, his journey marked by a series of letters from Paris, Lyons, Marseilles and Genoa. He was much loved in Leghorn and the Earle brothers in Liverpool recorded their joy at receiving a letter from him giving 'the pathetic account ... of the meeting between him and our much valued and old friend Sr Giuseppe Fantichi [the chief clerk].' He was soon to get some much-needed help. Two apprentices were indentured: a Mr Wilson, who travelled overland via Turin to Leghorn, where he arrived in March 'in high health and spirits', and J.J. Hirtzell, son of a merchant and old friend from Exeter 'who has determined on a voyage to Italy and to place himself under your care for some years'. Once Cailler and the two apprentices had settled in, Hodgson returned to Liverpool to enjoy his retirement.[23]

Many of the letters in the letter book are very short, just a few lines to notify the Italian house of some relevant piece of information or serving as a letter of introduction with a request to make the traveller's stay in Leghorn 'agreeable and as comfortable as possible.' Interspersed with these polite notes are great screeds, sometimes five, six pages or more, packed with instructions, advice, news, price lists and gloomy

22 Livorno letter book, D/EARLE/2/3, p. 37, 13 June 1802.
23 D/EARLE/2/3, 5 and 17 February 1802, 10 April 1802.

speculation on the diplomatic scene. The Earle brothers were never really assured that the peace would last for long and, although they were able to forget this from time to time, a spirit of pessimism runs through the letters and affected their commercial behaviour. Gloomy or not, the letters themselves suggest a much busier and more proactive trading environment than had existed in the days of Thomas Earle senior, when Leghorn was described by a visitor as a place where 'the forenoons are appropriated to business, the afternoons totally to pleasure'.[24]

The brothers were keen to drum up new business, while former customers and correspondents had to be wooed back after the Earles' five-year absence from Leghorn during the various French occupations. A circular detailing their business, no longer extant, was prepared and sent to potential customers all over the British Isles and also to France, once again a trading partner after many years of warfare, the United States, Hamburg, Amsterdam and Trieste, the gateway of Austria and other parts of central Europe to the Mediterranean. It was also thought a good idea to gain a few northern correspondents, so 'we shall ... make your name familiar in the Baltic.'[25] If any of these merchants should show a real interest, it was necessary to make discreet inquiries into their credit standing. Messrs John Shuback & Sons of Hamburg, for instance, were strongly recommended by a London house, 'as of the first rank and renowned for a scrupulous punctuality', while the American Mr Nimmo, owner of several ships, was certainly an honest man, but 'what his fortune is we are not yet exactly informed'. The Earles were also not quite sure about Monsieur Jean Guichard, formerly of Lorient but now of Paris, who had applied for credit of £3–4,000. It was necessary to make inquiries, 'as we do not know how he may have fared during the Revolution, though we know him to have been wealthy before that period.' They were informed by 'a very particular friend from Paris ... that Mr Guichard is very rich but is speculating.' Still some doubt there then, but none about Mr J.G. Turner of Liverpool about whom the Earles were asked by a London firm for an opinion: 'We advised them to have nothing to do with him. We look upon him (entre nous) as an adventurer.'[26] How easily a reputation could be destroyed in those days of personal credit.

24   MMM D/EARLE/8/3.
25   D/EARLE/2/3, 9 April 1803.
26   D/EARLE/2/3, 28 July and 27 November 1802.

Circulars may have brought in some business, but a personal visit was more likely to be effective. In Chapter Five, it was seen that in the early 1760s William Earle Sr occasionally went on business trips to London, Birmingham, the West Riding and other potential sources of orders. But this activity was completely eclipsed by Thomas and William Earle Jr, John Lewis Cailler and Thomas Leathom in the early nineteenth century. They all went on fairly frequent visits to London while Cailler, as a Manchester man, went quite regularly to his home town before his departure for Leghorn, when Thomas replaced him as the firm's Manchester man. Leathom too was to travel to Manchester and Birmingham. Elsewhere, the main areas visited were the West Riding of Yorkshire and the West Country, these journeys being described as 'tours' and written up after the event in 'minutes' for despatch among the partners and to Leghorn. The woollen cloth industry was an important market for olive oil imported from Leghorn, this replacing the natural grease washed out of the wool in the cleaning process. This was a big business: one clothier from Leeds planned to order 100 tons of oil in each shipment from Leghorn, but this was largely taken for granted and the main interest in these letters was to try and develop the market for Italian wool in Yorkshire and other centres of the woollen textile industry. The partners and employees in Italy were urged 'to obtain knowledge of the best mode of collecting wool in the several states of Italy' and also to send 'parcels' (samples) since informed opinion suggested that 'wool of all kinds will sell in England ... and wool will become a perfect article of commerce.'[27]

Tours to the West Country were also likely to include visits to clothiers, but they often started in Chester, where business could be conducted after enjoying breakfast with Mr Hodgson's sister, who lived there. The actual business was mainly done with the skinners and glove makers, who were encouraged to increase their purchases of Tuscan kid and lamb skins, some orders being substantial such as the 20,000 skins ordered by Rogers of Chester. Bristol would normally be included in the tour and here the visits were mainly to exporters of iron, lead and tinplate, all in demand in Italy, and also to shipowners who might be encouraged to direct their exports to Earle & Co. in Leghorn. However, the main focus of these West Country tours was the Newfoundland fish business which was organised and financed by merchants in a mass of

27 D/EARLE/2/3, 27 December 1801.

small ports in Dorset, Cornwall and Devonshire. Newfoundland cod was the most important 'English' export to Italy and the more of it sent to Leghorn and consigned to Earle & Co. the better, for then they would not only earn their commissions for selling the fish but also for putting together a suitable return cargo for England.

The letters, being written from England, have more to say about potential exports to Italy than imports, but the latter were also considered and the team in Leghorn was encouraged to seek out information and suppliers. Shippers were always keen to discover new bulk cargoes which could be used as ballast and one suggestion was salt from Trapani in Sicily or Cagliari in Sardinia. Salt was also a major export from Liverpool but there was no harm in sending it both ways, so the Livorno house was asked to send some current prices. They were also asked for information on the Sicilian brimstone (sulphur) business. 'We hear very contradictory accounts about the time of year when brimstone is to be had in Sicily, some say in February and others not till September', something one might expect a family who had been importing Sicilian brimstone for 40 years would already have known.[28]

One useful product which had been imported by the Earles before the French occupation and hopefully could be imported again was *pozzolana*, a volcanic ash whose name derives from Pozzuoli near Naples, though it could be obtained elsewhere in the Kingdom of Naples and the Papal States. This product was much in demand in the preparation of hydraulic cement. In the past, the Earles wrote to their representatives in Leghorn, it had been possible to get an exclusive privilege to export this material from the Papal States, 'by a proper tip to the prelato or cardinale who had the superintendence of this department of the public business.' Earle & Co. in Italy were instructed 'to discover how the Roman government now feels upon the subject', a task which might best have been undertaken by Joseph Denham, who, despite his girth and his age, was still in business in Civitavecchia.[29]

The main business of Earle & Co. was, according to the partnership agreement, 'to engage in the commission business and in the purchasing of goods and bills at Leghorn', an emphasis which is repeated in a letter of January 1803 regarding an application from Messrs John Lubbock &

28 D/EARLE/2/3, 20 March 1803.
29 D/EARLE/2/3, 9 February 1803; for some glimpses of Denham in the 1790s see FO 79/10; FO 95/5/6.

Co. to open up a correspondence with the Leghorn house. 'We replied that you chiefly devoted your attention to commission business.'[30] This policy was generally followed, most of the business of Earle & Co. being to sell cargoes coming into Leghorn on behalf of other merchants, fish for instance, and to arrange for the purchase of a suitable return cargo, earning commission in both cases. This was a low-risk policy since, once a deal had been contracted, the returns in the form of commissions were certain and not dependent on profits. The policy may have had a particular attraction during these uneasy days of the Treaty of Amiens, since the Earle brothers in Liverpool were reluctant to have capital tied up in goods in transit or sitting in warehouses in Italy, lest another French invasion make them vulnerable to seizure.

The capital of 50,000 Leghorn dollars mentioned in the firm's partnership agreement was instead invested mainly in bills. Some of these were the bills of travellers who needed cash to enjoy their visit to Italy, like Dr Cappie of York and his sisters, who were travelling 'with a view to winter in Pisa'. The Leghorn house was told to supply them with £150–200 should they need it, a service often offered. Earle & Co. were instructed to treat such visitors with courtesy, to pay them 'some attention' or 'shew them those civilities which will make their stay at Leghorn agreeable.'[31] Entertainment of prospective customers was an important aspect of business in Georgian times, just as it is today, and in this case the 'attention' could be enhanced by use of the firm's house in the Tuscan countryside and a box at the Leghorn theatre.

The firm was also encouraged to offer advances to merchants planning to export goods to or from Leghorn, this money up front often being sufficient to clinch an arrangement that the cargo be consigned 'to your address' and not to someone else's. Either T. & W. Earle in Liverpool or Earle & Co. in Leghorn would give the merchant an advance on the security of his cargo and receive a bill payable in so many weeks or months in return, this credit being supported if necessary by bills on Liverpool or London. These advances were often substantial, such as the £2,000 advance on the cargo of the American ship *Atalanta* sailing from Bristol to Leghorn, the debt to be secured by an insurance policy, or the two-thirds lent on a cargo of Manchester goods valued at £4,500. Since such advances were often paid in sterling and repaid

30 D/EARLE/4; D/EARLE/2/3, 29 January 1803.
31 D/EARLE/2/3, 13 October 1802.

in Leghorn dollars or *vice versa*, there was an element of speculation on movements of the exchange rate in the transaction, but overall it was likely to be a profitable business, provided of course that some research had been done into the debtor's credit standing.

By December 1801, when their Leghorn business started up again after its five-year break, Thomas and William Earle no longer owned any ships suitable for a Mediterranean voyage. The quick answer to this shortage of shipping was to charter, something they do not seem to have done before. Chartering could be arranged very quickly, so that right at the beginning of the letter book we find that two brigs, the *Mercury*, Captain John Mortimer, and the *Testimony*, Captain William Blackaller, have been chartered for Genoa and Leghorn, and Naples and Leghorn, respectively. On 8 December 1801, letters were sent to Leghorn conveying this information: 'We recommend him [i.e. Mortimer] to your good offices and request that you will give him every dispatch in discharging his cargo, not doubting you will have it in your power to procure him a good return freight.' The two ships sailed together on 22 December and were loaded with cargoes typical of those sent from Liverpool to the Mediterranean – coal, lead and lead ore, iron hoops, sugar, coffee, ginger, rum, tobacco and 22 barrels of bottled porter.[32]

Thomas and William's plan was to get 'a continuance of regularity and punctuality' by sending ships out to Leghorn in sequence in the hope 'that we may ere long secure a decided preference for the House in the trade'. So, these first two chartered vessels were followed by two more in May 1802, by another two in October and November, and finally by the *Shakespeare*, which sailed for the Mediterranean on 4 January 1803, 'quite full'. This ship belonged 'to our friends Messrs John & R. Gladstone', who were mainly Baltic merchants, and Earle & Co. were instructed to procure her a freight, preferably fruit from Italy and Sicily to St Petersburg. 'They would prefer that voyage to any other.'[33]

In addition to these chartered vessels, the Earles were busy buying ships for their own fleet. In a letter of 14 April 1802, they reported that they had 'purchased a very good vessel called the *Somerset* which we have laid on for Genoa and Leghorn to sail the middle of May'. The purchase of three other vessels was recorded in the letters: the *Britannia*, which sailed for Naples and the Fairs of Salerno in July 1802; the *Minerva*,

32 D/EARLE/2/3, 16 and 22 December 1801.
33 D/EARLE/2/3, 5 June 1803. John Gladstone was the statesman's father.

which sailed for Naples a few weeks later; and the *Pomona*, bought in December 1802 for a voyage to the Fairs of Aversa in company with the *Somerset* if she returned from her previous voyage in time. Aversa was inland from Naples and the Fairs held in April were attended by buyers from all over Italy and were a major market for Manchester cotton goods amongst other things.

In addition to handling the cargoes of ships chartered or bought by their partners in Liverpool, Earle & Co. in Leghorn were also busy disposing of cargoes carried by ships in which the Earles had no interest. In the early weeks of the new partnership, one can see the immediate benefit of touring the West Country and gaining the confidence of some of the local shipowners. On 15 December 1801, for instance, the brig *Jason* of Teignmouth sailed from Dartmouth 'with a cargo of codfish to your address' and on 5 January 1802 the American ship *Atalanta* sailed from Bristol for the same destination. The Leghorn firm was instructed in both cases to dispose of the cargoes to best advantage 'and procure a vessel on good freight for England'. Two other potential customers were being approached at approximately the same date: Mr John Newell of Bristol, who 'may probably send you a vessel of 100 tons if we can assure him of a return freight', and Mr Thomas Crokal, 'who goes out supercargo of the brig *Lochnell* bound to your port ... and shall be glad if he avails himself of your services for the disposal of the goods in his care.' Supercargoes were travelling merchants who handled the business side of a voyage, but they never seem to have been employed on ships in Earle ownership, where their role was undertaken by the captain in addition to his other duties, an obvious saving.[34]

The chartering of seven ships and the purchase of another four in the first year of the new partnership, together with a stream of vessels belonging to other merchants being sent 'to your address' would seem to imply that Earle & Co. were enjoying a boom and would continue to do so into the foreseeable future. But this would be a misleading assumption. The Peace of Amiens was signed in October 1801 and ratified in March 1802, but neither the British nor the French were satisfied that they had got what they wanted from the eight years of warfare and both sides regarded the Peace as no more than a useful breathing space.

Such uncertainty was hardly conducive to developing the Leghorn trade and the letters in the letter book reflect regular mood swings.

34 D/EARLE2/3, 13 December 1801.

Now, the letters are buoyant and the development of trade with New York or southern Italy or wherever is emphasised; and then a mood of pessimism takes over. On 27 December 1801, the brothers in Liverpool wrote that they 'do not like the complexion of the public prints [i.e. newspapers] written these four days ... caution is needed', but in the same letter they develop a scheme to corner the Italian wool market. On 20 February 1802, they are not easy at the delay in the ratification of the Treaty, 'nor with the disposition manifested by the French Consul [i.e. Napoleon] to make himself master of the greater part of Italy.' Earle & Co. in Leghorn are advised 'to sell, convert into cash and remit' everything possible. But, on 31 March, the Leghorn house is urged to 'rejoice ... in the final conclusion of the definitive Treaty of Peace.'

There followed a few months of optimism but, by 13 October 1802, gloom had set in again and a letter was despatched saying that 'we do not at all like the aspect of public affairs', though this did not stop the brothers in Liverpool demanding that enquiries be made as to 'what goods are likely to be shipped to the Fairs, particularly Aversa.' A week later, on 20 October, a 'private' letter was sent for the eyes of Mr Cailler only, enclosing 'our serious thoughts upon the present threatening aspect of public affairs.' Another private letter was sent off on 3 November as the Liverpool Earles were now sure that war was coming. The Leghorn house was ordered to 'sell, realize and remit' and to note that 'outstanding debts *may* be as much exposed to seizure and confiscation as goods in your warehouses.' But, in the next two letters they seem to have forgotten these fears. The focus is instead on a 'supply of eatables' and some dining tables sent out on the *Margaret*, the price of lead, the Newfoundland fish market and the possibility of shipping carriage guns to the Adriatic. 'Can you give us encouragement to send any and, if so, what caliber? The larger the cheaper they are with us.'[35]

The new year was, however, to see the return of gloom. Public affairs were very alarming by 13 March 1803, insurance rates to the Mediterranean had risen to 12 % and the Leghorn house was urged to send any rum or lead to Malta or Naples for the potential military and naval demand. The mixture of business as usual and near panic continues until the beginning of May, when William Earle was sufficiently alarmed to make his way to London, where he could hope to get the latest news at its sources, from Lloyds, the House of Commons and friends

35 All taken from the letter book D/EARLE/2/3 on the dates quoted.

in the know. 'I reached this place yesterday', he wrote to Cailler on 3 May from London. 'I wish it were in my power to afford you any consolatory advices upon public affairs. They look worse and worse every day [this last word crossed out and replaced with 'hour']. The crisis is fast approaching.' The letter ends with kind remembrances to Cailler's sister and the apprentices, and is signed 'Adieu, William Earle'. This may seem a bit melodramatic, but it was to some extent justified. Just two weeks later, the government announced that letters of marque against France would once again be issued and the peace was over, just 14 months after its ratification in March 1802. By the end of May, the French were once again at the gates of Leghorn and their newspapers declared that the Tuscan port was in a state of siege.[36]

Thomas and William Earle could console themselves with the knowledge that the Leghorn house had obeyed their order to minimise stocks in their warehouses. And the brothers had also inherited their father's firm belief in insurance. 'I have the satisfaction to add that all the property has been insured at premiums moderate enough, considering the alarms which subsisted at the time we did them.' Meanwhile, Cailler and his colleagues in Leghorn continued to sell off their remaining stocks, so that on 29 June he was congratulated on 'clearing your hands of every thing you had on sale.' By this date, the Earles could report that, apart from the *Pomona*, 'we have not a single ship of any description afloat at sea and until we hear from you ... we shall not think of business to the Mediterranean.' The *Pomona* was to trade in Venice, Sicily and Malta and only finally returned to Liverpool on 4 May 1804, 'after escaping many dangers from the enemy.'

By 11 September 1803, William Earle could refer to 'the late firm of Earle & Co.' in a letter to Cailler and, although there are letters to Cailler right up till January 1808, the Earle venture in Italy could be said to be over after half a century of successful trading. But such disappointments would deter neither the Earles nor the rest of the Liverpool trading community. If they could not engage in the slave trade nor in trade with Leghorn, they would have to look elsewhere – perhaps Malta, which was now a British possession, or further afield, such as South America, which was all the rage after the news reached London in September 1806 that Buenos Ayres had been captured by a British force. 'The object which now interests the mercantile world more

36 D/EARLE/2/3, 13 March, 17 May, 29 June 1803.

than any other', wrote William Earle to Cailler on 27 September 1806, 'is the opening of trade to Buenos Ayres, a vast number of ships are said to be in preparation in London ... and about 12 or 14 from hence, nearly the same from Bristol ... The young men here are all applying to the study of Spanish.'[37]

37 D/EARLE/2/3, 27 September and 7 October 1806.

CHAPTER TWELVE

New Horizons

> 'As Commerce is what renders every Country
> rich and consequently powerful; so the Merchant
> may be said to be the most useful Member of the
> Society in which he lives.'[1]

As the eighteenth century drew to a close, an advertisement appeared in the *Liverpool Advertiser* announcing the auction of 'that commodious and convenient house, with the stables, coach-house and warehouse behind it, situated on the south side of Hanover Street, now in the possession of William Earle Esq.' And, a week later, another notice announced the forthcoming sale of property in the same street belonging to his brother, Thomas: 'a dwelling-house, counting house, warehouse and stables for five horses and a double coach-house.' Also up for sale was a small adjoining dwelling house 'very suitable for the residence of a principal clerk.'[2]

Thomas was now 45 years old and William 39; both brothers were rich after two decades of successful trading and they were ready for the next stage in the progress of an achieving merchant, to acquire some of the trappings of a gentleman. One important feature of this was to purchase a country property and, for merchants of Liverpool, the most favoured places to do this were Toxteth and Wavertree to the south and south-east and Everton to the north, all very urban now but then still in the country, though not far from the hustle and bustle of the great port. Everton was the most frequented by rich merchants and was home to eight of the 20 leading slave merchants in 1800. 'The village of Everton', wrote John Aiken in 1795,

> commands an extensive prospect of the mouth of the river ... as well

1 Postlethwayt, 1757, p. 21.
2 *BLA*, 9 July 1798, 4 and 11 March 1799.

as of the opposite coast of Chester, and the northern part of Wales. This village has of late years become a very favourite residence, and several excellent houses are built along the western declivity of the hill.³

The Earle brothers had been happy to live next door to each other in Hanover Street, but they decided to place the whole town between their country residences. Thomas purchased 88 acres of farming land in Toxteth in 1798 and on it built a large stone house called Spekelands. The house has long been demolished but his grandson, another Thomas, described it in a letter written some 50 years after the house was built: 'quite in the country with tilth [cultivated land] on both sides and it had a very pretty lawn and flower gardens.' Gardening, a genteel pursuit, was a hobby of both Thomas and his wife. The house 'was of white stone and handsomely fitted up inside with a marble pavement to the hall and mahogany doors to the principal rooms'. It was a substantial property, which was valued at £12,000 in 1826.⁴

Thomas died in 1822 and his will gives some idea of the contents of this property: 'To my dear wife Mary Earle, all my household goods and furniture, plate, pictures, prints, glasses, china, linen, printed books and wearing apparel and also all my wine and liquors ... and all my carriages, carts, horses, cows, farming stock and implements of every description.'⁵ One learns more about the man from the unusually detailed obituary published on 16 July 1822. Thomas was described as 'the head of one of the oldest and most respectable mercantile houses in this town,' but his virtues went far beyond the success of the business he and his brother had built up. Like that other Thomas Earle, his uncle and father-in-law, he was famous for his hospitality to 'enlightened foreigners and strangers, to whom his house was at all times open.' And, in social life, 'Mr Earle was cheerful, courteous and hospitable; in manners polished; and, in conversation, engaging, possessing a mode of expressing himself peculiarly agreeable and not infrequently heightened by playfulness or pleasantry.'⁶

3 Aiken, 1795, p. 359; Pope, 2007, pp. 170–71.
4 D/EARLE/7/257, letter to Hardman Earle, 18 October 1855; Thomas, 1980, p. 29.
5 TNA, PROB 11/1663/73, will of Thomas Earle of Spekelands, 2 November 1822.
6 *BLA*, 16 July 1822.

Figure 11. Everton, 1817, showing the houses of successful merchants

His widow Mary continued to live in the house until her death in 1849, but before then there were major changes, as can be seen in the letter written by Thomas's grandson: 'The first thing, perhaps, which struck a blow to the exclusively rural character of the place was the formation of the Liverpool and Manchester Railway which passed through one portion of the fields belonging to the estate.' This was England's first proper passenger railway, with iron rails and a steam locomotive, and it opened in 1830, eight years after Thomas's death. One imagines that, if he had lived, he would have had mixed feelings about this development. As a Whig and an innovative merchant, he believed in progress, but as a country gentleman he might have preferred a little more peace and quiet. His widow and their son Hardman were at first opposed to the proposed railway, but this may have been a tactical move to maximise compensation, as Hardman later became one of the most active directors of the railway.[7]

Meanwhile, William Earle bought a house, or rather a villa, on the Netherfield Road at Everton. William died in Rome in January 1839, 'in his eightieth year', and his English possessions were speedily sold off by his executors. On 12 March 1839, the property was described by Messrs T. Winstanley, auctioneers, as a 'spacious dwelling-house, with pleasure gardens, hot houses, ample coachhouses, stables and outbuildings, to be let with immediate possession.' And, on 18 and 19 March, they auctioned 'the whole of the genuine household furniture, table services of china, glass, library bookcase, and other effects of the late William Earle Esq.' These effects included rich hangings and carpets, fine china and glass, mahogany dining-room furniture, display cabinets 'with marble tops and plates of glass over, 60 x 30 inches' and a London-built pony phaeton, painted green.[8]

Of greatest interest to those who attended the auctions may well have been 'the choice wines' sold on 19 March and the collection of pictures auctioned on 17 and 18 April at the Exhibition Rooms in Post Office Place, Liverpool. William was the grandson of John Earle, a man referred to by contemporaries as a 'wine merchant'.[9] But it seems unlikely that John ever had for sale as much wine as William had 'in the cellars

7 Thomas, 1980, p. 106. Large-scale maps of the railway show it surrounded by fields marked 'Mrs Earle'.
8 *Liverpool Times*, 12 March 1839.
9 See above, pp. 11–12.

of his late residence at Everton ... for his own use.' There were nearly 3,000 bottles, much of it fortified wine such as the 40 dozen of 'very choice port' and the 50 dozen of Madeira, but also including 18 dozen choice claret and many famous wines from further south, such as the '30 dozen Calcavella of a superior quality', a sweet wine from Portugal, or the 30 dozen bottles in quarts and pints of Falernian, a strong wine from the Bay of Naples which had been much admired and enjoyed since Roman times. And if Falernian with an alcoholic content of 15 or 16 per cent was not potent enough, there were also 20 dozen bottles of fine old rum and brandy.[10]

David Hancock, in his book *Citizens of the World*, notes that collecting art, like building houses, 'reflected, enhanced, and reinforced' the emerging gentility of successful merchants.[11] William Earle certainly did his best in this respect. Thomas had pictures and prints to leave to his dear wife Mary, but his brother William was a certainly genuine collector, the owner of an 'extensive and valuable collection of paintings by the most admired masters ... selected with much taste and judgment during a period of nearly 40 years in Italy and this country.' The sales catalogue listed 122 paintings by nearly 80 different artists, mainly Italian, Dutch and Flemish, but also some by Englishmen, mostly of Italian subjects, such as the 'two scenes in Italy' by Richard Wilson of Liverpool (1713–82), a pioneer of landscape painting in Britain. There was also a pair of paintings, 'The Bandit Chief' and 'The Bandit's Wife' by Charles Lock Eastlake (1793–1865), who became the first Director of the National Gallery in 1855. These two small paintings, each 14 inches by 18, were described as 'painted for Mr Earle', who was one of the artist's patrons.[12]

William Earle's collection also included pictures by far more famous painters than these, such as Rembrandt, who was represented by 'the head of a Dutch Admiral.' This was described as 'a genuine and powerful specimen' of the Dutch master's work, though it is of course impossible to say at this remove how accurate or genuine these attributions were. An certainly genuine and more powerful example of Rembrandt's work once owned by William, but not sold at the

10 *Liverpool Times*, 19 March and 16 April 1839.
11 Hancock, 1995, p. 347.
12 Earle, 1839 for the catalogue; about half the paintings are also listed in the *Liverpool Times*, 26 March 1839.

postmortem sale, was 'Portrait of a Man with Arms Akimbo', signed and dated 'Rembrandt, 1658'. This was bought by William in 1806 for £39 16s at the sale of the Liverpool banker William Clarke, a fellow resident in Everton. Two centuries later, in 2009, it was sold in London for just over £20 million, a record price for a Rembrandt. So, it seems fair to say that William's art collection was very impressive for a provincial merchant.[13]

A fortnight after the sale, the *Liverpool Times* printed 'the prices realised by the principal pictures', the highest being 250 guineas for 'St. John Baptising Christ' by Paris Bordone (1500–71) and £100 and 155 guineas respectively for 'a fine romantic landscape' and 'a landscape with ruins' by Salvator Rosa. Prices are listed for 22 paintings altogether, including 'Christ with the Doctors' by the Genoese painter Gioacchino Assereto (1600–49), which was purchased for £110 by a Mrs Jones 'as a present for a permanent Gallery of Art in Liverpool.' This painting, now described as a copy of the original Assereto, was indeed presented in 1843 by Mrs Benjamin Heywood Jones to the Liverpool Royal Institution, a precursor of the Walker Art Gallery, which opened in 1877 and now houses Mrs Jones's gift and five other paintings from William's collection.[14]

The neo-classical sculptor John Gibson (1790–1866) was another famous artistic associate and friend of the Earles, 'to whom he owed something in his early life', this being patronage and some financial support, which William shared with Roscoe and other Liverpool worthies. Gibson was born in Wales, but trained in Liverpool before moving to Rome in 1817 to study under Canova. One of his early successes was a monument to the memory of Anne, wife of William Earle. 'I have just finished one in marble to go to Liverpool', he wrote of this work in a letter to a friend in England. 'For this monument, Canova has given me great praise.' Gibson also produced bas-reliefs in memory of both Earle brothers, 'Justice Protecting Innocence' in memory of Thomas and 'William Earle, Esq., seated, reading the Bible.'[15]

13 For the Rembrandt and other information on William's art collection, many thanks to Xanthe Brooke of the Walker Art Gallery; Syers, 1830, p. 255.

14 For the prices paid at the auction see *Liverpool Times*, 23 April 1839. Many thanks to Xanthe Brooke for information on the paintings formerly owned by William Earle which are now in the Walker Art Gallery.

15 Earle, 1890, p. 49; Eastlake, 1870, p. 254; Sharples, 2004, p. 243. For the bas-relief of William see Figure 12 opposite.

Figure 12. William Earle the Younger (1760-1839), marble bas-relief
by John Gibson, showing him lost in thought reading a book

William Earle was described in legal documents as 'merchant of
Liverpool' but, by the early nineteenth century, he was also very much
a part of the Anglo-Italian art world, the world of the Grand Tour. This
is well illustrated by three letters in the Roscoe papers written in 1822
and 1823. In October 1822, William Roscoe wrote to his friend, Mr
Mathias in Naples, to tell him that he was sending him a book which
would be brought from Liverpool 'by my particular and highly respected
friend and townsman Mr William Earle who is leaving England with his
son [Charles] with a view of passing the winter in Italy.' In September
1823, Mathias wrote from Naples to thank Roscoe for the book and for

'the additional pleasure of the acquaintance of Mr William Earle and his family.' Mathias complained of the terrible summer heat of Naples, like a furnace, and remarked that the wise Earles had spent the summer 'in a beautiful country across the Bay, called Castellammare which is cooler than this city, and is pleasant on many accounts.' The final letter, written to Roscoe on 23 November 1823 by William Earle himself in a neat and attractive hand, refers to his journey south via Milan, Florence and Rome and the many learned and interesting acquaintances he made, a journey much embellished by his friendship with Roscoe. 'I must mention to you how much your name has done for me here.' This is not the letter of a Liverpool merchant, but of a connoisseur and man of the world who was very much at home in Italy.[16]

Country houses and picture collections are two good indications of the gentrification process upon which the brothers embarked from the 1790s. There were several others. In England, then as now, social aspirations might well be signalled by a merchant's choice of school, university and profession for his children. Thomas, who had been educated at Manchester Grammar School, had three sons and three daughters alive when he died in 1822. His eldest son, William, was sent as a boarder when he was seven to a fashionable school near Nantwich in Cheshire owned by a Mr Gretton. This was what we would call a prep school and was recommended by his father's friend Samuel Hodgson, who lived nearby. 'Mr Gretton's terms are 25 guineas a year including washing ... two boys lie in a bed. If a boy has a bed to himself he pays five guineas a year more.'[17]

Hodgson, in a delightful letter to Thomas, emphasised the healthy situation of the school, the social distinction of the fathers of the other boarders, the excellence of Mr Gretton's teaching, the kindness of Mrs Gretton and, perhaps most importantly, the rules that ensured that these privileged boarders were kept well apart from the plebeian dayboys who were paid for by the parish.[18] William, who sounds a lively and likeable lad in Hodgson's letters, later went to Charterhouse, still in its original London location and described by the Duke of Wellington as 'the best school of them all'. He was destined to become a merchant in the family tradition and school for him was followed by 'many continental tours'

16 LRO, 920 ROS 2673, 2675, 1322.
17 D/EARLE/11/7.
18 D/EARLE/11/7.

which were to make him a good linguist, like his father and grandfather before him. William was joined at Charterhouse by his younger brother Hardman, who was to be a railway magnate rather than a merchant and was to add further lustre to the family by becoming a baronet in his old age. Richard, the youngest son, was sent to St John's College, Cambridge and then went on to read successfully for the bar, though he made his career in the Colonial Office.[19]

Only two of Thomas's daughters, Ann and Jane, are mentioned in his will. The third daughter, Mary, was born in 1794 and, shades of Lydia Bennet, ran away against her father's wishes with Sir William Percival de Bathe, an Irish army officer whom she married in November 1820. There is a letter from her to Thomas in the Earle Collection, written when he was ill and she just about to embark for 'the uncertainties of a soldier's life'. Her letter is charming and full of affection for her 'dear father', who she hopes will soon be 'mounting your charger once again as the best and most *becoming* exercise you can possibly take'. All of which seems very sad as her affection did not reconcile her to her father, who strongly disapproved of her behaviour and cut her out of his will.[20]

Thomas's brother William had a smaller family, but they well exemplified his genteel aspirations. His only son Charles is described succinctly in the contribution to family history published by T. Algernon Earle in 1890. Born in 1798, Charles was educated at Eton and Trinity College, Cambridge. 'He never entered any profession, and devoted much of his life to sport. He was fond of hunting and a capital shot, and throughout his life was a great patron of cricket.'[21] No hint of the mercantile life in Charles, then; nor was there in the choice of husbands by William's two daughters. Elizabeth married a country gentleman, Joseph Ashton of Woolton, Esq., and Anne Mary married Colonel Caldwell of the Bengal Army. They were left £10,000 each by their father and both lived chiefly in Italy and died and were buried in Rome.[22]

The obituary of Thomas Earle gave much praise to his contribution to public life in Liverpool: 'To no individual, perhaps, is the town of

---

19 Earle, 1890; Pope, 2007, p. 179; Quick, 1990, p. 38; PROB 11/1663/73, 21 October 1820; Thomas's second son, another Thomas, died of typhus aged 17 while at school in Aberdeen. D/EARLE/2/3, 5 and 22 February 1806.

20 D/EARLE/7/15, undated, but written after her marriage.

21 Earle, 1890, p. 51; Pope, 2007, p. 179.

22 Earle, 1890, p. 51; PROB 11/1909/16, will of William Earle, 27 April 1839.

Liverpool under greater obligations for his public services than to Mr Earle.' He had been mayor in 1787, when only 33 years old, and for the rest of his life he was pressed, successfully, to give his name, time and money to a wide range of political, economic, social and charitable enterprises, such as the committee of Dock Trustees; the committee 'for obtaining a free trade to the East Indies' (successful in 1813); the Music Hall, of which he was one of the six directors; the Committee of the Lyceum, with its elegant circular library room; or the committee to consider erecting a public monument to Admiral Horatio Nelson, a project discussed on 17 November 1805 before 'one of the most numerous and respectable meetings ever remembered.'[23] William was not quite as active as his brother, but he did his bit, contributing to charities, sitting on various committees and proposing the Earl of Sefton as the Whig candidate for Liverpool in the 1818 election, as his brother had done for William Roscoe in 1806.[24] And, in *Gore's Liverpool Directory* for both 1800 and 1805, we find Mrs William Earle on the committee of the Ladies' Charity, 'for the relief of poor married women in childbed.'

Both brothers were also very active in volunteering and helping to pay for the defence of Liverpool and the Mersey against the not unlikely event of a French invasion. Ireland, too, posed a threat during these dangerous years, particularly in 1798, when a large-scale rebellion of the United Irishmen broke out. In May of that year, the *Liverpool Advertiser* reported that the Earles were making a very expensive contribution to the port's defence: 'We hear that Messrs. Thomas and William Earle are completely fitting up at their own expense a very formidable gun-boat of 60 tons burthen, carrying 24-pounders on her bows, for the public service.' We hear no more about this generous offer, so maybe the gunboat was never put into service, as the Irish rebellion was soon quashed and invasion fears focussed on the French army at Boulogne and the English Channel.[25]

Both brothers were certainly involved in the defence of Liverpool by land. In March 1797, the Liverpool volunteers were organised into six companies, one of which was commanded by Captain Thomas Earle. These companies were composed of 'respectable gentlemen, merchants,

---

23 *BLA*, 16 July 1822; Baines, 1852, p. 524; Sharples, 2004, pp. 11, 12, 151. The Nelson monument was unveiled in 1813.
24 Picton, 1907, i, p. 342; for Roscoe see above pp. 214–15.
25 *BLA*, 7 May 1798.

and the principle tradesmen and their sons, armed and clothed at their own expense.' After the Peace of Amiens, Captain Thomas Earle became Colonel Thomas Earle and was joined by Lieutenant-Colonel William Earle, both brothers being commanders of a battalion of Liverpool volunteers. During the general election of 1806, William was described in a squib as 'brave Colonel Earle, a man of manners silky', which may be some indication of his character, while his brother played a prominent part in the court martial of his adjutant, Captain Carmichael, for 'disobedience of orders and with addressing Colonel Earle in abusive language.'[26]

With so many civil, social and military duties, one might imagine that the brothers had little time for business, but they were still merchants first and foremost and were to trade actively until the death of Thomas in 1822, though never again on the scale of the 1780s and 1790s. Trading in the early nineteenth century required some serious consideration since, as has been seen, their last venture into the slave trade was the *Minerva*, which sailed for Cape Coast Castle in 1804, while trade with Leghorn and Italy generally was brought to a halt by the return of the French.[27] They would have to seek new horizons if they wanted to continue as overseas merchants. One possibility would have been privateering, a use of shipping which had been so successful in earlier wars. And, searching through the applications for Letters of Marque for the war against France from 1803 onwards and against Spain from 1805 to 1807, one does find such applications for eight Earle-owned ships, the three last slavers owned by the brothers and five other vessels trading to the West Indies or Berbice and back. But none of these ships declared a crew which could have done much damage to a serious enemy, most of them having just 12 or 15 men, and it seems probable that the Letters of Marque were acquired mainly to provide some protection from the hungry attention of the Royal Navy press gangs. Some Liverpool privateers did well in these wars, especially against the Spaniards, but the Earle ships were not among their number and one must assume that Thomas and William felt it unwise to try their luck once again after the successes of the American War of Independence.[28]

26 Baines, 1852, pp. 501, 515; Earle, 1890, p. 50; Jones, 1959, pp. 23–25.
27 See above chapters 10 and 11.
28 Applications in HCA 26/88–93, 26/100–102. For Liverpool successes and losses from notices in the Liverpool papers see Williams, 2004, pp. 385–429.

The opponents of abolition had predicted that the ending of the slave trade would cause mass unemployment and misery in Liverpool, so heavily did the port depend on the trade. But, in fact, this proved to be false and more harm was done to Liverpool's trade and shipping by the war and by Napoleon's continental system, which barred British ships from most ports in continental Europe. But this still left the rest of the world open to British shipping and, as David M. Williams showed 40 years ago, the owners of the Liverpool slaving fleet were quick to find new uses for their ships. The most important areas of re-deployment were the West Indies and the north-eastern part of South America, where newly conquered colonies provided markets for British goods and sources of cotton, coffee, sugar and other West Indian staples. The opening of trade with Argentina in 1806 and with Brazil after the flight thither of the Portuguese royal family a couple of years later provided further important destinations for British ships, while on the other side of the Atlantic, navigational and trading skills developed in the slave trade could be used to trade in other African products, especially palm oil. And Malta, Britain's new colony in the Mediterranean, had an important role in smuggling exports into the southern parts of Napoleonic Europe, a function performed in the North Sea by the German island of Heligoland off the mouth of the Elbe, which was seized by the British in 1807.[29]

Thomas and William Earle did not have slave ships to redeploy after 1807, as they had given up slaving three years previously. But, between 1804 and 1823, the ships they owned, seven in all, were similar to slave ships, well-armed, fast snows and brigs, of around 200 tons burthen.[30] Most of these ships gave good service, each undertaking four, five or more voyages before it was sold. As time passed by, the Earle deployment of shipping diminished, until in 1816 they had only two ships, the 200-ton *Westbury* and the 275-ton *Fairy*. And, for the last few years, they owned just one ship, the romantically named *Fairy*, which was eventually sold in 1823. All these ships had virtually identical ownership, just the two brothers, their partner William Leathom and, from 1812, when he was 25, William Earle the Younger, Thomas's eldest son.

29 Williams, 1973; Neal, 1969.
30 Data on shipping and voyages from Liverpool Ship Registers in MMM and Mediterranean Pass Registers in TNA ADM 7.

It is possible to identify 33 of the voyages made between 1804 and 1823 by these seven Earle ships. Twenty-two of the voyages, two-thirds of the total, were made from Liverpool to Berbice or Demerara in what is now Guiana, five to islands in the West Indies, four to other places in South America and there were just two voyages elsewhere, one to Newfoundland and one to the Mediterranean. Ships sailing to Guiana and Brazil brought home mainly cotton, but also other West Indian and South American staples such as sugar and coffee. The days of Guianese cotton were numbered, as competition from the southern states of the United States forced owners to abandon their cotton plantations. Between 1809 and 1824, 111 cotton estates were given up in Berbice and this trend was to continue.[31]

There is a postscript to the story of the connection between the Earle family and the colony of Berbice. Once cotton had been abandoned, cultivation was almost entirely confined to coffee and sugar grown along the first 20 miles or so on each side of the river that gave the colony its name, with vast areas of uncultivated land and jungle beyond the plantations and in the interior. The population of these cultivated strips were mostly slaves; in 1833, for example, there were 570 whites, many of them living in New Amsterdam, the capital of Berbice and the only real town, 1,651 free coloureds and free blacks and 19,320 slaves.[32] All this was very soon to change since, on 28 August 1833, the Slavery Abolition Act received the Royal Assent in the British Parliament. This dramatic change in the lives of the slaves had been the subject of debate for many years but, as with the Abolition of the Slave Trade in 1807, the weight of public opinion was such that emancipation seemed to be inevitable. The only questions remaining to be answered were when it would take place and the terms on which it would be granted.[33]

In the event, emancipation came into force on 1 August 1834 and the terms were very generous to the planters and other slave-owners. There was to be a period of six years during which the former slaves were required to continue to work as 'apprentices', receiving a daily wage of 1s and 4d for their compulsory six-day working week and working a total of 45 hours a week instead of the 54 hours a week

---

31 Thompson, 2002, p. 276.
32 Green, 1976, p. 13.
33 On emancipation in general and in Berbice see Thompson, 2002; Moohr, 1972; Green, 1976; Draper, 2010.

they had toiled as slaves, not much money but for most of them the first they had ever had to spend. Discipline was relaxed, though 'stripes' of the whip or several hours in the stocks were still available to chastise unruly, disobedient or lazy apprentices. And, most important of all, the former owners were to receive compensation for the loss of their 'property', an amazing £20 million to be distributed between the various colonies.

The administration of this complex piece of legislation was conducted by a body called the Slave Compensation Commission, who were, not surprisingly, flooded with real and fictional claims to a share in this £20 million bonanza. The records of this body have recently been fed into a database by a team at University College London and the results are now searchable.[34] The main item under the name 'Earle' was a sugar plantation of about 700 acres called Utile et Paisible, 12 miles up the west bank of the Berbice River. This was owned jointly by William Earle (the 75-year-old art collector), William Earle the Younger, son of Thomas (now deceased), and Thomas Leathom. They were the owners of 197 slaves and were to share compensation of £10,197 for the loss of this property. Since there was no counterclaim or litigation, this was settled on 30 November 1835, a very nice windfall.[35]

The Earles had not owned this plantation for very long. Sources which give the names of the owners of slave plantations show the owners of Utile et Paisible right up to 1834 as being 'The heirs of James Cully deceased and George Watson', Irish absentees represented by John Ross, a slave owner himself who acted for many absentees. So, since the Slavery Abolition Act was passed in August 1833 and came into force a year later, it might seem rather surprising that the Earles and Thomas Leathom should receive compensation for the slaves.[36] An explanation can be gleaned from the Berbice Plantation Papers, an assemblage of documents in the Earle Collection.[37] This is rather a ragbag, but there is one document that gives a clue as to what had been going on. This is a cutting from a Berbice newspaper of 9 May 1834 which reports the 'transport' [i.e. conveyance] of the plantation Utile et Paisible by John Ross, acting for Cully & Watson, 'in favour of T. & W. Earle & Co. of

34 Legacies of British Slave-ownership: http://wwwdepts-dev.ucl.ac.uk/lbs.
35 TNA, T 71/885 # 477.
36 TNA, T 71/445, p. 63; CO 116/153, p. 158.
37 MMM D/EARLE/5.

Liverpool, merchants.' There is also a letter from Ross, dated 17 July 1834, congratulating the Liverpool firm on having become proprietors of this sugar plantation. And, in amongst the Berbice papers, there are one or two much later observations that the plantation had been acquired in settlement of a bad debt.[38]

There are no details of this debt nor indeed, apart from the newspaper cutting, of the conveyance of the plantation, but it seems clear that the two William Earles and their partner acquired the plantation just before the 1 August deadline and so were able to claim and acquire the £10,000 compensation and use it to settle some debt Cully & Watson had incurred. They were hardly likely to have been the only people who took this heaven-sent opportunity to get the British taxpayer to reimburse money owed to them by dishonest or bankrupt planters and on the face of it they had been very clever. The only problem was that, in addition to the compensation, they acquired the plantation, whose name they quickly changed to a more patriotic 'Hanover Plantation'.

Since the elder William Earle was now resident in Rome and chiefly interested in adding to his art collection, his nephew William Earle the Younger and Thomas Leathom were the active partners in the company. They were merchants and knew very little about running a plantation, and their agents in Berbice did not give them very good advice. The fact was that there could hardly have been a worse time for ignorant absentees to take over a plantation than in the wake of emancipation. The best policy would have been simply to take the compensation money and then abandon the plantation. This is what many owners did. But the Earles found it difficult to behave like that and an unrealistic spirit of optimism runs through the surviving papers.

'The main fact of life in the free West Indies', wrote William A. Green in his book on emancipation in the sugar colonies, 'was that black labourers were unwilling to remain submissive and disciplined cane workers', once they were no longer slaves and even more once they were no longer apprenticed labourers, this second emancipation coming into effect on 1 August 1838, two years earlier than had originally been planned at Westminster. Coercion in its more unpleasant forms was now illegal and, in a largely unsettled colony like Guiana, there was plenty of vacant land on which the former slaves could live as peasants in villages, growing plantains and other foodstuffs, and working for wages only so

38 MMM D/EARLE/5/3/1; /5/5/1; 5/6/21; 5/10/16.

long as they needed to earn money for the few luxuries they could not grow or make themselves.[39]

In the face of such intransigent labour, planters either abandoned their estates or made efforts to bring in plantation workers from elsewhere who would work hard for the wages offered them. In a poor world there were many such people. Immigrants were brought in from Sierra Leone, Madeira and Barbados amongst other places and a major effort was made to attract free black labour from the northern United States. From the 1840s, the Guianese sugar plantation industry was to be saved by the import of huge numbers of indentured labourers, mainly Indian, working on terms similar to those granted to the slaves when they became apprentices following emancipation. T. & W. Earle did not import Indians, but their papers show them trying most of the other sources of labour and even dabbling in the business of transporting such labourers from New York and other American ports to Guiana. None of these schemes did them much good and, by the 1840s, they were desperate to sell or at least rent out their plantation though they were still reluctant to abandon it. Hanover Plantation looked like a very poor proposition and one instinctively agrees with the sentiments expressed in 1846 by William the Elder's son, Charles: 'It would be unwise to throw much more money after bad.'[40]

Not much more money was in fact thrown away on Berbice after 1846 but, by then, the plantation had almost certainly cost the Liverpool firm more than the £10,000 that the partners had received as compensation. As the century progressed, the documents surviving in the Berbice Plantation Papers become few and far between and members of the family in England seem almost to have forgotten about their sugar plantation in British Guiana, not surprisingly since the land had reverted to jungle or bush and the buildings had been knocked down to provide road-making materials. Every now and then the papers were turned over by an inquisitive member of the family, one of whom discovered in 1883 that Hanover was not the plantation's original name. 'Its real name is so different. It has only acted up to half of its name. It may be "paisible", but certainly is not "utile".' This judgment was confirmed in 1895 in a letter from a Mr Matthews, an officer of the Georgetown telegraph company who had visited Hanover

39 Green, 1976, p. 170.
40 MMM D/EARLE/5/10/4, 13 May 1846.

Plantation at the request of Sir Thomas Earle of Allerton Hall, the current head of the family. Matthews found the place all right, 'but the land being thickly covered with high bush and trees, it was impossible for me to go through it.' The inhabitants of neighbouring lands told him that 'there are no buildings or erections whatsoever on the property and no squatters working the land.' When Sir Thomas died in 1900, his executor 'took control of [Hanover Plantation] and closed it all up.' The Earle family's adventures in the Guianese sugar industry were over.[41]

The story of Hanover Plantation does nobody much credit and it has to be accepted that the Earles were no great shakes at managing plantations. But they were successful merchants and a very good idea of the trade of Liverpool as a whole and of Thomas & William Earle & Co in the twilight of their careers can be obtained from the Liverpool Customs Bills of Entry whose records begin in 1820.[42] This was a daily publication and each bill contained a list of all vessels coming into Liverpool and their last port of clearance, together with a full account of the cargo carried and the names of the consignees. The 1820 list gives a very good idea of the worldwide scope of the Liverpool trading empire. Liverpool now had ships coming in from Buenos Ayres, Calcutta, Manila, even Australia, though the old focus on America, the West Indies and Ireland had not been completely eclipsed. This was still a sailing-ship commerce, but was just about to change. Steam tugs already helped ships get out of the Mersey and steam packets offered smoky services for passengers to Bristol, Dublin and Glasgow and all ports between. But, once out in the open sea, sail continued to be master and this played into the hands of American ships and American masters, who dominated all routes except those reserved by law for the British. American ships were cheaper to produce, better designed and more efficient with lower man-ton ratios. They were also much better run, with lower levels of desertion and drunkenness than their British counterparts. American captains also received much praise for their ability to concentrate on the job. William Cobbett put it rather nicely, as he usually did: 'I never knew an American captain take off

41 D/EARLE/5/10/17, C.W. Earle to Sir Thomas Earle, 22 February 1883; /5/10/31, Matthews to Sir Thomas Earle, 20 March 1895.
42 Henceforth LCBE. I have used the microfilm edition produced by Microform Academic Publishers of Wakefield.

his clothes to go to bed during the whole voyage; and I never knew any other who did not do it.'[43]

The Bills of Entry show that the Earle brothers were the twentieth most important cotton importers into Liverpool in 1820, bringing in a total of 3,428 bales during that year.[44] Some of this came from ports in the United States, but most was from South America, mainly Brazil but including some consignments from Berbice. In amongst all the other shipments was the 275-ton *Fayry* (*sic*), the only ship owned by the Earles to appear in the Bills of Entry, which arrived in the Mersey from Maranham in Brazil on 24 March 1820 with a cargo entirely of cotton for 13 different importers, including T. & W. Earle, who received 1,100 bags. This shipment alone represented about one-third of their total imports of cotton for the year. The *Fairy*, the last ship owned by the Earles, made the voyage from Liverpool to Berbice or 'the Brazills' every year from 1812 to 1823.

Neither in 1820, nor in any other year, did the Earles focus entirely on just one type of cargo, be it slaves or cotton. The most important shipments apart from cotton were those made to a company usually called Earles & Carter. The Articles of Agreement of this partnership, dated 1 October 1798, show that there were four partners, Thomas and William Earle, Thomas Hodgson, and John Carter of Liverpool, merchant, probably a son or other relation of the Joseph Carter who had been an apprentice of William Earle Sr and was in partnership with him in several of his projects in the 1760s.[45] The partners were to 'carry on the business of a merchant and factor in partnership at Liverpool ... in the several articles of grain, flour, hops, butter and cheese and also import/export from the ports of the Baltic and Ireland.' Hodgson and Carter were to be the active partners and were to devote their whole time to this business from the Earle offices in Hanover Street. In 1804, the company became involved in seed crushing and the extraction of linseed oil, using a mill with stamping machines, which from 1810 was in the suitably named Oil Street. Linseed oil was used as a lubricant and also as a 'drying oil' in the manufacture of paint, while oilcakes fed to cattle provided a useful secondary demand. The firm was later

43 Williams, 1988, Cobbett quotation on p. 74. The Liverpool newspapers have many advertisements for steam packets.
44 Williams, 1969.
45 See above pp. 102–06.

described as 'the most extensive seed crushers in the country', one of the few examples of Earle investment in manufacturing.[46]

The entries for Earles & Carter in the Customs Bills of Entry show a firm very far removed from the focus on slaves, colonial staples and Mediterranean products that had previously characterised the business of the Earle family. There were at least ten consignments from the Baltic, but this was a very different business from that conducted by their uncle Ralph 60 or 70 years earlier. The main loading ports were Archangel, Dantzig and Konigstadt, from each of which the Earles imported mainly wheat, and Riga, which produced more mixed cargoes of oats, barley, linseed for their crushing machines and deals. The other main sources of cargo were Trieste, from which was shipped mainly Indian corn (maize) and linseed, and North America. Here, the Canadian ports were the most important, especially Quebec, from which came timber, flaxseed (i.e. linseed), ashes or potash and flour. Flaxseed and flour were also the main cargoes shipped from New York, while Wilmington, North Carolina, supplied Earles & Carter with turpentine, like linseed oil much in demand by the paint industry, though the product had many other uses. None of these shipments were made in ships belonging to the Earles, shipowning now increasingly becoming a specialist activity supplying a service to merchants.

Thomas Earle died in 1822, but his name, or rather initial, survived in a rather ghostly way in the company he had helped to create. So, in 1825, the next year for which the Liverpool Customs Bills of Entry have survived, there are still some entries made for T. & W. Earle, though the pattern of shipments had changed considerably from 1820 and quite a few of them were consigned to W. Earle rather than the company. In fact, it is not too fanciful to imagine that the new pattern reflected the interests of William, the surviving brother, a man who was perhaps not so devoted to business as his elder brother had been, was happiest in the Mediterranean and especially in Italy, and enjoyed drinking wines and storing them in his cellars and collecting things to display in his cabinets.

There were now very few entries in the Bills for the perhaps rather dull firm of Earles & Carter and none at all from the Baltic. There were also far fewer imports of cotton from either North or South America. On

---

46 MMM D/EARLE/4; Brace, 1960, pp. 47, 140; from 1860, the company became known as Earles & King.

the other hand, William seems to have developed a new and substantial trade in Egyptian cotton from Alexandria with one ship in May, one in June and one in December each bringing in over 1,000 bales of cotton. There was a revival of imports from Italy as well, mainly of silk, but including such old favourites as straw hats from Leghorn. The wine trade was also busy with entries from Trieste, Cadiz, Oporto and Bordeaux, and brandy from Le Havre. Oranges and lemons from Spain, Portugal and the Azores were also important in the weeks running up to Christmas as they had been throughout the trading careers of the Earles, from grandfather John onwards. But perhaps the most intriguing items are entries that seem destined to fill those 'fine display cabinets' which were sold at the auction following William's death. In April, a 'box of fossils and specimens' was shipped to William in the *Sampson* from Trieste and later in the year we find 'natural curiosities' and a 'box of minerals' coming from Hamburg, while on 16 December the *Corsair* arrived at Liverpool from Singapore, which had been ceded to the East India Company in the previous year. And on board, amongst many other good things, we find a box of minerals and 'four boxes of natural curiosities' for William Earle.[47]

William was 65 in 1825, an age at which men of his family would normally be retired or at least thinking of retirement. No doubt he continued to trade a bit, while spending more and more of each year in the warmer climate of Rome, but this seems to be a good place to bring to a close this biographical journey through the lives of three generations of the Earle family. The main focus has been on just six men, all merchants, who took the family from its fairly humble beginnings as brewers in late seventeenth-century Warrington to a distinguished place in the mercantile hierarchy of Liverpool, the fastest growing and most successful port of the age. Why should this family be so successful, while many others failed to make the grade and never got to live in a country house or send their sons to Eton or Charterhouse?

Few of their contemporaries would have predicted that it would be the Earles who did so well, since they certainly got off to a bad start. The very first of these six men, John Earle, must be considered a failure since even if one gives him credit for raising a trio of successful sons, going bankrupt twice is hardly a sign of success. There is not really

47 LCBE, 18 April, 6 May, 13 September, 29 October, 4 November, 16 December 1825.

sufficient evidence to state with certainty why John failed. He may just have been unfortunate, though to be unlucky twice is perhaps a sign of weakness or at least carelessness. So, what was it that saved his three sons and his two grandsons from repeating such carelessness?

One obvious factor, about which we know virtually nothing, was the importance of marrying a good or at least a rich wife. Since a bankrupt father was hardly able to do much to complete the education of his children or to launch them into the mercantile world, it is clear that someone else must have provided the means to do this and who else could that be but John's wife and her family. Mary Finch, John's second wife and the mother of his three merchant sons, was the only child of Ralph Finch of Chester and was described as an heiress. John certainly wasted some of her money in what seems with hindsight a period of extravagant trading following his marriage in 1710. But it seems certain that there was still money left to launch his three sons and to give them the traditional 'portion', the capital sum provided by relations to get a merchant started. It was also the Finch relationship that enabled John's eldest son Ralph to inherit the Willis fortune and estates in 1788.

Ralph's younger brothers, Thomas and William, may have received portions from their mother and her family, but they were probably fairly small and it is clear that they both worked very hard and with some risk to increase this capital and so give themselves a good start. William found the work of a slave ship captain distasteful, an 'over busy noisey trade', but it was the traditional way for young men in mid-eighteenth-century Liverpool to acquire business capital and so he made the most of it. Thomas increased his capital by his profitable (but potentially hazardous) connection in Leghorn with the successful privateer Fortunatus Wright, and also by his clever piece of business in buying the unwanted Royal Navy ship *Lowestoff* and selling her at a great profit to the Papal Navy. These were smart moves, and quite daring too, and it is noteworthy that when it came to their turn, William's sons were able to move into business with much greater ease and less risk.

The mention of John's extravagant trading after 1710 and its probable connection with his first bankruptcy in January 1719 prompts an investigation into the attitude of his children and grandchildren to risk. This is a subject central to the understanding of merchants and their success or failure and has recently been analysed by Sheryllynne Haggerty in her book on 'business culture' in late eighteenth- and early nineteenth-century Liverpool. She shows that merchants had various strategies to reduce risk, such as banding together in partnerships, shipping goods on several different ships and ensuring that these ships and goods were adequately insured. However, when summarising Liverpool as a whole, she can only say that merchants needed to strike a balance between prudence and risk, between being the sort of man who 'was rather too timorous a trader to make a fortune' and those 'who have naturally adventurous spirits, who are resolved to be all or nothing.'[48]

Where did the Earles lie on the scale between timidity and 'all or nothing' adventure? They were certainly not afraid of adventure, whether in privateering or trade, and they frequently show up as innovators or at least fast followers; in at the very beginning of the Liverpool slave trade, leaders in Italian trade, keen to develop whatever seemed a good idea at the time, the Spanish and Portuguese wine trade, the Shetland fisheries, the emigrant trade to Newfoundland, the trade between Liverpool and Archangel, cotton exports from Guiana, the Liverpool linseed oil business and so on. But, although adventurous and innovative, they were all careful, with the possible exception of John, a trait which can most easily be seen from the two surviving letter books, William senior's in 1760–61 and Thomas and William junior's in the early years of the nineteenth century.[49] These business letters can hardly be considered as literature; they are in fact rather dull. But they do give some insight into the character of the writer.

William senior was operating in a very difficult economic climate, the Seven Years' War, but his innate optimism comes through on nearly every page, even when things have gone seriously wrong. Difficulties were to be overcome and he was always sanguine and confident, quick to make the best of setbacks, always ready to look on the bright side. 'Things will soon come round', he wrote in the midst of one crisis, and this could be said to be his watchword. But he never forgot to be cautious as well as adventurous and optimistic. He was indeed a very prudent trader, never happy to have 100 per cent of any venture, always quick to check on the creditworthiness of any customer or potential partner, always insistent on being as fully insured as was possible. 'Run no risques' was another watchword and it was his ability to maintain

---

48 Haggerty, 2012, ch. 2, quotation on p. 43; see also Zahedieh, 2010, ch. 3.
49 D/EARLE/2/2 and /3.

a sensible balance between risk and adventure that ensured his success in the commercial world of Liverpool.

William's sons Thomas and William started business much richer men than their father, were better educated and were much more involved in public affairs, especially Thomas, who was probably the brightest of the six merchants considered in this book. He was also the richest, being credited with a personal estate of £70,000 in the probate duty records.[50] Such a figure must be considered a minimum valuation of his actual wealth, since it takes no account of his real estate in Liverpool and the surrounding country or assets held overseas and in any case is likely to be an underestimate. His and his brother's attitude to business, as revealed in their letter book, was rather more pessimistic than that of their father (with good reason) and even more careful. But they were still prepared to be adventurous and involve their firm in new business, especially in America, and after the demise of Livorno they were quick to move into new types of business, such as cotton importing and linseed oil manufacture. Nevertheless, they come across as less adventurous than their father and their uncle, both of whom had fortunes to make more or less from scratch. The obituary of Thomas, which has been quoted before, gives a very interesting summary of his character:

> Experience had taught him on all occasions to weigh well before giving his opinion, and his judgment was therefore respected, even by those from whom he differed. Probably the distinguishing features of his character were coolness in deliberation, and caution in action; which latter he may sometimes be thought to have carried to an extreme.

The implied criticism in this last comment strikes a rather strange note in what is otherwise a laudatory obituary. But, as long as it is combined with a spirit of adventure, it may well be that extreme caution is not a bad character trait in a merchant. It certainly does not seem to have done the Earles any harm.[51]

---

50 Pope, 2007, p. 210. His brother William's personal estate was valued at £45,000.
51 *BLA*, 16 July 1822.

Bibliography

The works listed are those which have been referred to in the Notes. Place of publication is London unless otherwise stated. Where there is a second publication date in parentheses, the second one has been consulted. For abbreviations see above pp. xv–xvi.

Ackroyd, Harold, *The Liverpool Stage* (1996)

Addobatti, Andrea, 'Il negozio della Sicurtà marittima a Livorno (sec. xviii)', *NSL* iv (1996)

Aikin, John, *A Description of the Country from Thirty to Forty Miles round Manchester* (1795)

Anderson, B.L. 'The Lancashire bill system', in W.H. Chaloner & B.M. Radcliffe (eds) *Trade and Transport: Essays in Economic History in Honour of T.S. Willan* (Manchester, 1977)

Anstey, Roger & Hair, P.E.H. (eds), *Liverpool, the African Slave Trade, and Abolition* (1976)

Ascott, Diana E., Lewis, Fiona & Power, Michael (eds), *Liverpool, 1660–1750: People, prosperity and power* (Liverpool, 2006)

Atti del Convegno di Studi, *Gli inglesi a Livorno e all'isola d'Elba (sec. xvii–xix)* (Livorno, 1980)

Baines, Thomas, *History of the Commerce and Trade of Liverpool* (1852)

Barker, Elizabeth & Kidson, Alex, *Joseph Wright of Derby in Liverpool* (New Haven, Conn., 2007)

Bates, Cristina, 'The role of British merchants in Livorno in the marble trade between Italy and Britain during the 18th century', paper read at Royal Holloway College in May 2006

Behrendt, Stephen, 'The captains in the British slave trade, from 1785 to 1807', *THSLC* 140 (1991)

Bellamy, Joyce M., 'A Hull shipbuilding firm', *Business History* vi (1963)

Bignamini, Ilaria, 'The Grand Tour', in Andrew Wilton & Ilaria Bignamini, *Grand Tour: The Lure of Italy in the Eighteenth Century* (1996)

Bignamini, Ilaria & Hornsby, Clare, *Digging and Dealing in 18th-century Rome* (New Haven, Conn., 2010)

Blinkhorn, William K., *A History of Whiston* (Northwich, 2004)

Boardman, James, *Liverpool Table Talk a Hundred Years Ago* (Liverpool, 1871)

Bolster, W. Jeffrey, *Black Jacks: African American Seamen in the Age of Sail* (Cambridge, Mass., 1997)

Borsay, Peter, *The English Urban Renaissance: Culture and Society in the Provincial Towns, 1660–1760* (1989)

Boswell, James, *Life of Samuel Johnson* (1790, 1965)

Brace, Harold W., *History of Seed Crushing in Great Britain* (1960)

Brewer, John, 'Whose Grand Tour?', in María Dolores Sánchez-Jáureghi & Scott Wilcox (eds), *The English Prize: The Capture of the Westmorland, an Episode of the Grand Tour* (New Haven, Conn., 2012)

Broadbent, R.J., *Annals of the Liverpool Stage* (Liverpool, 1908)

Brooke, N., *Observations on the Manners and Customs of Italy* (Bath, 1798)

Brooke, Richard, *Liverpool as it Was: 1775 to 1800* (Liverpool, 1803)

Burton, Richard, *The Apprentices' Companion* (1681)

Butterworth, William, *Three Years Adventures of a Minor* (Leeds, 1822)

Campbell, John, *A True and Exact Description of the Island of Shetland* (1750)

Chalklin, C.W., *The Provincial Towns of Georgian England* (1974)

Chalklin, Martha, 'Ivory in World History – early modern trade in context', *History Compass* 8 (June, 2010)

Chandler, George, *William Roscoe* (1953)

Checkland, S.G., 'Finance for the West Indies, 1780–1815', *EcHR*, 2nd ser. x (1958)

Chitty, Mike, *Discovering Historic Wavertree* (1999)

Chorley, Patrick, *Oil, Silk and Enlightenment: Economic Problems in 18th-century Naples* (Naples, 1965)

Clemens, Paul G.E., 'The rise of Liverpool, 1665–1750', *EcHR*, 2nd ser. xxix (1976)

Clendenning, P.H., 'William Gomm: a case study of the foreign entrepreneur in 18th century Russia', *JEEH* vi (1977)

Colley, Linda, *The Ordeal of Elizabeth Marsh* (2007)

Collyer, Joseph, *The Parent's and Guardian's Directory* (1761)

Corbett, Sir Julian, *England in the Seven Years' War*, 2 vols (1907)

Costello, Ray, *Black Liverpool: The Early History of Britain's Oldest Black Community, 1730–1918* (Liverpool, 2001)

Coughtry, Jay, *The Notorious Triangle: Rhode Island and the African Slave Trade, 1700–1807* (Philadelphia, 1981)

Craig, Robert & Jarvis, Rupert, *Liverpool Registry of Merchant Ships* (Manchester, 1967)

Crow, Hugh. *The Memoirs of Captain Hugh Crow* (1830, 2007)

Cruickshanks, Eveline et al. (eds), *The House of Commons, 1690–1715* (Cambridge, 2002)

Cryan, Mary Jane, 'La saga dei Denham: una famiglia irlandese nel Lazio settentrionale', *Rivista* (2005)

Currie, William Wallace, *Memoir of the Life, Writings, and Correspondence of James Currie* (1831)

Curwen, Samuel, *The Journal of Samuel Curwen, Loyalist*, ed. Andrew Oliver (Cambridge, Mass., 1972)

Dalton, Henry G., *The History of British Guiana* (1855)

D'Angelo, Michela, 'Nel "Britannico Nido"; la communità inglese a Livorno in età moderna', in *Scritti di storia per Gaetano Cingari* (Milan, 2001)

Davies, K.G., *The Royal African Company* (1957)

Davis, Ralph, *The Rise of the English Shipping Industry in the 17th and 18th Centuries* (Newton Abbot, 1962)

Defoe, Daniel, *The Compleat English Tradesman* (1726–27)

Defoe, Daniel, *Reformation of Manners* (1702)

Defoe, Daniel, *A Tour through the Whole Island of Great Britain* (1724–26, 1962)

Del Nista, Mauro, 'Giardini' della Congregazione Olandese-Alemanna (Livorno, 2004)

Derrick, Samuel, *Letters Written from Leverpoole* (Dublin, 1767)

Dickens, Charles, *Great Expectations* (1860, 2002)

Donnan, Elizabeth (ed.), *Documents Illustrative of the Slave Trade to America*, 4 vols (Washington, D.C., 1930–33)

Draper, Nicholas, *The Price of Emancipation: Slave-ownership, Compensation and British Society at the End of Slavery* (Cambridge, 2010)

Duffy, I.P.H., 'English bankrupts, 1571–1861', *American Journal of Legal History* xxiv (1980)

Duke, Antera, *The Diary of Antera Duke, an Eighteenth-century African Slave Trader*, ed. Behrendt et al. (Oxford, 2010)

Dumbell, Stanley, 'Early Liverpool cotton imports and the organization of the cotton market in the 18th century', *EJ* 33 (1923)

Earle, Hardman Arthur, *Earle Pedigree* (1929)

Earle, Peter, 'Age and accumulation in the London business community, 1665–1720', in N. McKendrick & R.B. Outhwaite, *Business Life and Public Policy* (Cambridge, 1986)

Earle, Peter, *Corsairs of Malta and Barbary* (1970)

Earle, Peter, *The Making of the English Middle Class: Business, Society and Family Life in London, 1660–1730* (1989)

Earle, Peter, *Sailors: English Merchant Seamen, 1650–1775* (1998)

Earle, T. Algernon, 'Earle of Allerton Tower', *THSLC* 42 (1890)

Earle, William of Everton, *Splendid and Genuine Collection of Pictures* (Liverpool, 1839)

Eastlake, Lady, *Life of John Gibson, R.A., Sculptor* (1870)

Edinburgh New Dispensatory (1797)

Edwards, Michael M., *The Growth of the British Cotton Trade, 1780–1815* (Manchester, 1967)

Enfield, William, *An Essay towards the history of Leverpool* (Warrington, 1773)

Erskine, David (ed.), *Augustus Hervey's Journal ... 1746–1759* (1953)

Falconbridge, Alexander, *An Account of the Slave Trade on the Coast of Africa* (1788)

Faulkner, Harold Underwood, *American Economic History* (New York, 1960)

Feinberg, Harvey M., & Johnson, Marion, 'The West African ivory trade during the 18th century', *IJAHS*, xv (1982)

Fiennes, Celia, *The Illustrated Journeys of Celia Fiennes, 1685–c. 1712*, ed. Christopher Morris (1982)

Filippini, J.P., *Il porto di Livorno e la Toscana (1676–1814)*, 2 vols (Naples, 1998)

Fisher, Roger, *Heart of Oak; the British Bulwark* (1763, 3rd ed., 1771)

Flavell, M. Kay, 'The enlightened reader and the new industrial towns. A study of the Liverpool Library, 1756–1790', *British Journal for 18th-century Studies*, viii (1985)

Fleming, J., *Robert Adam and his Circle in Edinburgh and Rome* (1962)

Ford, Brinsley, 'The letters of Jonathan Skelton', *The Walpole Society* 36 (1960)

Ford, Brinsley, 'Thomas Jenkins: banker, dealer and unofficial agent', *Apollo* vol. 99 (June 1974)

Forde, Daryll (ed.), *Efik Traders of Old Calabar* (Oxford, 1956)

Frattarelli Fischer, Lucia, 'Il bagno delle galere; schiavi a Livorno fra Cinque e Seicento', *NSL* viii (2000)

Fremantle, Anne (ed.), *The Wynne Diaries*, vol. ii, 1794–1798 (1937)

Galani, Katerina, 'The Napoleonic Wars and the disruption of Mediterranean shipping and trade', *Historical Review* vii (2010)

Gee, Joshua, *The Trade and Navigation of Great-Britain considered* (1729)

A General and Descriptive History of Liverpool (Liverpool, 1795)

Gibson, T. Ellison, *Blundell's Diary: selections from the diary of Nicholas Blundell Esq., from 1702 to 1728* (Liverpool, 1895)

Goodwin, Lorinda B.R., *An Archaeology of Manners: the polite world of the merchant élite of colonial Massachusetts* (New York, 1999)

Green, William A., *British Slave Emancipation: the sugar colonies and the great experiment, 1830–1865* (Oxford, 1976)

Guida-Inventario dell'Archivio di Stato di Livorno (Rome, 1961)

Guarnieri, Gino, *Livorno marinara* (Livorno, 1962)

Guglielmotti, Alberto, *Gli ultimi fatti della squadra romana, dal 1700 al 1807* (Rome, 1884)

Haggerty, Sheryllynne, *'Merely for Money'? Business Culture in the British Atlantic, 1750–1815* (Liverpool, 2012)

Hancock, David, *Citizens of the World* (Cambridge, 1995)

Hanway, Jonas, *An Historical Account of the British Trade over the Caspian Sea* (1753)

Harriott, Lt. John, *Struggles through Life*, 2 vols (1808)

Harris, J.R. (ed.), *Liverpool and Merseyside* (1969)

Hayward, Horace A., 'The British Factory in Livorno', in Atti del Convegno di Studi, *Gli inglesi a Livorno e all'isola d'Elba (sec. xvii–xix)* (Livorno, 1980)

Hervey, Augustus, *Adventures Afloat and Ashore of a Naval Casanova* (2004)

Heywood, Thomas (ed.), *The Norris Papers* (Manchester, 1846)

Hill, Susan J., *Catalogue of the Townley Archive at the British Museum* (2002)

Hochschild, Adam, *Bury the Chains: the British struggle to abolish slavery* (New York, 2006)

Hodson, J.H., 'The letter-book of Robert Bostock, a merchant in the Liverpool slave trade, 1789–1792', *Liverpool Bulletin*, iii (1953)

Holmes, Michael, *Augustus Hervey: a naval Casanova* (Bishop Auckland, 1996)

Howard, John, *An Account of the Principal Lazzarettos in Europe* (1791)

Howman, Brian, 'Abolitionism in Liverpool', in David Richardson, Suzanne Schwarz & Anthony Tibbles (eds), *Liverpool and Transatlantic Slavery* (Liverpool, 2007)

Hulton, Ann, *Letters of a Loyalist Lady* (Cambridge, Mass., 1927)

Hunt, Leigh, *Autobiography*, 3 vols (1850)

Hutchinson, William, *A Treatise on Practical Seamanship* (1777, 1979)

Hyde, F.E. et al., 'The cotton broker and the rise of the Liverpool cotton market', *EcHR* 2nd ser. viii (1955)

Hyde, F.E. et al, 'The port of Liverpool and the crisis of 1793', *Economica* n.s.18 (1951)

Hyde, F.E., *Liverpool and the Mersey: An Economic History of a Port, 1700–1970* (Newton Abbot, 1971)

An Impartial Collection of the Addresses ... Published at Liverpool during the Election ... in November 1806 (Dublin, 1806)

Ingamells, John (ed.), *A Dictionary of British and Irish Travellers in Italy, 1701–1800* (New Haven, Conn., 1997)

Inikori, J.E., 'The import of firearms into West Africa, 1750–1807', *JAH* xviii (1977)

Jarvis, Rupert C., *Customs Letter-Books of the Port of Liverpool, 1711–1813* (Manchester, 1954)

John, A.H., 'Miles Nightingale, Drysalter: A study in 18th-century trade', *EcHR* 2nd ser. xviii (1965)

Johnson, Marion, 'The Atlantic slave trade and the economy of West Africa', in Anstey Roger & P.E.H. Hair (eds), *Liverpool, the African Slave Trade, and Abolition* (1976)

Jones & Wright, *History of the Election for Members of Parliament for the Borough of Liverpool, 1806* (Liverpool, 1806)

Jones, Sir Clement, *John Bolton of Storrs, 1756–1837* (Kendal, 1959)

Jones, Robert E., 'Getting the goods to St Petersburg: water transport from the interior, 1703–1811', *Slavic Review* 43 (1984)

Kaplan, Herbert, *Russian Overseas Commerce with Great Britain during the reign of Catherine II* (Philadelphia, 1995)

Keene, Charles A., 'American shipping and trade, 1798–1820: the evidence from Leghorn', *JEH* xxxviii (1978)

Kellenbenz, Hermann, 'The economic significance of the Archangel route from the late 16th to the late 18th centuries', *JEEH* ii (1973)

Kennedy, Ludovic, *Nelson's Band of Brothers* (1951)

Kenworthy-Browne, J., 'Matthew Brettingham's Rome Account Book, 1747–1754', *The Walpole Society* (1983)

Lambert, Sheila (ed.), *House of Commons Sessional Papers of the 18th Century* (Wilmington, DE, 1975)

Langton, John, *Geographical Change and Industrial Revolution: coalmining in south-west Lancashire, 1590–1799* (Cambridge, 1979)

Latham, Frank A., *Timber Town: a history of the Liverpool timber trade* (1967)

Law, Robin & Strickrodt, Silke, *Ports of the Slave Trade (Bights of Benin and Biafra)* (Stirling, 1999)

Lightbody, Hannah, *The Diary of Hannah Lightbody, 1786–1790*, ed. David Sekers (Liverpool, 2008)

Lo Basso, Luca, 'Livorno, gli inglesi e la guerra corsara nel Mediterraneo occidentale nella seconda metà del XVIII secolo', *NSL* 15 (2008)

Lockhart, Audrey, *Some Aspects of Emigration from Ireland to the North American Colonies between 1660 and 1777* (New York, 1976)

Longmore, Jane, 'Civic Liverpool: 1680–1800', in John Belchem (ed.), *Liverpool 800: Culture, Character and History* (Liverpool, 2006)

Longmore, Jane, 'The urban renaissance in Liverpool, 1769–1800', in Elizabeth Barker & Alex Kidson, *Joseph Wright of Derby in Liverpool* (New Haven, Conn., 2007)

Lovejoy, Paul E. & Richardson, David, 'Letters of the Old Calabar slave trade, 1760–1789', in Vincent Caretta & Philip Gould, *Genius in Bondage: Literature of the Early Black Atlantic* (Lexington, KY, 2001)

Lovejoy, Paul & Richardson, David, '"This Horrid Hole": Royal authority, commerce and credit at Bonny, 1690–1840', *JAH* 45 (2004)

Lovejoy, Paul & Richardson, David, 'Trust, pawnship, and Atlantic history: The institutional foundations of the Old Calabar slave trade', *AHR* 104 (1999)

Luzón Nogué, José M, *El Westmorland* (Madrid, 2000)

Lyon, David, *The Sailing Navy List: All the Ships of the Royal Navy, Built, Purchased and Captured, 1688–1860* (1993)

Macartney, George, *An Account of Russia in the Year 1767* (1768)

Manners, John, 5th Duke of Rutland, *Journal of Three Years' Travels … in 1795, 1796, 1797* (1805)

Mannion, John J., *The Peopling of Newfoundland* (1977)

Marriner, Sheila, *The Economic and Social Development of Merseyside* (1982)

Marshall, J.D. (ed.), *The Autobiography of William Stout* (1974)

Martin, Bernard & Spurrell, Mark, *The Journal of a Slave Trader, 1750–1754* (1962)

Masefield, G.B., 'Crops and Livestock', in E.E. Rich & C.H. Wilson (eds), *Cambridge History of Europe*, vol. 4 (Cambridge, 1967)

Moohr, M., 'The economic impact of slave emancipation in British Guiana', *EcHR*, 2nd ser. xxv (1972)

Morgan, Kenneth (ed.), *An American Quaker in the British Isles: The Travel Journals of Jabez Maud Fisher, 1775–1779* (Oxford, 1992)

Morgan, Kenneth, *The Liverpool Customs Bills of Entry (1820–1939)* introduction to the Microform Edition

Morgan, Kenneth, 'Liverpool's dominance in the British slave trade, 1740–1807', in David Richardson, Suzanne Schwarz & Anthony Tibbles (eds), *Liverpool and Transatlantic Slavery* (Liverpool, 2007)

Moss, Dr William, *Georgian Liverpool: A Guide to the City in 1797*, ed. David Brazendale (Lancaster, 2007)

Muir, Ramsay, *A History of Liverpool* (1907)

Neal, F., 'Liverpool shipping in the early 19th century', in J.R. Harris (ed.), *Liverpool and Merseyside* (1969)

Newman, Jennifer, '"A very delicate experiment": British mercantile strategies for financing trade in Russia, 1680–1780', in Ian Blanchard et al. (eds), *Industry and Finance in Early Modern History* (Stuttgart, 1992)

Newton, John, *An Authentic Narrative of some Remarkable and Interesting Particulars in the Life of the Rev. John Newton* (1764)

Norris, Robert, *Memoirs of the Reign of Bossa Ahadee, King of Dahomy* (1789, 1968)

Northrup, David, *Trade without Rulers: Pre-colonial Economic Development in South-eastern Nigeria* (Oxford, 1978)

Oldham, James, 'Insurance litigation involving the *Zong* and other British slave ships, 1780–1807', *Journal of Legal History* 28 (2007)

Pagano de Divitiis, Gigliola, *Mercanti inglesi nell'Italia del Seicento* (Venice, 1990)

Pagano de Divitiis, Gigliola, 'Il porto de Livorno fra Inglhilterra e Oriente' *NSL* i (1993)

Parsons, Sarah, '"A Conversation of Girls": Wright and the British visual culture of slavery, 1760–1800', in Elizabeth Barker & Alex Kidson, *Joseph Wright of Derby in Liverpool* (New Haven, Conn., 2007)

Peet, Henry (ed.), *The Earliest Registers of the Parish of Liverpool (St Nicholas's Church) ... 1660 to 1704* (Rochdale, 1909)

Peet, Henry, *Liverpool in the Reign of Queen Anne, 1705 and 1708* (Liverpool, 1908)

Picton, J.A., *City of Liverpool: Municipal Archives and Records, 1700–1835* (Liverpool, 1886)

Picton, J.A. *Memorials of Liverpool, Historical and Topographical* (Liverpool, 1907)

Pope, David, 'The wealth and social aspirations of Liverpool's slave merchants of the second half of the 18th century', in David Richardson, Suzanne Schwarz & Anthony Tibbles (eds), *Liverpool and Transatlantic Slavery* (Liverpool, 2007)

Postlethwayt, Malachy, *The Universal Dictionary of Trade and Commerce* (1757)

Powell, J.W. Damer, *Bristol Privateers and Ships of War* (Bristol, 1930)

Power, Michael, 'Councillors and commerce in Liverpool, 1650–1750', *Urban History* xiv (1997)

Price, Jacob, 'Credit in the slave trade and plantation economies', in Barbara L. Solow (ed.), *Slavery and the Rise of the Atlantic System* (Cambridge, 1991)

Priestley, Margaret, *West African Trade and Coast Society* (Oxford, 1969)

Puig, Amador Mari, 'Cors i comerc a Menorca: la commercialització de les preses (1778–1781)', in Goncal López Nadal, *El comerc alternatiu* (Palma de Mallorca, 1990)

Quick, Anthony, *Charterhouse: A History of the School* (1990)

Radburn, Nicholas James, 'William Davenport, the slave trade, and merchant enterprise in 18th-century Liverpool', M.A. thesis, Victoria University of Wellington (2009)

Rathbone, Emily, *Records of the Rathbone Family* (Edinburgh, 1913)

Reed, Gordon, *Introduction to the Earle Collection* (Marlborough, 2009)

Richards, W.A., 'The import of firearms to West Africa in the 18th century', *JAH* xxi (1980)

Richardson, David, 'The 18th-century British slave trade: Estimates of its volume and coastal distribution in Africa', *Research in Economic History* 12 (1989)

Richardson, David, 'Profits in the Liverpool slave trade: The accounts of William Davenport, 1757–1784', in Anstey Roger & P.E.H. Hair (eds), *Liverpool, the African Slave Trade, and Abolition* (1976)

Richardson, David, 'West African consumption patterns and their influence on the 18th-century slave trade', in Henry A. Gemery & Jan S. Hogendorn, *The Uncommon Market: Essays in the Economic History of the Atlantic Slave Trade* (New York, 1975)

Richardson, David, Schwarz, Suzanne & Tibbles, Anthony (eds), *Liverpool and Transatlantic Slavery* (Liverpool, 2007)

Roberts, B. Dew, *Mr Bulkeley and the Pirate* (1936)

Rodger, N.A.M., *The Command of the Ocean: A Naval History of Britain, 1649–1815* (2004)

Sánchez-Jáureghi, María Dolores & Wilcox, Scott (eds), *The English Prize: The Capture of the Westmorland, an Episode of the Grand Tour* (New Haven, Conn., 2012)

Sanderson, F.E. 'The Liverpool abolitionists', in Anstey Roger & P.E.H. Hair (eds), *Liverpool, the African Slave Trade, and Abolition* (1976)

Sanderson, F.E., 'The structure of politics in Liverpool, 1780–1807', *THSLC* 127 (1977)

Schwarz, Suzanne, *Slave Captain: The Career of James Irving in the Liverpool Slave Trade* (Liverpool, 1995)

Scoresby, William, *An Account of the Arctic Regions*, 2 vols (Edinburgh, 1820)

Sekers, David, *A Lady of Cotton: Hannah Greg, Mistress of Quarry Bank Mill* (Stroud, 2013)

Sellers, Ian, *Early Modern Warrington, 1520–1847* (Lampeter, 1998)

Sharples, Joseph, *Liverpool (Pevsner Architectural Guides)* (2004)

Sheridan, R.B., 'The commercial and financial organization of the British slave trade, 1750–1807', *EcHR*, 2nd ser. xi (1958–59)

Smith, Adam, *The Wealth of Nations* (1961)

Smith, Rev. Jeremiah Finch (ed.), *The Admissions Register of the Manchester School, vol. i: 1730–1775* (Manchester, 1866)

Sparks, Randy J., *The Two Princes of Calabar* (Cambridge, Mass., 2004)

Stanley, H.M., *The Congo and the Founding of its Free State*, 2 vols (1885)

Starke, Mariana, *Letters from Italy*, 2 vols (1815)

Starkey, David J., *British Privateering Enterprise in the 18th Century* (Exeter, 1990)

Stewart-Brown, R., *Liverpool Ships in the 18th Century* (Liverpool, 1932)

Stobart, J., 'Culture versus commerce: societies and spaces for élites in 18th-century Liverpool', *Journal of Historical Geography* xxviii (2002)

Stonehouse, J., 'A Nonagenarian', *Recollections of Old Liverpool* (Liverpool, 1863)

The Stranger in Liverpool (1816)

Syers, Robert, *The History of Everton* (Liverpool, 1830)

Taylor, Eric Robert, *'If we Must Die': Shipboard Insurrections in the Era of the Atlantic Slave Trade* (Baton Rouge, 2006)

Taylor, James Stephen, *Jonas Hanway, Founder of the Marine Society* (1985)

Thomas, R.H.G., *The Liverpool and Manchester Railway* (1980)

Thompson, Alvin O., *A documentary History of Slavery in Berbice, 1796–1834* (Georgetown, Guyana, 2002)

Touzeau, James, *The Rise and Progress of Liverpool, 1551 to 1835* (Liverpool, 1910)

Trivellato, Francesca, *The Familiarity of Strangers: The Sephardic Diaspora, Livorno, and Cross-cultural Trade in the Early Modern Period* (New Haven, Conn., 2009)

Trevelyan, Raleigh, *Princes under the Volcano* (1972)

Troughton, Thomas, *The History of Liverpool* (Liverpool, 1810)

Ultimieri, Davide, *Livorno: feste di popolo e di sovrani (1621–1798)* (Livorno, 2012)

Walker, John Frederick, *Ivory's Ghosts: The White Gold of History and the Fate of Elephants* (New York, 2009)

Warnier, Jean-Pierre, 'Slave-trading without slave-raiding in Cameroon', *Paideuma* (1995)

Webster, Anthony, 'Liverpool and the Asian trade, 1800–1850', in Sheryllynne Haggerty, *'Merely for Money'? Business Culture in the British Atlantic, 1750–1815* (Liverpool, 2012)

Wilkins, Frances, *Manx Slave Traders* (Kidderminster, 1999)

Williams, David M., 'Abolition and the re-deployment of the slave fleet, 1807–1811', *Journal of Transport History* n.s. ii (1973); reprinted in Williams, *Merchants and Mariners* (St. John's, Newfoundland, 2000)

Williams, David M., 'Liverpool merchants and the cotton trade, 1820–1850', in J.R. Harris, *Liverpool and Merseyside* (1969) and Williams, *Merchants and Mariners* (St. John's, Newfoundland, 2000)

Williams, David M., *Merchants and Mariners* (St. John's, Newfoundland, 2000)

Williams, David M., 'The rise of United States merchant shipping in the North Atlantic, 1800–1850s', in Clark G. Reynolds (ed.), *Global Crossroads and the American Seas* (Missoula, Montana, 1988)

Williams, Gomer, *History of the Liverpool Privateers and Letters of Marque, with an Account of the Liverpool Slave Trade* (1897, 2004)

Yarker, Jonathan & Hornsby, Clare, 'Buying Art in Rome in the 1770s', in María Dolores Sánchez-Jáureghi & Scott Wilcox (eds), *The English Prize: The Capture of the Westmorland, an Episode of the Grand Tour* (New Haven, Conn., 2012)

Zahedieh, Nuala, *The Capital and the Colonies: London and the Atlantic Economy: 1660–1700* (Cambridge, 2010)

Index

Printed and bound by CPI Group (UK) Ltd, Croydon, CR0 4YY

06/06/2023

03224569-0001